Will Randall was born in ... ... London. He taught languages in the West Country for ten years before going to live in the South Pacific. His first book, *Solomon Time*, was the story of his experiences there, and since then he has lived in, among other places, India (*Indian Summer*, 2004), Africa (*Botswana Time*, 2005) and numerous parts of France (*Another Long Day on the Piste*, 2006). He continues to travel, teach and write, and is currently resident in Boston, Massachusetts.

Visit the author's website at: www.willrandall.co.uk

Praise for Will Randall

For *Botswana Time*
'This is a good-humoured book, written by a man who went to Botswana with an open heart. The result is a wonderful, amusing and affirmative book about that remarkable country, filled with laughter, colour, and simple decency. Bravo, Mr Randall. Bravo'

Alexander McCall Smith, author of
The No.1 Ladies' Detective Agency

For *Indian Summer*
'Many great writers have written about their time in the East; Somerset Maugham, E. M. Forster and Rudyard Kipling among them. Even if he never writes about India again, Will Randall should be added to this illustrious list'
Daily Express

'Randall kaleidoscopically evokes his changing perceptions of the country's extraordinary diversity in a travelogue full of sensuous detail, humour and poignancy'   *Observer*

ANOTHER LONG DAY ON THE PISTE

WILL RANDALL

ABACUS

First published in Great Britain in 2006 by Abacus
Reprinted 2007 (twice)

A CIP catalogue record for this book is available from the British Library.

ISBN 978-0-349-11933-5

Typeset in Palatino by Palimpsest Book Production Limited,
Grangemouth, Stirlingshire
Printed and bound in Great Britain by Clays Ltd, St Ives plc

Abacus
An imprint of
Little, Brown Book Group
Brettenham House
Lancaster Place
London WC2E 7EN

A Member of the Hachette Livre Group of Companies

www.littlebrown.co.uk

This is a book for anyone who believes that what goes up must come down – preferably in one piece.

Acknowledgements

Mountain villages are populated by friendly folk with a common purpose – having a good time without breaking anything. There were, however, a number of people who went out of their way to help me and I would like to thank them here. Angus Rumbold masterminded the whole operation. Had it not been for him there would not have been a book. Gavin Larsen organised getting me about in one piece, and he and Tom Babbington always remain jovial good company. Matt Symonds, a great fixer and great fun, definitely sorted me out. Elsewhere, Will Palmer came to my rescue when technological disaster struck, and Peter and Margaret of Friends in France did their best to keep my floundering efforts going.

Everyone at Little, Brown and, specifically, Abacus, is always incredibly supportive. Tamsyn Berryman has a sharp eye for detail and an encouraging enthusiasm for my books. Kirsteen Astor does a brilliant job reminding me what day of the week it is and making sure I am in the right place at the right time. Time and again, Duncan Spilling produces attractive, imaginative cover designs. Richard Beswick is renowned and remarkable for his cool insights and comforting confidence.

My agent Kate Hordern keeps my contractual affairs in order with admirable efficiency, making sure all the while that I knuckle down when needs must. Her listening ear and cheerful good advice are always much appreciated. Richenda Todd knows how books work and always alerts me in a kindly way to any faults that I may not have spotted myself. Tanya Demidova has again provided wonderful illustrations from the barmiest of suggestions.

Finally, the encouragement of family and friends is what makes a seemingly hard task so much easier. I am very grateful to them all.

WR
St Jean-de-Luz, France
June 2006

Contents

Prologue

Snowing was not the word.

Dumping it or flogging it down, perhaps.

Whatever the correct terminology was, within the few moments since I had disappeared off into the trees, a near-clear sky had clouded over completely. Soft white flakes the size of my thumbnail were tumbling down thickly. Already they were forming little mounds on my shoulders that cascaded down my front as I struggled as usual with my gloves and ski sticks. Visibility was now alarmingly limited.

Only just a little earlier, as I had come round the last bend, I had gazed down, with some relief, on the pretty view of the village of wooden chalets surrounding the simple church, its copper cupola reflecting the last of the sun, which had still been just visible across the valley before it disappeared behind Mont Blanc. I had been looking forward to unsnapping my skis outside the Café de la Poste, propping them up in the little rack beside the woodpile, loosening the fastenings on my boots and clomping through the door, up to the bar – a cowboy in thermal waterproofs. Before long, after a certain amount of whooshing and shooshing from the steam-powered machine beneath the great Art Nouveau mirror, the ever-cheerful Jimmy would slide a steaming glass cup of *vin chaud* down *le zinc*, the pitted metal top of the bar. Relaxing on a stool, I would take the time to inhale the delicious aromas of cinnamon, orange, cloves and red wine.

Unfortunately, due to my unavoidable pit stop, I was still halfway up a mountain in a blizzard. I could scarcely see the end of my skis and my companions not at all. To add to my woes, it was fast getting dark.

A combination of the altitude, the cold, one too many fizzy drinks and the vicious bumps of a particularly alarming mogul field, which I had absolutely hated and should in no way have allowed myself to be conned into attempting, meant that once back on the regular piste it had been necessary to answer a rather urgent call of nature. With the quietest of hisses my friends, imagining, I think, that I was going my own way, had headed on down the hill as I shot off into the woods that fringed the path. Had they waited for me, they would have quite rapidly realised that all was not in fact well. The dull thump of human being into a very solid, rather spiky pine tree, had been accompanied by a clattering of skiing equipment and a particularly choice, really quite satisfying, series of obscenities that had actually gone some way to making the pulsing bump on my forehead feel rather better. This minor accident had, unfortunately, done nothing to relieve the pressing reason for my departure from the not so straight and rather narrow path.

Skis, and rather more particularly their bindings, are contrary bits of kit. They are more than happy to part company with your boots when you are travelling at speeds in excess of fifty miles an hour downhill, abandoning you mid-mountain before hurtling off either down a ravine or into the softer body parts of any other skiing casualty in the vicinity. However, when you're lying with one leg up a tree and the other seemingly straight out behind you, will they budge? Er, no.

Finally, after a great deal of huffing and puffing, which caused steam to come out in little spurts from the top of my jacket, I managed to extricate myself and rather dizzily stand up. At which point I promptly sank to mid-thigh in a snow-drift. There was, however, absolutely no time whatsoever to reposition myself. A most unseemly flurry of hat, gloves, goggles, sunglasses, clips, zips and fasteners followed before my mission could be accomplished. Some few minutes later I reappeared from the trees on all fours, much relieved, a ski in each hand, my poles trailing behind me. By the time I had got myself reassembled it was snowing really hard.

Still, I was very much in one piece and operational – except that my goggles had fogged up – but then, when didn't they? Now all I had to do was get myself to the bottom of the mountain and into the eminently more suit-able environs of the Café de la Poste. The only significant impediment to my plan was that, and I hardly liked to admit it to myself, I had never actually skied this side of the mountain before and had next to no idea how to nego-tiate my way back down into the resort. Visions of a fifteen-mile walk in the rain lower down the valley wearing ski boots and being splashed by the headlights of non-stopping traffic, or being picked up by a merciless taxi driver who charged only in multiples of one hundred Euros, made me groan almost as loudly as I had when I'd inadvertently slapped my goggles back on to my forehead and its Quasi-modoian lump.

Well, I thought to myself, the only way is down.

Whistling, fairly cheerfully, I pushed off. Within a few yards I was covered from head to toe in thick fresh snow. How I used to laugh when I saw people coming down the

mountain resembling mobile snowmen. How ridiculous
they appeared! Glancing round, I prepared myself for a
good old giggle at all the serious skiers looking perfectly
ludicrous. My desire to laugh was unfortunately disappointed. There was nobody else covered from head to toe
in snow. In fact, there was nobody else.

Burrowing into my sleeve I finally got hold of my watch.
Blimey, it was past five o'clock – not surprising then that
it was beginning to get dark and the mountain was now
deserted. Whistling a little more loudly and a little more
cheerfully, I carved some fairly tidy turns down to the next
corner. It was a shame really that there was no one around
to admire them.

Idly wondering how you went about building an igloo,
I skied down another narrow path whose uphill side was
thickly wooded and whose downhill side was – as far as
I could see in the thickly falling snow – a precipice. Splin-
tering away from the strangely geometric, frozen wall to
my right, a chunk of ice fell across the mountain path.
Somehow, despite the increasing precariousness of my position, I felt annoyed by the way it had spilled out, spoiling
the polished neatness of the piste. Puffs of snow spray,
diamond dust in the dying of the day, scorched my cheeks
and blurred my already rather watery eyes. The next few
hundred metres, which I covered without incident, enjoying
in a funny way the solitude of the mountain, brought me
to a T-junction. There was a signpost with arrows pointing
in both directions, but as they only indicated the names of
the pistes, always, it seemed to me, drawn from mysterious sources in the French Alps, I was none the wiser. How
much more sensible it would have been, how much easier
my choice, if one of them had read 'Very easy route to the
bottom' or 'Café de la Poste' and the other pointing in the
opposite direction something like 'Nightmare black run'

or 'Treacherous winding path along ravine'. No, instead there was a wooden cut-out of a blue chamois pointing one way, and a picture of a startled-looking Alpine rabbit on *raquettes* pointing the other. Cursing my decision to have folded my piste map into a rather effective paper dart rather late on in the café the night before, I wearily inspected my several dozen pockets for a coin to toss. Eventually, I located a one Euro piece – from Belgium, I noticed in passing. The Queen of the Belgians had a rather pleased-with-herself look, I thought, as I flicked the yellow piece out of my gloved hand. Bet she had never been stuck up a mountain all on her own miles from anywhere, left to fend for herself as the night drew in, the temperatures plunged and the woods began to stir. My Euro coin disappeared into a snowdrift.

By now it was really snowing thickly and it was not even possible to see the glimmer of the lights of the village, which should have been twinkling below me in a most welcoming fashion. This, I did realise, was bad news. I had been hoping to be able to orient myself by them. A decision had to be made quickly, and I knew from bitter experience that once I had chosen one path or the other there was no going back. I would have preferred to end up in Switzerland rather than walk back up the hill.

Eventually I decided to turn left for no better reason than that the slope seemed to be a little less steep. As happened at the end of most of my days skiing, self-preservation kicked in. No longer was I flush with adrenalin, excited to be up here in the mountains breathing the fresh air and thrilling at the wind in my remaining hair. Now all I really wanted to do was to get to the bottom without twisting, tearing, stretching or breaking any part of myself. And then I wanted only to rid myself of the ridiculous contraptions strapped to my feet as quickly as I realistically could, and put them as far out of sight as possible. On my return to the village I would always feel rather like a sailor hitting dry land after an extended trip out at sea – a little giddy at first, but then confidently aware of the fact that perfectly flat dry land was what I had been best designed for. On this particular evening I was more careful than ever. Fortunately there had been plenty of fresh snow over the last few days and this latest fall made for very easy skiing conditions. The temperature had not yet dipped much below freezing, and so far there had been none of the bone-shaking clattering that you experience trying to turn on sheet ice. For now, there was just the infinitely soft support of powder.

Some people have an innate, highly honed sense of direction which leads them unerringly to their destination.

I am not one of those people.

Normally I am just content to follow the tips of my skis but, despite this happy-go-lucky sense of adventure, that in the past had served me so well, now I was under the distinct impression that I was not on my most direct route to a *vin chaud*.

Below me in the gloom I could make out a circle of silvery snow surrounded nearly entirely by the darkness of trees. As I approached I could see strung high above their tops the spiky outline of a chair-lift. It was not moving, and as I reached its bottom I could see the snow beginning to stick to the panes of glass in the door of the *remonteur*'s little hut and to a wide, red metal shovel leaning beside it. Skiing and side-stepping around the clearing I desperately tried to find the onward route. Twice round I went, and then a third time, rather quicker as a distinct sense of panic began to gurgle up inside me for the first time. The only way out appeared to be either back up the hill the way I had come or down a single track through the trees, most probably used by animals as they migrated over the mountains in the summer.

Gazing back up at the glowering mountain, I realised that my choice was an easy one. Sucking in a couple of lungfuls of air, I put my skis together and set off down the path. As it only measured a few inches across with deep snow on either side, attempts to steer and regulate my speed were all but impossible. I prayed that my route would not be blocked by any disorderly roots under which my skis might become embedded, my forward trajectory thereby, no doubt, catapulting me into yet another pine. Wriggling in and out of the trees, following the natural contours of the terrain, I travelled faster and faster, and the run developed into a surreal arcade game in which I had no control over the direction I took – as if I had not yet put my money in the slot.

At the very moment I thought that any hope of stopping without contact with a solid object was impossible, the slope took a slight upward turn, just enough to slow me down to a reasonable speed, and I burst out of the forest into the open; from darkness into light, or rather a growing gloom. For a thrilling moment, seeing the wide stretch of glittering snow, I believed myself to be back on a manicured piste, needing now only to sally down through the finishing arch to the adulation of the crowd, but the powder puffing around my knees made me realise that my homecoming was not going to be quite so quickly applauded. Still, the wide open space meant that this field was cultivated in the spring and summer and therefore I must now at last be at a relatively low altitude.

Sitting back on my skis, trying to lift my tips above the surface, I traced virgin tracks that, as I glanced back over my shoulder, carved themselves in thick black lines in the moonlight. So shallow was the incline that on a couple of occasions I feared grinding to a halt. The thought of having to shovel my way through the drifts was one of the most depressing yet. Somehow though, every time I thought I was about to come to a standstill, a little dip in the ground, unseen beneath my skis, carried me on. By now, the light was so bad that the view of trees and snow below me had become entirely monochrome, a jumble of lumpy shapes and random spindly fingers of branches. It was now almost impossible to judge distances and on more than one occasion I came dangerously close to disappearing back into the forest at the edge of the field. Not having enjoyed my first experience of the woods in the dusk I stopped, backed up and tried to remain out in the open.

By now I was very tired. My thighs were burning, swollen, so it seemed, to twice their normal rather unimpressive thickness. Even though they felt like they were on fire, the rest of me suddenly felt frozen cold. Somehow the mountain air was managing to pierce the umpteen layers of vests, T-shirts, shirts and jumpers, and the sweat that had poured from me as I wrestled my way out onto the piste was now running icily down my back.

To my alarm, I recognised that the control that I had over the direction of my skis, never anything near total, was now nothing more than feeble. Each turn required immense concentration and exhausting effort, and I was forced to come to a halt every few dozen yards. My breath, deep and quick, came puffing out of my mouth in great clouds that would not have embarrassed a narrow-gauge Alpine steam engine. As I panted, leaning heavily on my ski sticks, I became aware that I was shaking not simply through physical exhaustion but also because I was beginning to get quite frightened.

Pushing images of frozen moustaches, grey-white, icy faces, and stiff motionless limbs out of my mind, I stumbled around until my skis were again facing down towards where I imagined the village to be.

In the half-light, the surface of the mountain appeared to be tablecloth smooth but I knew this to be nothing more than a mirage. In the daylight, every contour would be clearly visible, but now I had to try and relax enough to ride any invisible bump, hillock or mogul. Leaning forward against all my natural instincts, I bent my knees a little further trying to absorb any nasty shocks with my aching legs.

Momentarily, I thought that I had skied off the edge of a cliff as my internal organs, operating on some different system of gravity to the rest of my leaden body, rose in my stomach. Several minutes later, or so it seemed, my skis came back to earth in surprising unison and I suddenly, rather fancifully imagined that I might have achieved a jump of a medal-winning distance. Instead of raising my arms in recognition of the applause of a phantom crowd, I swung myself to a halt. Feeling delighted that I was still upright, I thumped my ski sticks back into the freezing surface. As I did so, I suddenly sensed, to my alarm, that I was sliding rapidly backwards. Turning and desperately urging my skis to once again become parallel with the slope, I over-compensated and found myself lurching back down the hill like an out of control, spinning Formula Two racing car. Losing my balance I flew forwards over the front of my skis, praying in that split second that my bindings would release me. With two dull clicks, they reluctantly did so, but not before a flash of white, sodium light burst in my knee and rocketed up to explode with excruciating pain in my brain. The agony was not much soothed by the cold crystals of snow that scoured my cheeks as my face hit the ground with an audible whack and my nose burst open.

For a few seconds I lay there before realising, at one and

the same moment, that I could not move my left leg and that the strange, almost comfortingly warm, metallic taste on my tongue that then filled my mouth with a gush was my blood.

Blood.

Bloody hell.

Bloody skiing.

1

Settling Back Down

November is no time to start undertaking any kind of new enterprise. Nobody is interested. People are looking forward to Christmas with great excitement – particularly if they are under eighteen or in retail. Of course, most sensible grown-ups await the holiday's arrival with a certain lurking sense of nausea brought on by an excess of commercialism. Christmas lights have been up in the high streets since early September, and everyone lurks in their offices, wary of the 'Great Day' and displaying signs of the early onset of dyspepsia at the thought of steroidal, watery turkey, carbonised chipolatas, bread sauce, and brussels sprouts of all things.

From the top of the London bus where I was slumped, I could see forward-thinking shoppers buying thoughtful presents for loved ones. No doubt they would be taking them home and keeping them prudently in the bottom of a cupboard until it was time to pull them out with pride and watch the sheer joy of the recipients as they tore back the wrapping paper to reveal their hearts' desires. My own memories of roaring round the shops at four o'clock on the afternoon of Christmas Eve made me grimace. In a cold sweat, I would reach for whatever sort of rubbish I could lay my hands on, confident only that whatever it was could at least be recycled by the receiver to other distant relatives until its use-by date.

Jesus, I thought, shaking my head.

Trudging back to a flat that I owned, but in which I had never spent, until just recently, a night, I pondered what it was that I might apply myself to once the 'festive season' was over. There was certainly no point in doing anything concerning my long-term future until the spring. All that worried me now was what I should do until then. Travels fairly far and wide over the last five years, that had taken me from the shores of the South Pacific to the slums of India, had left me a little out of practice when it came to organising my daily life into a regulated European timetable.

This time I was out of Africa, still bearing with some pride the remnants of a bush tan on my arms and legs – not that these were on display as, shivering, I put the key into the lock of the communal front door. Stumbling over piles of dusty junk mail and up the worn stairs to the second floor, pulling open the poppers of my padded jacket, I set about unlocking the several clunking and snapping locks that I had recently had fitted to the door. Once inside, various bolts shot, I collapsed onto the small sofa and gazed at where the television would have been had it not been stolen.

Discovering the shattered front door of the flat on my return from the airport had depressed me, but not as much as the discovery that the neighbour upstairs, a young civil servant who worked across the river at the Ministry of Defence, had ignored it for a whole week. Simon had an immensely annoying habit of checking his watch every couple of seconds whilst I spoke to him, as if he was in a huge rush to get back to the office and prevent World War 3. In such haste had he been that he had walked past the scene of the intrusion for 'oh, about seven days now – I first noticed it on the day of our audit'. When I enquired why it was that he had not thought fit to take any action, he just shrugged, as if I was barmy to think that it was anything to do with him, checked his watch again and shot down the stairs. Through a soot-smeared window I had watched him clip off down the street to the bus stop with a curious high-kneed gait.

Something about London air has a strangely anaesthetic effect on me, which meant that after I had relocked all the locks from the inside I promptly fell asleep and was only woken some time later, my head hanging over the edge of the sofa, by the *peep-peep peep-peep* of a newly purchased mobile phone, which flashed and vibrated and played music but was extraordinarily unhelpful when it came to making a telephone call. Unable to locate the pocket into which I had slipped it before the ringing stopped, and finding only a 'missed call' message when finally I laid my hands on it, I gave up, chucked it onto my coat and snoozed off again.

But it wasn't long before some other bastard was trying to get hold of me.

'All right, Mr R?'

Despite my grogginess I recognised the youthful saluta-tion.

'Hello, Matthew, how are you?'

'Yeah, fine, mate, fine. Just chilling with a few mates, Hutchy and a whole load of other people. All good. Anyway, heard you were back. What's occurring?'

'Well . . .'

Matthew was one of a number of my former students who had kept in touch with me over the last five years since they and I had left a particularly pleasant school in the West Country. Although I had been on a worldwide 'walkabout' (in the aboriginal rather than royal sense) and they had gone on to further studies – most of them by now having left colleges and universities – they had been assiduous in letting me know of their progress, their plans, their hopes and aspirations, which more often than not were rather more concrete than my own. Not only was I flattered that they should wish to remain friendly but I was also proud that they would often ring to ask my opinion about their next step.

Since we had left school I had decided that, as they were no longer my direct responsibility, I would refrain from passing comment about what they planned to do, but I did try to give them as much balanced information as I could. More often than not the advice that I provided was based on a number of my own disastrous decisions and their even more hopeless outcomes. Really I only hoped that they would find themselves a niche in life which would provide them with as much enjoyment and satisfaction as mine had. I had begun to realise as I approached my forties that the achievement of contentment and fulfilment was more often than not entirely serendipitous. Perhaps it was true too, however, that to an extent, it is possible to make your own luck. My counsel came at no cost of course – still, it would be nice, even if the thought was a little selfish, if some of my former students eventually became restaurateurs, bar and yacht owners, lawyers, financial wizards and finally nursing home proprietors.

On this occasion, Matthew was after advice about how he should perform at an interview for an insufferable-sounding job in financial marketing – whatever that was. As the marvellous Mr Jolly, my bank manager and inter-mittent friend, could testify, I was hardly well qualified to provide Matthew with any sensible suggestions. He seemed grateful enough for what I had to say, although at one stage he did snort with derision (yes, I can only describe it as such) when I muttered something about a suit and tie.

'Yeah, cheers for that then, mate,' he made to end the conversation. No doubt he was off to his next exciting social engagement.

'Okay, Matthew, look after yourself. Don't do anything I wouldn't do,' I replied rather patly, but as the convention required.

'Leaves me a pretty free hand then! Hey, by the way, you'll never guess who's sitting in my flat right now – says he wants to have a word with you.'

'Who?' I asked rather nervously, dreading that it might be one of the very few – fortunately very, very few – of my past students who had been so adolescently painful that I really had no desire to be in contact with them again.

There was a little giggling and a thump as the mobile telephone was chucked across the room at the other end.

''Ello, sir!' Another cheerful voice greeted me.

'Jimmy?'

It always amazed me that despite the time that had passed and the growing up that had been done, by these young-sters at least, I always seemed to be able to recognise a voice or face and, even more astonishingly, remember a name.

All very *Mr Chips*, I am sure.

'Hi, hi, sir! How are you doing?'

'Fine, thanks, fine! Good to hear from you.'

'Yeah, yeah, yeah, totally! Cool, sir.'

I was about to suggest to him that he need not be quite so formal when I remembered an episode that had taken place when I was first stepping out as a teacher. One of my former students had returned to show off his long hair, his fancy pack of cigarettes and his alcoholic breath. Grinning he had approached me as I stood, feeling bored, on 'dinner duty' in the cafeteria. He wasn't a bad lad, although it always did surprise me that the pupils most likely to return to their

Alma Mater were invariably the ones who had complained most about the pettier aspects of school life, and who had forever been telling me how much they were looking forward to leaving.

'All right, sir?' he had said.

'Fine, thanks, but you don't really have to keep on calling me "sir"!'

'So what should I call you then?'

'Oh, I don't mind, you can call me what you want . . .'

Young I was, and inexperienced.

'Okay, then, baldy.' He had grinned and the sniggers had echoed across the steaming hot plates.

So now if Jimmy wished to remain on the formal side then perhaps it was no bad thing.

'You're back from the mountains then, Jimmy? How's it all been going?'

'Yeah, cool, cool, thanks, yeah, yeah, yeah, totally cool.'

'Cool then?'

Jimmy, in a flurry of enthusiasm, did not notice the irony.

'Yeah, yeah, yeah. So you've been off and away then, sir?'

Only then did it strike me that I had not spoken to Jimmy since the day we had left school. It felt like yesterday. So much common experience shared in the past meant that it was pleasantly easy to pick up where we had left off.

'Yes, I have been around and about a bit,' I laughed. In the five years since I had sold my home near Taunton complete with its rather Luddite, circular-dial telephone, information technology had developed so astonishingly that I was now finding a laptop and a mobile phone almost indispensable. So easy was the spreading of gossip world-wide that I had managed to keep abreast of everybody's developments and they of mine even if I had not seen or spoken to them in person.

Young Jimmy had decided against setting off down the fairly well-worn path from school into higher education, deciding instead that the funds that this would require would be much more wisely invested in seeing something of the world. His girlfriend and he had 'done' South-East Asia but the social pressures of life on the Koh San Road and a three-times-a-day diet of Pad Thai had meant that they had finally parted company – she in the direction of a commune in southern India and the arms of an apparently extremely hirsute German with a degree in packaging, he to go and look up some of his friends who were doing a season in the Alps. They were inevitably 'cool, yeah, pretty cool'.

'So where are you living then, Jimmy?'

'Oh, just crashing at some mates' for the moment trying to earn some dosh so I can get back up the mountains. Should be heading out there again in a couple of weeks.' I could hear the eagerness in his voice. 'Gonna be amazing.'

'Great. Sounds like you're pretty happy with things then?'

Just slightly, very slightly, I noticed a strange wistful note of something that might, perhaps, have resembled envy in my voice.

'Yes, I am, thanks. How about you, sir? What your plans then?'

Happily, before I had the chance to break into another bravura performance of bluster, he went on.

'Know what, sir? Know what you should do? You should come on out. There's going to be quite a few of us out this season. It's a place called Mont St Bernard. You ever heard of it? No? It's great. Going to be a blast. Loadsa skiing, boarding whatever. I'm going to get into parascending and that. Nightlife is excellent! Loads of pulling and drinking cr, I mean, après-ski, know what I mean?' He laughed. 'Yeah, yeah. Go on! You should, you know; it will be a laugh, seriously, mate.'

'Yes, I'm sure it will. But I'm a bit old for all that sort of thing . . . anyway, I've got to get a few things sorted out here.'

'Oh, yeah? Like what kind of stuff?' he asked laughing.

Oh, the perspicacity of youth.

'No, anyway, I really do reckon I'm a bit old for all that now, don't you?' After all, I was bloody nearly forty.

'No way, rubbish. How old are you now? Bet you're not even fifty yet. You're younger than my dad and he still skis. Don't be such an old fart, sir.'

'Go for it – you're only young once,' I heard a voice holler from somewhere in the background.

'Yeah, yeah, go on. Might never get the chance to do it again, sir.'

True.

How very true.

2

The Only Way Is Up

S tartled snowflakes were swept into the Café de la Poste as the front door swung open to allow yet more revellers over the threshold one busy evening in early January, several weeks after my arrival in Mont St Bernard. As the sparkling crystals were snuffed out by the unexpected warmth with which they were greeted, so the customers' cheeks glowed evermore rosy as they clustered around the brass and ceramic beer pumps. For now, the atmosphere was cheerful and relaxed. The period that described itself as après-ski more often than not slipped into that all-important part of the French day: Aperitifs, or '*L'Apéro*' as it was more fondly known. It was generally a quiet time. Only later did things become a little more excitable. After a few weeks in Mont St Bernard I was beginning to feel the rhythm of the days.

Most people, having enjoyed their skiing, were now feeling the benefits of the clear mountain air and the warm sunshine, and had built up healthy appetites. Before long the small bar would be filled with jostling skiers, the separate groups easy to discern at the high round tables. In the corner furthest from the front door, under an enamelled shield advertising a particularly treacly type of Belgian beer brewed by some extremely cheerful, chubby-faced monks, sat the *pisteurs*, the piste-bashers, bearded and leathery. They were today's equivalent of the woodsmen who had inhabited the mountains before the arrival of the chair-lift and the *chocolat chaud*. Unlike the rest of the clientele, these men, and they were all men, were just about to begin their work. Not that this in any way diminished their enthusiasm for the little balloon glasses of pastis, which shone, jaundiced, in the light of the electric-candle lamps that sat on each table. Soon they would leave in the direction of Chez Patrice, where they would consume quantities of one of the eponymous owner's heartier dishes, perhaps *une daube* – tender lumps of beef nearly as large as their fists stewed in a rich sauce of wine, carrots and onions – served up alongside huge bowls of shiny tagliatelle. All this of course would be washed down by quantities of *La Mondeuse*, the light red wine of the Savoy, poured into glazed brown pitchers from a petrol-pump arrangement on the wall by the door to the kitchen. Later, filling their flasks with one of the numerous *eau-de-vie*, brewed locally and, as far as I knew, totally illegally, they would head for their vast piste-bashing machines, start them with a roar of black diesel smoke and zoom almost vertically up the mountains. Here they would drive around at an incredible speed at angles that defied mathematics until dawn rose, upon which they would return to the bar of the Café de la Poste for coffee and the obligatory *petit blanc*, a sharp glass of cold white wine. Gruff always, friendly more often than not, they had all come over to shake our hands that evening, and once again I admired the way that they looked so effortlessly the part: their *salopettes*, warm, hand-knitted pullovers smelling powerfully of hand-rolled-cigarette smoke and sweat, their jerkins, scuffed leather boots, their gloves moulded to their hands, were all worn as a second skin, a birthright. The comparison with the outfits of the couples and families sitting at the other tables was almost comic.

Most of the tourists, all here from Saturday to Saturday, would not have looked more uncomfortable or out of place had they arrived in the bar dressed as scuba divers, guards at Buckingham Palace or ginger-haired Scotsmen in kilts. Actually there were a few ginger-bewigged Scotsmen in kilts drunk in one corner but they were avoided by the assembled company, including the normally all-embracingly affable Jimmy. The other punters, as we *saisonniers* patronisingly referred to them, were kitted out in clothes that had either been hired or bought at short notice. For the main part, their outfits were too bright, too light and, in a certain number of cases, worryingly tight. The visitors were joined occasionally by one of the numerous ski instructors, who were usually found grouped around a pinball machine. This pinging, whizzing, flashing and whirring contraption sat next to the impressively 1970s jukebox that provided the 'sounds' until the dismal disc jockey turned up with his cardboard boxes, turntables and appalling taste.

Like the *pisteurs*, the ski instructors dressed the part but their outfits were better cut and altogether more stylish. Their professional duties over, they hovered around the younger female section of the patrons, chatting up, often in appalling English, any or all of the girls.

As usual, at the heel of the bar, which they had colonised at the beginning of the season, sat a group of young people who, even with the best, most laid-back, liberal, let it all hang out, smart-huh-who-cares-about-smart will in the world, was one of the scruffiest, hairiest, sloppiest, shaggiest and possibly most unhygienic collection of youngsters it had ever been my mixed fortune to meet. When I had come in they had greeted me with all kinds of bizarre hand and arm movements which included quite a lot of snapping, shaking, bobbing and jerking, and cries of *Yo dude, how's it going?*

Laughing, I had responded with some complicated hand gesture of my own, which made it look to any uninitiated observer that I was about to go off and answer the telephone. They were a good bunch really.

Soon the instructors left on their way to a *réunion*, which seemed to take place at least weekly and which seemed to involve gargantuan quantities of food and unnerving amounts of *bonhomie*. My next-door neighbour, the farmer's wife, had promised me some more rabbit *ragoût* and before long I would be heading back up the hill, to warm my hands at her wood-burning *Petit Godin*, to eat sumptuously and listen to yet more tallish tales from her husband.

Occasionally, of course, the Russians would appear. Then the atmosphere would change perceptibly – not for the better.

More than once, sitting in the bar, I had remembered, not without a wry smile, the reasons behind my decision to make my way to the little ski station of Mont St Bernard, halfway down La Vallée Profonde between the villages of Issy and L'Abbas.

Old fart!

After the call had finished, I had laughed at Jimmy's well-meant rudeness.

Old, indeed.

Honestly, young people today.

Although I had not really been piqued by Jimmy's jibes about my age, it had set me thinking about all the sporting ventures in which, in a few years' time, I would certainly be too decrepit to take part. Not by nature particularly thrill-seeking or risk-taking, I did carry, as we all do, a few trophies of moments of attempted sporting derring-do, a sort of catalogue of the competitions and combats we have undertaken over the course of the years. My left knee still continued to make a noise like a firecracker every time I flexed it fully, a reminder of a particularly hectic netball competition in Devon; my right shoulder still bore the hazy brown mark of a graze picked up as a result of a fall from a particularly belligerent donkey somewhere in Spain; there is a large dint in my right shin after an unsuccessful exit from a dugout canoe in the Solomon Islands, and across the bridge of my nose there will forever be a small scar that I acquired aged eight from a drinking fountain during a particularly hard-fought water-spitting competition against a rival school on a trip to the Tower of London.

Thankfully, I have never chosen to undertake any of the more obviously dangerous sports. My parents, keen equestrians, had between them broken, twisted, snapped or generally mistreated nearly all the various components that make up the human body. One brother had retired from parachute jumping, an experience that would leave him pale and mildly shaking every time he was asked to recount it. Wishing to keep his feet more firmly on the floor, he had taken up marathon running. Thus, he annually ran the risk of being run down by tens of thousands of people all dressed in varyingly ludicrous outfits, ranging from the rather slower knight in suit of armour and pantomime horse to the speedier but no less absurd long distance runner. One of my closer friends had undergone a fortunately fairly short-lived fascination with bare knuckle fighting. He had not joined a club or organisation and just seemed to pursue his interest whenever the mood took him – often fairly late on weekend evenings.

No, I had always been much too sensible to undertake any of these sports. Apart from anything else, they all scared the living daylights out of me.

a variety of snowboards and surfboards, all in their own special zip-up bags. Attached to the ends of the roof rack on either side of the car were dangling two mini-skis, about a foot long, like two ostentatious dangly earrings.

'So, is this your lot then?' asked Guy, attempting to be as undismissive as possible as he squeezed my small plain hold-all into a last corner of the back of the car. 'You'll be getting all your gear out there then? New shit for the season, yeah?' he said as we set off.

'Yeah . . .' I supposed. I hadn't really thought about my wardrobe apart from buying a woolly jumper and a pair of pretty comfortable boots. (I had been cold ever since I got back from Africa.) Clothing, even in my most influenceable periods, all of them under the age of thirty, has only ever been of practical use to me: warding off the cold or protecting my fragile self from prying, possibly slightly amused, eyes. I was only slightly less astonished by the prices of 'designer' clothes than I was by the fervent, burning desire people had to own them. Apart from feeling deeply shocked about the inequities between the profits of the vendors and the remuneration of the manufacturers, I could not find any part of me that was at all moved by the subject of fashion. Skiers, though, and more particularly snowboarders, were, I knew, more concerned than anybody to get just the right thing. Not having the heart to disappoint my fellow traveller, I muttered something about giving it some thought.

'Cool, cool.' Guy grinned as we lurched out onto the M25 in a thoroughly under-25 fashion, before changing the subject to one that left me even more bereft of interest. 'So, you been doing quite a lot of working out then? Which gym do you use when you're in London?'

'What?'

Visiting a gym seemed to be a very distant concept. Actually, I couldn't really remember having visited one since I

owned those little plimsolls with elastic sides – and that
must have been before I could tie my shoelaces for myself.
Of course, I hadn't had any problem performing that particular task for years. (Well, at least since the morning of the
Thursday before last following an impromptu farewell celebration at my brother's place which had involved several
bottles of something called *Rakia* from Bulgaria.)

'Oh, you gotta, mate. Vi'al, man, if you wanna do any
sort of aerial stuff. You can get really radical if you have
good upper body strength.'

'Really?' I said, expressing as much interest as I could,
in the full knowledge that I had just gone up a size in
trousers. 'How do you mean aerial stuff? Aerial?'

'Yeah, you know: "Threes", "Sevens", "Flips"? Yeah?'

'Yeah, yeah, dude . . .' I mumbled.

Having no idea what he was talking about, I returned
my attention to the map-reading which was the only responsibility that Guy had specified when he had offered to give
me a lift.

'Here, here, turn off here! Oops, sorry!'

'Oh, get a grip, dude!' he yelled as we scooted between
lanes.

'Okay,' he said quietly, after we found ourselves back on
four wheels. 'Now, come on, let's wake up shall we, William?
Concentrating. Come, on, let's try and sit up properly, shall
we?' As Dover flashed up on another sign we both laughed
at the tables turned. But I did imperceptibly squirm a little
straighter in my seat.

An hour later, the sun was rising over the French coast
and despite the relatively humdrum nature of the trip so
far, I recognised lighting up within my chest that warm
glow of anticipation.

Here we go again, I smiled. Another little adventure.

Probably settle down in the spring.

Somewhere in the course of Guy's motoring education he had become confused and clearly believed that it was in France and not in Germany that there was no speed restriction on the motorway. As cheerfully as my insides would allow me, I grinned as we zoomed past surprised-looking families, commercial travellers and the occasional police car. Under normal circumstances I might well have waved, but my hands appeared to be otherwise engaged gripping various parts of the car's upholstery. In no way adding to my sense of personal security, Guy spent much of the time travelling through the Pas-de-Calais reciting a list of disasters that had befallen him on the road over the last few years. My own motoring career was about as chequered as a motor-racing flag, so I did have some sympathy with him. Unnecessary, though, I thought, to refer quite so regularly to cutting tools.

As he then went on to describe a medical handbook's worth of recent skiing injuries, I stared out of the window, admired the mournful flatness of Picardy and wondered about the public transport options. Fortunately, after his early flush of motoring zeal, my co-pilot seemed to relax and it was much easier to hear what he had to say as the wind noise around the shuddering car reduced and we slowed to a speed that, in a court of law, would probably not have been an imprisonable offence.

Although by now I had pretty much abandoned any attempt at map-reading, we knew that we were headed for Geneva before heading eastward and upward into the French Alps and the Haute Savoie. The châteaux of Champagne whizzed past in a blur, and before long we found ourselves in the soft hills of Burgundy heading towards Beaujolais.

'So what kind of gear are you going to get yourself then, Will?'

Closer now to our destination, Guy's thoughts had turned

to winter sports. With great relish he had just been telling me how he had broken his collarbone for the third time last season. On that occasion too, he had had to be cut out – there appeared to be a pattern developing here – but this time it was from some skiing outfit that he had doubled his student loan to purchase.

'You know what kit you're going to be skiing in?'

'Er . . . how do you mean?'

'You know! What make of ski jacket, pants? All that stuff.'

'Actually, I've got absolutely no idea.' It hadn't even crossed my mind. 'Sorry.' Somehow it suddenly felt as if this was something for which I ought to be apologising. 'So what kinds of different ones are there then?'

Guy scratched the makings of a goatee beard and gave this question some serious thought. 'Well there is . . .' and he proceeded to reel off a list of different brand names and their various attractions, most of which seemed to be that they were either cool or wicked. At least I think this was what he was going on about. He may have just been talking gibberish.

'Can't I, you know, just find a normal one? You know, something, well, normal. Nothing fancy.'

'Normal? What do you mean a normal one?' Guy sounded utterly bemused.

We had just left the Autoroute de Soleil at Macon before it headed down to Lyon and the Côte d'Azur and were now heading eastward towards the Swiss border. As we transferred from one motorway to the next via some nausea-inspiring roundabouts I happened to spot an absolutely vast, French shopping centre.

'*Ici Hypersport!*' read a huge blue and white sign. '*Promotion ski!*'

'Quick, in there. Just the place. Bound to be able to find something.'

'You serious? It will all be total crap in there. It will all probably be really . . .' Here he took a deep breath, '. . . cheap.'

'I know. Just the place. Go on, quick.'

With only a little less hooting of horns than is normally heard from an Italian wedding procession, we successfully crossed three lanes of traffic, left the main road, rode a central reservation with disdain and ended up halfway inside a trolley shelter.

Hypersport was just the place. Row upon row of logo-less clothing hung under the bright lights of the warehouse; to my further delight most of the ski jackets and trousers seemed to have tags attached to them that announced that savings were to be made. Guy looked positively weak. What was more, the overhead strip-lighting must have had a bad effect on him as he had now put on a pair of impenetrable sunglasses and was looking nervously around him. Eventually, after I had asked one of the sales assistants a couple of peculiarly inane questions and was holding out a lilac one-piece jumpsuit – only really to see if I could count the number of zips that it had – Guy decided that he needed to step in and stop me making a fatal fashion mistake.

Quite expertly, he pointed out the various pros and cons of the different models available and I did start to see that there were a number of reasonably important practical decisions to be made. On the other hand, I didn't really see that it mattered particularly how baggy my trousers were. According to Guy baggy was good.

Hmm. I would see.

Finally, we found an outfit that complied with Guy's fairly rigorous list of prerequisites and narrowly squeezed itself into the tight financial parameters laid down by my bank manager friend, Mr Jolly.

'Right then, what about all the other bits and bobs – like

gloves and goggles and all that sort of thing?' Now that I was here I wanted to get it all out of the way as quickly as possible. Guy, who had now recognised his ascendancy in the domain of ski accessories, would not hear a word of it.

'No, Will. You've got to remember that your gloves, your goggles and all that – that's the most important stuff. You've seriously got to get them from, like, a more professional place,' he said, as he looked rather disdainfully at the yawning staff in their Hypersport tracksuits. Realising he was probably right, I only purchased the ski outfit and we continued on our way.

'Bloody brilliant going off like this don't you think?' Guy's cool-as-ice mask slipped awry as he was overcome with the excitement of getting back on the road. As he changed gear with rather ruthless enthusiasm, grabbed some chewing gum, checked his hair in the rear-view mirror, had a sip of his drink and turned up the stereo to a door-bulging volume, seemingly all at the same time, I smiled in agreement.

Twenty years suddenly fell away and although I am no great nostalgist, I settled down into my seat and wrapped myself in reminiscence.

My parents, both enthusiastic and able linguists, were always keen that my brothers and I should have the opportunity to share the enjoyment that they had derived from speaking foreign languages. Both of them were well travelled, and many meals spent round the table in the evenings after school involved our mother and father regaling us with tales of exotic locations and experiences. So it was that we struck a familial happy medium – I was despatched 'on exchange' to various more or less exciting destinations, and my folks could quietly sigh with relief and smile at the thought of a couple of weeks of relative calm and quiet. As a boy I could talk the hind leg off any animal you care to mention, and as a teenager I could argue the toss at such length that it would have had all of the saints of the British Isles heading by the coach-load for Beachy Head. Adulthood seems, sadly, to have had little restraining effect on me. (Now perhaps is the moment to apologise publicly to the countless hundreds of my pupils in the past – poor, browbeaten, captive audiences.)

Soon, I realised that something as incidental as mastering a foreign language was not going to stand in the way of communication with the host families – for the main part in France and Germany – that welcomed me into their homes. Shell-shocked, their relief was palpable when they eventually returned me to the airport or train station; grandparents, uncles, aunts, cousins, even distant relatives were usually all in attendance, I suspect now, to ensure that I was really going.

My first excursion abroad alone began on my ninth birthday, the blow softened by an impromptu party thrown by the air hostesses on the British Airways flight to Frankfurt. Fantastic cake and fizzy orange, which I was not allowed at home, had us all in a state of high excitement when we touched down. The cabin crew and I were not quite dancing the conga out of the Arrivals Hall but I was certainly in high spirits when I was met by the mother of my new little exchange-partner friend. These were only slightly diminished when we reached the familial home, an imposing, slightly austere, modern German mansion in the pine-forested foothills of the Unterbergen Mountains. A rather military atmosphere surrounded it like a perimeter fence, and indeed it transpired that one of the umpteen Generals von Immernackt had saved the Duke of Wellington's bacon at some military engagement, as I was reminded innumerable times during the course of my stay. Struggling with my oversize suitcase up a flight of sweeping and well-swept steps, I followed Frau von Immernackt through the hefty carved-oak doors into a hall of marble, smoked glass and rare carpets. This was to be the first and last time that I was to find myself in this room – it being reserved for special occasions, which I personally was not again to warrant, but it was still an impressive moment. Standing amidst this finery, in a line arranged in descending height, were the von Immernackt offspring, all six of them. At their head was their father. Apart from the youngest and only female child, all the others wore matching lederhosen outfits and felt hats. Even at the age of nine I recognised the incongruousness of the moment as I approached in faded-blue flares and sandals (it was 1975). As I shook hands with each in turn, they clicked their heels and curtly nodded their heads. Delighted, I attempted to replicate the gestures which resulted in a rather sore neck and knee. When I reached the little girl, I was completely thrown by her swooping curtsy; nonetheless I didn't think my own effort in response too bad at all. This was amazing – it was just like the Von Trapp family, just like *The Sound of Music*. I wanted to tell them so but I didn't know the German for 'sound'. Actually, at that moment in my life, I didn't know any German at all.

The first afternoon slipped away quickly as I was shown about the place by a carrot-haired, freckled, skinny boy my age called Hans Detlof, who was to become one of my best childhood friends. He (and all five of his siblings) went on to become tax lawyers for the European Union although I don't remember him mentioning this as a childhood dream when we first met. He showed me his extensive glam-funk record collection and then *Abendessen* was announced by the ringing of a small gong at about six o'clock. We sat down to a meal of strange but by no means unpleasant soup, and sandwiches of smoked cheese and ham. This was all right.

All right until Frau von Immernackt, a shapely woman in her forties, appeared in the dining room entirely naked apart from a pair of dark-blue tinted goggles that she wore high on her forehead. *'Sauna und Sonnenlamp!'* she announced. So, perfectly naturally, we seven children trooped down into the basement, removed all our clothes and filed into the sauna where we sat on wooden benches, sweated profusely, and tried, in my case at least, not to stare. All this was just a prelude to being made to stand in a state of equal undress, aside from the compulsory blue goggles, in a ping-pong room, there to be irradiated with a small infra-red lamp by the lady of the house as we turned on our tippy-toes. Good for you apparently.

This of course took place nearly thirty years ago and it is to be hoped that I will make a full emotional recovery in the near future. In fact, I continued to return to the Von Immernackts' for several years after that, and Hans Detlof came to spend numerous holidays with us during which he was more often than not happily engaged weeding the flowerbeds or mowing the lawn after he somewhat unwisely let slip to my mum that he enjoyed 'the nature'.

Other trips, for the improvement of my French and my parents' general mental well-being, included staying with a family of firemen in Paris and spending a fortnight in a creeky château inland from Biarritz. This trip seemed from memory to have involved a meal that went on for about two weeks, and to which had been invited innumerable, often rather beautiful, cousins. The beach at St Jean-de-Luz was my first introduction to topless sunbathing, a pastime that I still pursue with enthusiasm today. Occasionally, the exchanges were tiresome and generally involved someone bespectacled and bashful called Frederic who didn't like anything at all from the food downwards, but mostly I had a wonderful time. So these adventures did eventually have the desired effect of making me semi-decently fluent in a couple of foreign languages – which subsequently provided me with a teaching career for the better part of ten years. It was also the period of my life during which I first contracted my incurable wanderlust, the symptoms of which seem to get worse by the year.

In the September of the year of my O-levels it was decided that a quick German refresher course was needed, partly because I was to be examined in that subject at the end of the year, but also because it was quite possible that I was about to render my family responsible for involuntary homicide. Why this should have been the case, why I was as I was at that age, I have spent the best part of the rest of my life trying to understand. My mother reached for the telephone and rang the Von Immernackts. Unhappily, it transpired that Frau von Immernackt was unwell – perhaps suffering from sunlamp irradiation. In any case, the prospect of me hoving over the horizon was clearly too much for her in her weakened state. Sadly, the exchange would not be able to take place that year – perhaps I would like to go and stay with the village vicar's son?

After peace was eventually restored to our home, various household items repaired or replaced and I was finally allowed back out of my room, my parents agreed that they would see if they could find an alternative.

Within a matter of days, through some invisible connection, my mother had made a new contact.

'What about Austria?'

'Dunno.'

'You'll be able to go skiing if you go over Christmas!'

Huh, a reason not to get me any presents I supposed.

'Whatever . . .'

And so it had begun. My first visit to Austria.

Skiing, sun, snow and, yes – now, as Guy and I zoomed

on closer to our destination, my whole being seemed to flip itself up and around and about and inside and out – of course, Susannah.

Further reminiscences were suddenly jolted out of me as Guy took another rather wild pull at the steering wheel. Due to his great enthusiasm he had reduced a journey that should, I felt, have lasted at least a couple of days, to a matter of a few hours. Before long, and after only a handful of near-death experiences, we found ourselves crossing the arching bridge at the end of Lake Geneva from where, for the first time, we could see the crests of the foothills of the mountains. Sunlight lit them invitingly and burst into a spectrum of colours where it fell across the fine spray of the giant jet of water that fountains from the middle of the lake. Perhaps because this was only our first view of the mountains, or perhaps because of the charioteering driving style of my chauffeur, I had, as yet, had no time to think of anything but self-preservation. It was only now that I sensed the thrill of imminent arrival. Within an hour, according to Guy, we would be arriving in the village. No rush, I told him as we left the city and found ourselves remarkably quickly on a winding mountain pass. Dark-grey granite cliffs on either side had been carved into by a turquoise-blue mountain stream that tumbled down along the side of the road whose course had no choice but to follow the natural terrain. Huge pine trees, hanging, it seemed impossibly, from the steep slopes, cast their final shadows across our path. Before long it was dark enough for Guy to turn on a pair of huge rally spotlights which, I was relieved to note, did not seem to draw out of him any further competitive streak. Sadly the same could not be said for the other would-be skiers who, despite the fact that their cars were at least as loaded down with equipment and bodies as ours was, were clearly in a hurry to reach their destinations. There was no shortage of buses, minivans and lorries roaring down the mountain to increase their excitement as they overtook us preferably on a blind corner or a hairpin bend. This time the hooting of horns did not appear to be a demonstration of annoyance, but rather an expression of the exhilarating driving conditions. Even Guy looked quite impressed.

Just as it became fully dark we arrived in the small town of Issy, where the lights of the shops and cafés were beginning to twinkle. Driving down the main street we arrived at a T-junction. To the right was signed: *L'Abbas 8 km, Mont St Bernard 5 km.* Slowly we climbed the relatively straight stretch of road, the car's headlights glinting off numerous billboards advertising a variety of accommodation and, almost without exception, depicting people young and old having tremendously good fun on acres of perfect snow. It was only then that it dawned on me that so far the only place any snow had been seen was on these hoardings, and I was reminded of the many times when I had headed up into one corner of the mountains or other with my heart in my mouth at the prospect of arriving in a ski resort devoid of its most important ingredient. To date, luckily, I had never been disappointed and Jimmy, who was already living there, had assured me that one of the major attractions of Mont St Bernard was that it was without fail covered in 'shedloads of the white stuff'. I remained on tenterhooks, however, as past travel experiences had sadly taught me that I have the strange capacity of arriving in places where, for the first time ever in living memory, things are not following their normal course.

Guy, despite being younger and altogether more optimistic about life than me, had also noticed that we were looking at a distinctly less than wintery wonderland. As we pulled out onto a small wooded plain, he muttered under his breath rather colourfully what he would be doing to the unfortunate Jimmy if the skiing conditions were not what they might be. Poor Jimmy, I thought. He had never pretended to have any godlike qualities – in fact, rather the opposite – he was most distinctly human.

Below us now, as we came round the final bend, laid out like a matchstick model, was the mountain village and ski resort of Mont St Bernard. In his description of the place Jimmy had been nothing less than accurate. It was charming.

One of the big complaints about French ski resorts, made particularly by people who do not necessarily go skiing just to go skiing – that is to say those who are just as interested in what happens off the piste as they are in what happens on it – is that many of the buildings of the more modern ski stations are hideous. When skiing as a pastime moved from the eccentric to the public domain and there was a vast expansion of interest in the 1960s, a number of mountain valleys that had hitherto been troubled by little more than passing goatherds found themselves transformed into mini housing estates. Whilst a great deal of care and attention was paid to opening up as many ski runs and lifts as possible, next to none was paid to the architecture of these new holiday destinations. Consequently some of the most famous resorts in France resemble the film set of a Marseille gangster movie complete with concrete tower blocks and lots of metal shutters.

Mont St Bernard had, on the other hand, never been designed with skiing in mind. Since the establishment of the hamlet in the seventeenth century it had been little more than a collection of wooden farmers' chalets, which had only played host, until the 1930s, to itinerant sheep herders, priests and contrabandists. Today, we could see that although it had been much enlarged it still retained its original character.

Around a small white stone church, with a strangely Eastern domed roof, were grouped a number of fairly large two- and three-storey Alpine hotels, and stretching away down the two parallel main streets were beautifully constructed log cabins with long sloping roofs and intricately carved balconies. Smoke twisted up from chimneys, the only stone part of these constructions. The scene was as peaceful as a Christmas crib. For the time being.

We pulled up in the main car park outside the oddly out of place neoclassical town hall and stretched cramped, and in my case slightly shaky, legs. Guy called Jimmy on his mobile – a brief conversation that involved the use of 'dude' seemingly every other word.

'Okay dude, he's going to be here in a minute – he's just coming down from his place. He's on his way to work. Says why don't we just go along with him and he can sort us out with somewhere to stay afterwards.'

Knowing Jimmy of old, I hoped he was going to be reasonably prompt – it not being one of his most prominent characteristics – as it was noticeably colder at this altitude. My breath misted in the evening air and, leaning back against the car, I watched it disappear upwards towards a clouding sky.

Outside a small pizza restaurant, a man dressed in full chef's whites was cooking crêpes, diaphanous and some eighteen inches in diameter, on a flat metal skillet. A gaggle of small children, all dressed in matching pneumatic ski suits, stood beside him as he expertly spread the pale yellow batter in wider and wider circles. I queued up and finally ordered one for me and one for Guy, who was industriously checking over his beloved vehicle. Warming my hands by the hot plates, I realised that I was enjoying the whole performance just as much as the youngsters.

As I looked on, I was suddenly surprised by how thrilled

I was to be here, as thrilled as I had been on my first visit to the mountains.

'Skiing will be great fun, you'll see, William,' my mother had said.

'Don't care . . .'

My parents, being sensible people, took me at my word and tickets were soon booked.

Secretly, as the day approached, I became increasingly excited by the prospect of this, my longest trans-European trip. I naturally kept this eagerness carefully disguised behind an impressive façade of scowls and grunts, even though in a back corner of the school library I had pored over the narrow concentric rings that fell over the Austrian Alps, imagining what real mountains might be like. *A Beginner's Guide to Skiing* was covertly perused in my bedroom, some of the more seemly material that had been read there for some time. I practised some of the poses as depicted in the black and white drawings of bearded skiers, and even launched myself like an Olympic ski-jumper from my desk, body straight like an arrow, until I hit my bed. Once recovered, I greeted the adulation of an imaginary crowd by punching the air and holding my golden statuette aloft. Then it was time for supper.

Eventually, the end of the autumn term arrived and after my parents had negotiated the triennial stand-off about my school report and what had been said at the parents and teachers meeting – I could normally tell how things had gone by how hard my dad slammed the car door on their return – it was time to pack.

I learnt that the family with whom I was to be staying ran a small block of apartments in a little ski resort near Salzburg. They had recently played host to a distant relative of mine who had been receiving treatment to some failing part of themselves and with whom they had struck up friendly relations. They had one son called Günter, who had been asked to join the Austrian Ski School and wanted to become a doctor. I, on the other hand, was having the utmost trouble hanging on in my present school. I was also utterly bereft of any idea of what I might like to do after I, voluntarily or otherwise, left full-time education. As a result I had already built up something of a sketchy dislike for this goody-goody Günter. No doubt I would be able to cope with him with cool Anglo-Saxon disdain and a couple of German one-liners. Hans Detlof had had a pretty impressive stock of these – a number of which I had noted down with surprising application. Most involved references to the profession of the victim's mother or their resemblance to parts of their own or others' anatomies.

Actually I was, at the age of fourteen going on fifteen, acutely nervous and insecure; I was just exceedingly good at covering it up, or at least so I thought. Kissing my mum goodbye on the platform at Victoria late one evening, I boarded the night train for Paris with a small suitcase, presents for my hosts, some of my favourite sandwiches and a handsome and undeserved amount of pocket money from my dad in my new wallet.

This was the old way to get across Europe: the train and then the midnight ferry-crossing from Portsmouth, with miles to walk from the train station to the boat, which was unfathomably awful once boarded. The unreasonably uncomfortable armchairs were more often than not abandoned in favour of the rear of the luggage racks, where I protected myself from the idly tossed bag by trying to sleep underneath someone's rucksack. Before we had even cleared English waters, the reek of vomit from the last set of inbound passengers had been masked by that of those heading for the French coast. Normally, I managed to hook up with some older teenagers setting off with their Eurorail passes secreted about their persons. Although I sounded as if I was about ten years old and looked not a great deal more mature than that, I was a little better travelled than most of them. Not that we weren't all pretty much scared witless most of the time. The difference was that they had beer and I had a thermos of orange squash. On occasion, I would convince a seedy-looking girl somewhere off the Isle of Wight to swap some of my barley water for a small can of Watney's Pale Ale. Quite often she looked surprisingly relieved.

Paris is full of long, grey shaking shadows at five o'clock in the morning, and alive with rats, junkies, prostitutes and thieves – all grey too – a negative of the colour and vibrancy of the streets and boulevards in the daytime. For a fifteen-year-old it was very scary.

Never have I clutched things so tightly. Not daring to stare, but snatching quick glances nonetheless, it was also extremely exciting. In the streets of Paris somewhere near the Gare de Lyon, in the early hours of the morning having missed my train, I smoked my first filterless Gitanes, drank my first slug of red wine from a plastic bottle and, coughing and spluttering, tried to catch a few hours' sleep in a smelly doorway, holding onto my backpack like it was the rock of Gibraltar.

As luck would have it, all my connections were easy on the way down to Austria. There were quite a number, and I got a little thrill from changing a pound in each different country and minutely inspecting each coin and note that I received, wondering what the strangely moustachioed men and the women with aprons and metal-rimmed spectacles might have done for the betterment of their compatriots to have their faces portrayed on the Lire, Franc, Deutschmark and Schilling notes that I tucked away in my shiny, stiff wallet.

When finally the train from Italy arrived in the mountains and valleys of Austria, and the rails and then the trains themselves became narrower and narrower, I gasped and pointed and snapped with my cheap Kodak camera in a totally uncool way. Yeah, but I didn't care because they were so astonishingly MASSIVE and so amazingly BIG, and anyway I didn't know any of the other equally excited tourists, so for once I didn't mind what they thought of me. It wasn't just the size of the mountains though – I was completely bowled over by how remote they appeared. How untouchable they seemed, how unmarked, how unbesmirched – this a word I had learned in English with that Mr Whatever. Puffs of cumulus nimbus (a term gleaned from Miss Thingy who taught me geography and who, being the only female teacher at school, was FIT) around the peaks of these gigantic rocks proved to me not how low the clouds might be but how mighty these mountains were. If anyone sitting on the beige leatherette bench seat next to me in the little clunking toy train had pointed out of the narrow, open, sliding window up into the sky and told me that before a week was out I would be up there as high as those clouds, I would have laughed a short sardonic laugh – a sort of 'Yeah, right' kind of laugh. In the event, a week later, looking down from above, laughing in any manner whatsoever was the very last thing on my mind.

Soon the train was clickety-clacking its way out of Salzburg station and the conductor, dressed in an ornate brocade and black uniform with a hat that barely fitted through the folding doors between compartments, made an announcement from the Bakelite phone at the end of the carriage. Despite his large moustaches and his sing-songy Austrian accent, I managed to decipher that he was welcoming us aboard. This struck me as strange as I had now been on a train for so long that I struggled to remember a life outside the European railway network, but it was a nice friendly greeting for the Salzburgers who had climbed on board loaded down with huge wicker baskets and hampers, which all seemed to contain quantities of teatime refreshments. Before long, I found myself being offered a huge slice of cake that tasted of what I have subsequently realised was caraway seed. I didn't like it much, but it was nice to feel included by these merry-makers.

Where are you off to, they asked. Where are you from? Are you going skiing? Have you been before?

I did my best to field these kindly questions.

'I am going to Gastein,' I replied.

'Oh yes, where in Gasteinerland?'

'Well, just Gastein.'

'But that is the area – Gasteinerland. Which station? Badgastein? Bad Hofgastein? Dorfgastein? Sportgastein?'

'I don't know.'

'Perhaps you should go to Dorfgastein,' said one.

'Perhaps Bad Hofgastein,' suggested another.

Oh, no.

Looking out of the train window, I realised as I caught sight of my pale reflection against the gathering gloom outside that this was my worst nightmare. I always checked I was on the right train. This was the right train; I just didn't know where to get off. Shading my face from the other passengers I stared a little more intently at myself and tried to feel a bit more grown up.

'Right,' I said to the compartment and to no one in par- ticular. 'So which is the station in the middle?'

Bad Hofgastein.

OK, cool, Bad Hofgastein it was going to be. It would probably be the right one, and if no one was there I would just ring their house. I had the number. Closing my eyes I practised a few phrases in my head and wondered whether I should adopt a tone of mild outrage at being kept waiting or whether I should say how terribly sorry I was that I had buggered up – *einen Fehler gemacht*. That cheered me up a bit.

Until I remembered that they probably wouldn't be at home as they would have already left to come and meet me at some or other unidentified station.

When, eventually, the train pulled into Bad Hofgastein station, I should have been bowled over by the picturesque scene: the quaint railway building, the snowflakes and the steam of a Frankfurter stall caught in the lamplight. Instead, I was just panic-stricken as I disembarked with hordes of Austrians returning home for the festive break.

'*Viel Glück!*' called the cake eaters, who were travelling further down the line, and they raised their plastic cups of warming *Glühwein*, the German version of *vin chaud* – mulled wine – as they pulled away with a crackle of sparks from the overhead cables.

When all the kissing and hugging had stopped and my fellow disembarkees had wandered off with their elated friends and relations, I was left alone, quite alone, apart from the rather apologetic stationmaster who was packing his briefcase for home. I approached the antiquated public telephone and, fumbling for the correct change, tried not to cry.

I was summoned back to the present reality of Mont St Bernard by the *crêpier* proffering my order in two paper wraps with a cheerful smile. Narrowly avoiding being run over by a small tourist train that seemed to chug in perpetual circles around the centre of the village, I tried to lick hot runny chocolate from my wrist before it trickled down the sleeve of my new ski jacket. Just as Guy and I were finishing off the last sweet mouthfuls and licking our fingers, the diminutive but jaunty figure of Jimmy appeared from a side street.

'Oh *man*, so good to see you. How are you doing, dude?'
He grabbed me in a Paddington Bear hug and slapped me
forthrightly on the back. 'Yeah, yeah, yeah, yeah. This is so
cool!' His wholehearted enthusiasm made me smile almost
as much as his wispy attempt at a beard and the trendily
crumpled and slightly stained jeans that appeared to be
attached to his person somewhere just above his knees.
Despite the coldness of the evening, he was only wearing
a T-shirt advertising motor oil and a baseball cap upon
which was perched a small black woollen hat normally
favoured by safe breakers.

'Did Guy tell you? I've got to go to work now – just over
in that bar over there, yeah? You guys can have a few beers
and then, after I'm done, you can come back and kip at my
place. Yeah? It's cool, loads of people are going to be staying
there.'

'So what have you got then? Some sort of chalet?' Guy
asked, intrigued, understandably so as he was planning to
share it with Jimmy and find himself some seasonal work.

'Well, not exactly a chalet, no . . .' Jimmy smiled. 'But you
know, it's pretty cool. Just leave your stuff in the car, it'll all
be fine,' he added with his normal cheerful optimism.

Guy looked a little nervous about leaving his gear on top
of his car, but such was Jimmy's enthusiasm that he
shrugged and followed us. I didn't really have very much
to lose apart from a woolly jumper that I was not particularly fond of – oh, and the bottom half of my new ski suit,
but if the average thief in Mont St Bernard was as fashion-
sensitive as these guys then I thought it unlikely that they
would take a fancy to them.

We made our way across the little square, for the first time
taking in the pretty decorated windows and the warm, attractive interiors, and then threaded our way between some metal
tables and chairs that were laid out in front of the Café de

la Poste, Jimmy's place of work. It was still early and the café, a wide deep room with a low vaulted ceiling, was all but empty. A long metal-topped bar at the far end was lined with enamel and brass beer taps, and behind these was a great wall of patterned glass and shelving on which stood dozens, no, hundreds, of different shaped bottles filled with every conceivable colour of liquid. The main room was furnished with small round wooden tables and chairs interspersed by much taller round counters at which customers could stand and drink, helping themselves from small bowls of peanuts and olives that were already laid out.

A number of Jimmy's colleagues, dressed much as he was in jeans and T-shirts – a kind of unofficial uniform – were busy polishing glasses and wiping down surfaces, sweeping the floor and spinning beer mats out onto the tables.

Imposing behind the bar, his knuckles resting on *le zinc*, stood a large, middle-aged man with a greying crew-cut and enormous, well-manicured, up-turning, dark-black moustaches. His ruby complexion had been provided as much by the products that he purveyed as by the years spent in the mountains. He remained quite impassive as the three of us approached the bar and, even after he had been cheerfully introduced as '*mon patron*, Gaston' by Jimmy and had grasped and wrung our hands, remained splendidly indifferent to our arrival.

Despite the fact that Guy and I, as we discussed later, found him distinctly scary on first meeting, we had to suppress our giggles when we first heard Gaston and Jimmy communicate. Gaston, it became clear, spoke next to no English, and Jimmy's French was blushingly hopeless. As I had taught French for years, I winced at his efforts. My embarrassment was only slightly relieved by remembering that I had not taught his class.

Most of the time employer and employee hoped to get their respective messages across by pronouncing words in their own language with the accent that they believed to be of the other. Were this system not effective, they would then slip into a combination of mime, gesture and, more often than not, simple linguistic invention. They just made words up. Gaston also seemed to think it effective to take swipes at his staff – not ever, I believe, with the real intention of connecting, but rather because he seemed to think it might reinforce whatever instruction he was trying to deliver. So it was that most of the barmen and women of the Café de la Poste spent their working hours ducking, side-stepping and weaving about.

Somewhat alarmed to discover that Jimmy's shift did not finish until two o'clock in the morning, some eight hours away, for the umpteenth time in my life I resolved to pace myself. Our first drinks were free, a welcoming gesture from Jimmy that was greeted with an inscrutable shrug from Gaston.

Guy and I made our way for the first but, I knew then, definitely not the last time, to some seats at the window. From here we could see the evening crowds beginning to mingle in the narrow street. Just as we were about to wish each other good health, out of the corner of my eye I glimpsed the first white snowflake float down, like a baby goose feather.

'Gonna be one and a half tonight up top,' announced one of the barmaids, who had a ring through her nose to which you could have moored a small rowing boat. 'Going to be totally awesome tomorrow.'

'Cool, cool,' Guy enthused.

'Cool, cool,' I enjoined dutifully, and then looked back out of the window rather mystified. For a long while nothing more was said. Falling snow must surely be one of the most entrancing sights that the natural world has to offer.

Once in my teaching life, two boys, both adopted, one from the Congo and the other from Mali, had arrived in England at the beginning of one winter term. There was obviously a great deal for them to learn, a great deal to which they needed to adjust. It could have been a difficult time for them but pleasingly, with a resilience perhaps borne from earlier experience, they took everything in their stride, until one day during morning break it began to snow. Both boys skidded to a halt in the playground where a rough and tumble football match had been charging to and fro. They stood motionless, arms outstretched, like two beatific statues, allowing the flakes to land on their hands and on their heads, on their shoulders and, with a slight squint, on their noses and the tips of their tongues. When the bell rang the other boys and girls raced to scoop up balls and bags and headed towards their respective classes, but these two, their faces raised to the sky, did not budge. Watching them from my classroom, I smiled, recalling my own first experiences of snowfall and let them be. Normally they would have been coming to my French class, but this occurrence was clearly far more magical than anything that might take place in my lesson.

Eventually my attention was drawn away from the view from the window at the Café de la Poste and back to the increasingly steamy atmosphere at the bar. Here Jimmy was dispensing a pharmacist's variety of concoctions, whirling bottles, glasses, ice and shakers like a circus juggler before, whistling cheerily, he manipulated the levers, switches and valves of the coughing coffee machine like an old-fashioned engine driver. This particular drink only appeared to be dispensed to customers no longer capable of consuming anything else on offer. Come midnight this certainly represented the greater proportion of the population of the pub.

To date 'the punters', those people who had decided to

stump up their hard-earned cash to be given a good time in the mountains, had not yet turned up in any great numbers, it being early in the season. Instead, the assorted ski reps, shop and hotel owners, chalet girls, ski technicians (known to the wider world as ski bums), lift operators, restaurateurs, cooks, barmen, waiters and waitresses, and of course the mighty piste-bashers, all English and French in equal number, had congregated in the bar to make the most of the calm before the storm.

The talk was mainly of what had happened over the course of the summer: the trips taken, and the new, cool places discovered. Experiences were shared, gossip gossiped and bitching bitched as all these men and women, young and youngish *saisonniers* – seasonal workers who travelled from snow to sea and back again every year – took pleasure in catching up with old friends for the new season. Of course, there was always a section of the community who said that this was going to be their last year and that soon they were going to settle down, but if they had already been a *saisonnier* for more than six years nobody believed them and just tried to get them to buy the next round.

With a certain degree of embarrassment, I am forced to admit that I am unable to give a clear account of my first evening in Mont St Bernard. Suffice it to say that apart from slight sniggers at a later stage in the evening, caused by my clear inability to strike any ball on the snooker table and my most sincere conviction that there was something wrong with the cue, I came away from the Café de la Poste with my dignity relatively intact. Of course, fresh air can be the making or breaking of a long evening's drinking, but I will never forget discovering, as we stepped through the door, that it was still blizzarding outside and that the snow was already just over knee-deep. Initially, due to my comparative maturity, I decided that I would refrain from kicking it up into the air, but then I thought, stuff it, and ran around like a lunatic. Why not?

'What a dump!' cried Guy joyously, and bundled little Jimmy into a snowdrift.

On arrival at the latter's home, I might have exclaimed much the same thing but with rather less cheer. For we soon discovered that Jimmy did live in a chalet – or, to be more precise, in the garage of a chalet. Once he had swung open the up-and-over metal door we were greeted by a scene before which Hieronymus Bosch would have set up his easel with enthusiasm. Rucksacks, ski boots, ski jackets, salopettes, goggles, gloves, sweet wrappers, loo rolls, pizza boxes, small tin cans, large tin cans, enormous tin cans, makeup, cigarette packets, ashtrays, the contents of ashtrays, some Bolognese sauce, underwear, swimwear and footwear had all been jumbled up in a massive mess and sprinkled liberally over an assortment of unconscious human bodies in various stages of undress and degrees of physical inti-macy.

'Anywhere you like! Oh man, it's just so great to have you here! Yeah, yeah, yeah, cool,' thrilled Jimmy, as he swung the garage door closed and lit a lethal-looking gas fire.

'Great to be here,' I replied with surprising enthusiasm, just as I was realising I had never seen so many socks in my life.

They were everywhere and, after I had found my patch of floor space and closed my eyes, they trampled their malodorous way through my dreams like a thousand marching cartoon characters.

3

Getting Sorted

For a reason quite unknown to me, it has always been the case wherever I have skied that people insist on waking up absurdly early. When at home, I am quite sure that most of them spend the early hours of the morning clinging desperately to their mattresses thinking of every conceivable reason why they need not quite yet get out of bed. Given a bit of altitude, everyone is bouncing around before seven in the morning. As you blunder down the corridor from the bathroom in the vain hope that you may be able to relocate your bed for another few minutes' snooze, people appear in doorways in order to perform inappropriate stretching exercises unsuitably attired, whilst others compare energy bars and discuss carbo-loading and slow-release diets before appearing at breakfast fully kitted out, bobble hats and goggles firmly in place. Where once a bowl of cornflakes and a quick cup of tea would have sufficed, now everyone without exception eats yoghurt and fibre and fruit and whole grains and bran, and maintains that they love it. After a battle to get to the one lavatory with its feeble flush and non-existent ventilation, all and sundry start noisily clomping out in ski boots before coming back three or four times to get bits of forgotten but vital kit. Hurrying voices get shrill and pillows pressed firmly over ears are rarely enough sound-proofing against the levels of excitement. For heaven's sake, the ski lifts won't be open for another hour.

That first morning in Mont St Bernard, however, it is true that I had absolutely no problem whatsoever in rising the moment it was light. I was out of the garage door as soon as I had worked out how to operate its latch and swing it up and over. Once out in the snow I gulped in huge lungfuls of mountain air. Assessing my present state of health, I diagnosed a bad back almost without doubt due to my having slept over the top of my holdall and a terrible giddiness caused by gas poisoning: propane from the heater had combined in a potentially lethal mix with methane supplied by my fellow *garagistes*. My blinding headache could have been put down to any number of different causes, but I strongly suspected something called a Yellow Peril which had involved a Pernod depth charge, one of several fanciful concoctions created and served by Jimmy just *'pour la route'* the night before. Still, things could have been worse and once I had managed to clap a pair of Boots sunglasses to my nose, I began to appreciate the stunning scene in front of me. Snow lay a foot and a half deep on the streets of the village and on the long sloping roofs of the houses. Guy's car had all but disappeared from view. On either side of the village I could see where the ski pistes threaded their way through the thick white pines in great swooping curves. In contrast the black parallel lines of the chair-lift cables ran straight up to the summits of the mountain crests from the very centre of the village. A gentle breath of wind blew little eddies of snow round the feet of the few other early risers, who seemed for the main part to be retired ladies in fur coats taking small curly dogs for their morning constitutional.

After slipping and sliding up the small slope from the garage door, I made my way down the high street with as much decorum as I could muster and dived into the first *salon de thé* that I came across. With a smile, the friendly owner plied me with croissants, coffee and some fizzy aspirin until I felt a little better. Thanking her profusely, I realised that it was not only my body that seemed to be operating below par but also my brain. This was almost the first time in the better part of seven years, my travels having not taken me to any Francophone countries, that I had spoken any French. While I did not suffer from any hesitation caused by timidity or embarrassment, what was rather more serious was that I simply could not remember the words. Luckily, like most of us who have learnt a foreign language, I was well practised in delaying tactics, but even I began to think that the amount of *'Bof . . . euh . . . bof . . . vous savez . . . bof . . . hein . . . bof . . .'* was a little excessive. The kindly woman kept smiling and nodding and smiling and nodding and doodling on her order pad with the unmistakable body language that read: 'Could you just bloody get on with it.'

Speaking foreign languages is just like riding a bike: once you get the hang of it you never forget. I am not sure if this is based on any linguistic or scientific fact but it's a comforting belief. I was keeping everything firmly crossed that I might find the same logic was applicable to skiing. Anyway, there was no particular rush to get involved in all that. After all, I was going to be in Mont St Bernard for ages. No need to dash out there and start zooming around like a madman. Probably spend a few days getting the feel of the place and once I knew my way about . . . well . . . then I could have a think about it.

'Where did you go, man? We've been looking all over for you. Jimmy thought maybe you didn't like staying at his place so you'd legged it. Ha, ha!' Guy was being very loud.

'No, no, no! No, I just thought I would probably have a quick look around. Just suss the place out a bit. You know what I mean, dude?' (It was in that very moment, despite my weakened state, that I made a solemn promise to myself that I would never, ever, as long as I lived employ the word 'dude' again. I am happy, no, proud, to say that so far I have stuck to my word.)

Guy and two matching mates had launched themselves through the door causing a rather startled ringing of the bell that had Madame hurrying nervously from the back kitchen and stopping in her tracks when greeted by three characters she clearly believed were there to do her no good. Once I made it clear to her that they were acquaintances of mine and it was safe to let them enter, she stood back and watched with wide-open eyes as they bounced themselves into three chairs around the sunlit table at which I was sitting.

'By the way, Will, this is Aubrey. You remember him – he was in the bar last night?'

'Yes, er . . . of course, yes.'

'Awright?'

Aubrey stuck out an impressively bejewelled hand and took mine in his before manipulating it in a number of weird and wonderful directions, which at one point made me wonder whether double-jointedness might be required, before hooking his thumb around mine and floating our two hands down to the table like a butterfly. It was really very strange.

'Hi, Aubrey.'

It was a bit unfair of Guy to have expected me to recognise any particular one of his friends as most of them looked exactly the same. Still, he was friendly enough, this Aubrey, despite his patchy facial bristles and an uncomfortable-looking bit of metal sticking out just below his lower lip. Longish hair that he had pulled, patted, pushed and poked at great length until eventually it ended up looking a complete mess could not disguise his friendly smile. Most of the rest of his face was covered by an enormous pair of sunglasses, and so, I discovered, it was to remain, night and day, for much of the rest of the season. Guy and he had been introduced by Jimmy who, after he had removed an elaborate disguise of sunglasses, woolly hat and headphones the size of dustbin lids, revealed himself to be the fourth member of our breakfast party. They all seemed to have rapidly become buddies – friendships no doubt born out of their common interests.

'So are you ready then?' asked Guy, after the three of them had polished off a large pile of pancakes and half a dozen croissants.

'Yeah, come on, let's get going,' enjoined Jimmy enthusiastically, happily unaware of the fact that he was now sporting a hot-chocolate moustache rather more impressive than his natural one.

'Get going where?' I asked, stifling a rather childish giggle. He did look very funny. Really I should have told him, but then so should the others who were also smirking in a thoroughly unhip fashion.

'We're going to help you get the rest of your gear. You know, skis and everything. Probably come in quite useful, don't you think?'

Rising above this rather infantile sarcasm, I paid the bill, dragged my new jacket back on and attempted to do up at least some of the fastenings.

Once back outside in the snow, Aubrey bid us farewell, or at least grunted, 'Cheers then boys, later kids, yeah?' and made his way down the main street with a gait more suited to a Milan catwalk. As he went, apparently to start up the kitchens of the chalet where he was resident chef, he fired a few peculiar but not particularly vulgar hand gestures at passers-by – no matter that they were complete strangers. As he rounded the corner scratching imaginary records in the air, Guy sighed with admiration.

'What a dude!' he breathed, before turning his attention back to my equipment problems. 'Okay dude, sir, let's get you sorted out.'

'So what makes you guys think you're the experts? Who do you think you are? Franz Klammer and Jean-Claude Killy?'

'Who?'

My rapier wit felt somewhat blunted.

'Come on. We haven't got all day and it'll probably be getting busy in there right now.'

Although I was rather under the impression that we did have all day, if not all week, if not until somewhere around about Christmas, I allowed myself, as usual, to be swept along by other people's enthusiasm. As we crunched through the snow, the real snow, I remembered from our shared car journey the importance that Guy gave to the sartorial side of skiing. Now we found ourselves gazing into the window of one of the many ski outfitters whose shops took up the ground floors of a number of the larger chalets in the middle of the village.

'This is the one that Aubrey was talking about,' confirmed Guy, taking a step back and looking at the name over the door. 'Yeah, this is the one. Chez Guinbert. It sounds like they've got the best stuff in town. All the latest makes. Aubrey says that the bloke who owns it is the mayor of the village and his brother owns all the big hotels in Mont St Bernard. It seems like the bloke's son must be a half-decent skier because he's been picked not just for the French ski team in his age group but also the snowboarding team. Yeah, I bet he must be pretty good.'

'Probably a tosser,' opined Jimmy, and we cheerfully agreed.

'But apparently his sister's a stunner,' Guy added, as an afterthought, and we pondered this point in silence as he pushed open the door with a jangle of cow bells. Kicking our boots against the outside wall to dislodge thick cakes of snow we stepped inside.

'Jeez, look at some of the shit they've got in here. Hey Guy, have a look at these 120s. Pretty rad, huh? They had these in Snow and Rock before I left. Awesome. You should get some of these, Mr Ran . . . I mean, dude,' Jimmy waxed lyrical. Guy and he went into further raptures about a number of other items, the net result of which was that they suddenly appeared to stop speaking comprehensible English. Leaving them to it, I had a wander around the shop.

In the eight years that I had not been skiing the equipment seemed to have changed out of all recognition. Once the length of skis went some way to denote how good a skier you were, and I remember having yearned for a pair two metres long – almost a rite of passage into adulthood for a boy skier. Despite the fact they were an absolute pain to carry around, weighed a ton, caused no end of hassle with other skiers in cable cars and were extremely ungainly once attached to your feet, I could have kissed the first pair that I ever received. Somehow they were proof that, in the eyes of snowbound society at least, you were deemed to have reached some level of admirable competence. Although, in my case, this was in no way borne out by my performance on the piste. Now, though, it seemed that the shorter your skis were, the more likely you would be able to impress on the slopes. It did seem very unfair, though, that the prices had increased in inverse proportion to the skis having shrunk. As usual, I hunted round for a bargain.

Seated behind the counter was a girl in her early twenties dressed in a red, white and blue ski suit. She was breathtakingly pretty. She smiled at me; she was just about to talk to me; I was just about to talk to her.

'Can I help you, *monsieur*?' asked a soft voice in French from behind me. Turning around, I found myself looking at some photographs of young men and women skiing dangerously fast and hazardously close to a cliff's edge. Then I realised I was being addressed by a small elderly lady, with a grey bun, sitting in a rocking chair next to the long john rack and grappling with some rather intricate knitting.

'*Euh . . . Bof . . . Oui . . . Bof.*' Eventually I managed to burble the fact that I was interested in buying myself a variety of bits of equipment.

Gloves and a hat were quickly decided upon. Somehow, I couldn't face wearing the stretchy man-made fibre tops that I was informed were *respirable*, but decided nonetheless to buy a couple of pairs of long johns as the old lady told me it would most certainly be very cold in December and January. Very good quality, she explained to me, grabbing the waistband and the crotch and pulling rather violently in opposite directions. Right, good. I'll take them. Now, I also need some boots and skis.

'Oh, for that you will have to speak with my grandson, Nicolas. He does all the fittings. It is his speciality. That is him in the picture you can see. *Nicolas, viens voir!*'

Over the counter were a number of photographs of people achieving Alpine greatness in what appeared to be a plethora of different disciplines. The particular photograph that she had pointed out showed a young man wearing a helmet and dressed in an extremely professional-looking ski suit wielding aloft an enormous silver cup that seemed to be almost the same size as he was.

This we soon discovered was not the optical illusion it at first seemed to be. After a few moments – Madame having rung a bell hidden under the counter – a secret door on the wall, which had at first appeared to be a large poster, opened up and the young guy in the picture stepped out. Not all mountain men were six foot six it appeared. Indeed Nicolas appeared to be closer to five foot five. *Le petit Nicolas* in fact.

His diminutive size seemed to have done nothing to dull his natural cheerfulness. With a smile he made his way to the racks of skis and asked me, in French, what it was that I required. Only then did I realise that I wasn't at all sure. It clearly was not as simple as buying one pair of boots and one pair of skis. Turning to Guy and Jimmy for their expert advice, which they had in no way been shy about proffering earlier, I now found them looking grumpy at the other end of the shop. They could not help themselves glancing up at the numerous photographs of the trophy-toting young man and back at his physical embodiment standing behind a selection of different boots. They obviously hated him.

So it was that I put myself in the hands of the ski champ.

'Now, Nicolas, I do want to buy some boots and I do want to buy some skis. But what I don't really want to do is spend a lot of money.' I smiled at him complicitly, and he smiled back at me with a slight frown.

'But you must get the best thing for the job, *monsieur*,' he replied. 'What kind of skiing will you be doing?'

'What kind?'

How many kinds were there?

'Well, just downhill, I guess.'

Nicolas smilingly categorised me as a joker, wandered off and came back a few minutes later with a number of large cardboard boxes of boots. After a little grunting and

puffing, I eventually managed to strap myself into a rather
fancy black and silver pair. After all the hassle it had been
getting into the blasted things, I toyed with the idea of
leaving them on, possibly for the rest of the season. Now
they were on they were really quite comfortable. Expensive
but comfortable.

'Now, what about some skis?' I lowered my voice lest
the other two should hear me and whispered, 'Cheap skis,
you know, *pas cher*!'

Nicolas didn't look terribly impressed, but he did admit
that they had some second-hand ones left over from last
season. 'You know the ones people sell back to the shop if
they get injured pretty badly. No more skiing for them.'

'Right . . . I see. Well, can I have a look at some anyway?'

Much the cheapest was a broad orange pair by a manu-
facturer that I was pretty sure I had heard of.

'What about these then? They look pretty good. They
would be okay, wouldn't they?'

'Oh, these are freestyle skis. For doing the tricks. You see,
they have this double lip.'

I had been planning to ask him why it was that this
particular pair seemed to have turned-up tips not just at
the front but also at the back.

'So what is that for, then?'

'Oh, of course, that is so that you can ski backward in
the same way as you can ski forward.'

'Ski backward? Why on earth would anybody want to
ski backward?'

'Oh, because if you have these skis you are freestyle.'

'Oh, is that right . . .'

Finally, based entirely on financial rather than stylistic
criteria, I decided to buy them. They were quite a nice
colour anyway. When I had paid the heart-sinking bill, and
Nicolas had put everything together and tested the strength

of the binding release on the skis, Guy and Jimmy finally deigned to come over, with only the curtest of nods in his direction, and helped me scoop up my various packages.

Only once we had got out were they able to express their opinion about what I had bought. But not before they had delivered their opinion on another aspect of the shop that they had noticed.

'Cor, sir . . .' Guy sometimes lets his otherwise implacable coolness slip in moments of high excitement. 'Did you see that guy's sister? She was totally fit. And I mean totally.'

'Yeah, she was awesome, sir,' added Jimmy unconsciously, his goatee wiggling with excitement.

After a few minutes they managed to regain their composure and turned their semi-professional eyes to my purchases.

'Bionic 270XS, last year's colour but good condition. Excellent binding. Second-hand, only about two weeks' use. What did you pay for them then? Jimmy cast his expert eye down the line of my skis. 'I would reckon about four hundred Euros.'

'Three hundred and fifty Euros.'

'Bargain, mate. But you never said . . . I didn't know . . . Had no idea you were up for pulling a few tricks.'

'Yeah,' continued Guy, 'you never said you were a freestyler.'

'Didn't I?' I mumbled, as I wiggled my fingers in my new gloves. 'Yeah, well, you know . . .' Play it cool, I thought.

Why not?

All that I needed now in order to be 'fully kitted out' was a ski pass. Anybody who was proposing to work through the course of the season could apply for a *saisonnier* pass, which was significantly cheaper than the normal tariff. Guy and Jimmy had every intention of applying for one and, not wanting to waste any time, had obtained what appeared to be a photocopied letter from Gaston suggesting that he would have some employment for them in the near future. 'You should get one too you know, it's a hell of a lot cheaper and you never know you might well be doing some work while you're here.'

After what I had just spent at the ski shop, I had every intention of looking out the Mont St Bernard Job Centre at the earliest opportunity but, sadly, for the time being I had no way at all of proving my intended industriousness.

'You're bound to be able to blag it,' laughed Guy, and Jimmy nodded in agreement. 'You can speak French so you'll never have any problem, I reckon.'

Leaving the boys to enjoy what they believed to be a well-earned beer, I sought out the ski-pass offices. Shuffling forward in a queue that had swollen in direct proportion to the amount of snow that had fallen the night before, I wasn't sure that I shared their optimism. Still, it was worth a try and it was quite true that I would be there for the remainder of the season.

Having spent quite a lot of time in countries where queuing is not so much a national pastime as a full-time occupation, I no longer suffer from the agitation of waiting. Sliding deeper into my thoughts, I idly investigated my new jacket and had discovered four new pockets by the time I rounded the last corner of the queuing system that had been laid out in the ticket agency. Patience was, unfortunately, not a virtue that had been bestowed in any great measure on the character in the fur coat standing in the queue ahead of me. Ever since she had stepped neatly in front of me as we arrived simultaneously at the end of the queue, she had been huffing and puffing and shaking her wristwatch as she muttered in a none too quiet Anglo-Saxon fashion about what a busy person she was and about how many things were left for her to do before 'my guests arrive'. As she shuffled forward she yanked on a lead to which was attached an off-white toy-poodle-type dog and it scooted along behind her.

When she arrived at the little glass window, she was greeted with a smile and a pleasant '*Bonjour, madame*' by a young student blinking behind his metal-rimmed glasses. Due to the imminent arrival of her guests she clearly had no time for such pleasantries. Instead, she flicked a credit card into the shiny metal bowl and said loudly, probably unnecessarily loudly, 'three ski passes for adults for one week' in English.

Whilst the task requested was performed, she had time to turn and bestow on me a small lipsticked smile and fiddle slightly with her matching fur earmuffs. Probably because of these, she was unable to hear the reply of the student behind the counter. Pointing over her shoulder, I signalled that her attention was required. Reaching into her handbag, also fashioned out of some unknown dead animal, she pulled out a gold pen and as she turned said equally loudly, 'Marvellous, where do I sign?'

'No, *madame*, I am very sorry, but it is not possible. You see each ski pass needs to have the picture of the person on it. So now we have a webcam so we can take pictures of all the skiers and then they go automatically on the pass. So your friends will need to visit us after they arrive.' As he explained, the man, blinking with discomfort in front of this imposing, unkind woman but still desperate to be helpful, wrote the word WEBCAM on a piece of paper in front of her lest she had not managed to understand his explanation.

We were probably all taken aback by the reaction. Pretty soon we realised that the woman in the fur coat didn't give a monkey's about any bloody camera. These people didn't have time to mess around coming into some sort of grotty office. They were only here for a week and they were going to get in as much skiing as was possible. Jesus!

'*Ze meunkey?*'

Very fortunately, the student's pronunciation was not sufficiently Inspector Clouseau-like for me to have a laughing fit, but the fur coat's next outburst was almost enough to have me holding my sides although I'm not sure whether this was because I wanted to laugh or be sick.

'Monkey? I'll give you a bloody monkey. *You* are a bloody monkey. You know that? You are a bloody monkey. Can't you speak any English at all? Isn't that what you're paid for?'

I felt duty-bound to intercede. Battling against natural cowardice, I was just about to suggest that I might act as an interpreter when the woman in the fur coat turned on her heel and strode out of the building, leaving a series of particularly crude expressions hanging in the misty air. As she swung through the automatic glass doors, her pooch lost its footing on the wet-tiled floor and whizzed, legs splayed, in a wide arc on the length of its leash. Unable to stop, it crashed head first into a breeze-block wall. Collectively wincing at the impact, the other onlookers and I gawped in astonishment. We could practically hear the birds tweeting.

Rather than soothe the poor creature, the Fur Coat hoiked it up by its collar, like a dead lamb on a meat hook, and stomped off into the street. Holding out an imperious hand, which caused the tourist train to stop dead on its tracks with a *ding-dong* of its toy bell, she disappeared into the crowd.

When it came to my turn at the counter, it was with a fair degree of embarrassment that I admitted my nationality. Ironically, of course, this unpleasant interlude played in my favour as so flustered was the poor man behind the glass that he did not even for a minute question my eligibility for a season pass. I think he was just relieved that I smiled at him.

Hardly had I the time to grab together all my various pieces of kit and stick my new ski pass in my mouth, for want of anywhere else better to put it, than my companions were urging me back in the direction of Jimmy's garage. This gave me the opportunity to dump any unnecessary paraphernalia, change into my new ski boots and, with a quick glance around at the various piles of clothing and equipment that seemed to be gently moving on their own, realise that despite Jimmy's generosity it was high time for me to find somewhere else to stay. Without wishing to offend my host, I still thought it sensible to mention the idea to him at this early stage and so I muttered something about not wishing to outstay my welcome or cramp his style. Whatever, whatever, yeah whatever, man, was his considered response, but he must have absorbed the information through his headphones because when a matter of minutes later we found ourselves in the queue for a six-seater chairlift, he hailed Aubrey who had just thundered down the slope behind us on a snowboard.

Technology had advanced since my last trip on one of these chair-lift contraptions and it was now no longer necessary to put your ski pass into a machine. Instead it was automatically read electronically through my pocket as I approached the turnstile, which then turned in a most welcoming manner. This was a vast improvement on the days of having to fumble for the pass attached to a piece of elastic around my neck and stick it in the slot whilst I dropped my gloves. Without fail, as I reached down to pick them up, the plastic card would be released to spring back and cut my chin with one of its sharp edges. So delighted was I on this occasion that I had escaped physical injury, I dropped my gloves anyway, but after only the most minor of kerfuffles I managed to catch up with the others.

Aubrey, punching my hand with his gloved fist, smiled at me, his lip stud wiggling, and drawled, 'Yeah, probably be able to sort you out, mate, no worries, easy!'

'Oh, great. Thanks, mate,' I mumbled but before I had time to discover what it was that he was going to sort out the herd of skiers moved on.

Shuffling along with the others, I reached the line at which to stop and wait to be collected by the chair-lift. As I did, I noticed a group of small boys and girls, perhaps nine or ten years old, arriving from some distance to queue up behind us. Like all youngsters born on skis they were amazingly agile; using their skis like skates for extra speed, they slid through the ticket barriers almost without slowing. For some reason they seemed very keen to catch us up. Then I realised that it was something about me that had caught their eye.

Why me?

Having heard me speak in English, they naturally presumed that I spoke no French and made no effort to conceal their conversation.

'Look at those skis he's got, the tall blond guy,' said one.

'Where?'

'Over there, at the lift. The one who hasn't got much hair.'

'Wow, amazing. Those are definitely the best you can get if you want to do tricks and stuff.'

'Look at that ski outfit he's got. What make do you reckon that is?'

'*J' sais pas.* Dunno. Doesn't seem to have a label on it. Maybe he got it custom-made.'

'Yeah, maybe, let's keep up with him. He'll probably do some stunts that we can try and copy.'

'You reckon he can do a 720?'

'Maybe, but he does look a bit old.'

'Follow him anyway? *D'accord?*'

'*D'accord!*' they chorused.

Pulling the safety bar down over my head and donning my new woolly hat, I very much hoped I was right about my 'riding a bike' theory.

As we were swept up and away, I felt the light wind whisk across my face. Before long the landscape opened up below us and brought to mind my first arrival in the mountains.

4

Slip-sliding Away

When, then, back in Badhofgastein, I had realized that I had clearly got out at the wrong train station and had eventually worked out how to operate the public telephone, I discovered, as I had feared, that there was nobody at home as the entire family had left the house to come out to meet me. Rightly guessing that I had got out of the train too soon rather than too late, my host family had followed the railway track back up the valley, calling in at each station as they did so. Two stops up the line, they found me feeling chilly and rather sorry for myself, but fortunately no longer tearful. Bundling me up with comforting words they drove me back home. Such was the kind and attentive nature of the Sumann family that I very quickly forgot my woes and promptly fell in love with Austrian *Gemütlichkeit* – a word summoning up a warmth and welcome and general well-being that is difficult to translate into English. Günter's father was a jolly, moustachioed man who worked as a physiotherapist at the hospital and was consequently very rarely left twiddling his own thumbs, and who also volunteered for the mountain rescue team. His mother managed the home, which included two holiday flats. They were both extraordinarily attentive to my comfort and happiness, for which, after a lapse of more than twenty years, I must now thank them.

Günter, although almost exactly my age, was considerably more grown-up than I and when we practised shaving in the mirror of the bathroom that we shared, it was actually worth his while taking the plastic safety cover off his razor. Without a second thought, he happily lent me all his spare and outgrown equipment, and took great pride in selecting for me just the right pair of skis from the extensive collection that the Sumann family kept in the cellar.

He was an outstandingly fine skier, and as he spent the summer months mountain climbing he was also staggeringly fit. His winter holiday was partly filled by a training programme for the Austrian Ski School, and the family decided that, as a complete beginner, it would be a good idea for me to take some lessons for the first week of my stay. So it was that when my morning lessons and his training were finished, we would meet in the village at lunchtime and go home for *Germknödel*-eating competitions before setting out again.

Germknödel, it must now be said, are a creation of which the Austrian people should truly be proud. Huge dumplings the size of small cabbages, they are filled with a delicious variety of fillings: jam, fruit compote, or – my own personal favourite – cinnamon and sugar. Gently steamed in buttermilk they are a meal in themselves, and although it must be nearly two decades since I last ate one, I remember them with the same fondness as I do the places I have most enjoyed visiting or the most entertaining people I have ever met.

Although I remember my first steps on skis with nothing but great enjoyment, surely of all sports this must be the one that seems to a beginner the hardest to master. First, your feet are locked into boots that allow them next to no movement at all – apart from a little toe wiggling. Then, to hinder your progress further, two long and, at the time of my learning in the early 1980s, heavy planks of wood are clamped to your feet in order to render the most minor motion either to the left or right or indeed backward or forward nigh on impossible. When, finally, you do find yourself vertical and facing in the right direction – which takes some people days, if they have not already given up – you realise that the biggest mistake you can make is to start to move. For once that happens, whatever little control you had over who you were, what you wanted from life and when you wanted it, is no longer in your own hands. Initially, the only way to prevent yourself from running at alarmingly high speed into the inevitably wide range of solid objects ahead of you is to hurl yourself bodily to the ground – a remarkably unnatural thing to want to do.

Skiing is undoubtedly the one sport that can produce more unexpected language from normally perfectly nicely spoken people than any other, and they always remain impressively unapologetic. Somehow it is all par for the course; were that same person to use even a tenth of the same bad language in any other walk of their lives relatives would become strongly concerned about the onset of Tourette's Syndrome. On a ski slope nobody seems to notice, possibly because they too are all swearing themselves into a state of apoplexia.

Suddenly, one day, and there is something almost mystical about this revelation, most people realise how skiing works. As if it were yesterday, I can remember my skinny legs in skin-tight ski trousers, wobbling hopelessly, careering from one crumpled heap to another until suddenly they understood the mechanics of the whole operation and miraculously, yes, *eureka*, I could ski. It is extremely rewarding to finally reach the stage of being able to stay more or less upright. From the moment that you have at least some control about the general direction in which you are heading, progress is very rapid. Although, let's face it, there are plenty of people who never reach this stage, throw their skis in a hedge and go home with the intention of taking all future holidays in Holland.

By the end of the first week in Austria I felt confident enough to accompany Günter and his best buddy Max, another very welcoming boy whom I liked right from the word go, and we sped around the mountains, meeting new friends and learning new tricks. Although, of course, being a teenager, I was studiously careful not to look astonished or amazed by anything that I encountered, I could not help one day but gasp, as from a ten-foot bank on one side of the mountain path along which I was skiing, Günter and Max appeared airborne, silhouetted against the dazzling spotlight of the sun, flew over my head, turned a full circle in the air and landed some twenty or thirty yards further on down the mountain. Luckily, by the time I met them at the bottom of the next lift, I had regained my impassive cool.

Perhaps what does make all the moments of madness in the early days of learning to ski so worthwhile is how incredibly funny human beings can be quite against their will. Without too earnest a consideration of the sadistic side of human nature, surely I'm not the only person who grips their sides and roars with laughter when someone does something that has obviously really hurt? No, I am not.

More positively, learning to ski can do wonders for your self-confidence because, it seems, there is always someone more useless than you – unless of course there isn't. Certainly, Günter was an extremely kind teacher and halfway through my stay I had become a fairly decent skier, had made a whole band of new mates and could even speak semi-reasonable German.

That was before the guests turned up. After that everything changed.

The first two weeks of my visit to Austria had flown by and I had been extremely happy. Christmas was on the horizon and, for the first and last time, I already had in advance a number of wrapped presents – gifts that my mother had tucked into my bag for the family. Part of me thinks that possibly one of them was a pot of Marmite but the rest of me likes to think not.

On the morning of Christmas Eve skiing was cancelled as the house was decorated from top to toe for the celebrations that evening. A real Christmas tree was erected in the sitting-room and duly decorated. The table was laid for the goose that was already roasting slowly in the oven. There were people arriving. I knew that from the number of places laid, but due to a momentary lapse of my language skills I had failed to cotton on to who exactly they were. From what I had gathered they were from Düsseldorf and were here for a holiday but whether they were friends or paying guests I was unsure.

In the middle of the afternoon, just after I had managed to fit in one more Germknödel that, by now, Günter's mother was producing pretty much continuously, his father returned from the train station and I heard the noise of enthusiastic greeting in the hallway. As I emerged from the kitchen, I very, very vaguely recollect noticing a husband and wife in cordial embrace with Günter and his mother. That part of the scene though was blurred and fuzzy at the edges, but crystal clear in the centre was the most beautiful person I had ever seen.

She smiled at me.

Blushing, I did a double-take.

She really did smile at me, I thought as I dashed back into the kitchen and closed the door behind me, my cheeks flushing furiously.

The remains of my Germknödel held no interest for me now.

Günter and Max were in full training for the under-sixteen championships that were taking place just the other side of Salzburg. Initially, at least, I was their keenest supporter. Christmas Eve had been and gone but the festivities had done little to improve my image in the eyes of Susannah – for that was the name of the beautiful German girl from Düsseldorf who had come to stay, and who now occupied ninety-eight per cent of my waking thoughts and a pretty large percentage of my sleeping ones too. Frau Sumann, Günter's mother, had been a wonderful hostess and everything to make the evening celebration go with a swing had been put in place. When we had all appeared at seven o'clock in the main hallway of the small block of flats, Susannah looking stunning in purple leggings, Günter and I had been given the task of opening a number of bottles of raspberry Sekt, an Austrian sparkling wine. Without being given specific instructions to do so we had filled our glasses as regularly as we did those of the other guests. By the time we were ready to sit down at the table I was extremely tipsy, and, in the process of trying to make my way to the table, had got involved in some of the decorations, the net result of which was a loud electrical pop and complete darkness. After Günter's father had reappeared from the cellar with his screwdriver and light had been restored, I was discovered trying to keep myself and the Christmas tree upright. With some sympathy, the general consensus of opinion was that I should go rather prematurely to bed.

Although slightly hazy about the events of the evening

before, I did still realise that I had heaped myself with enough embarrassment to have blown my chances with Susannah, at whom I was trying not to stare absolutely every second I was in her company. Luckily, because she was such a nice girl, she seemed happy enough to be alone with me when, on occasion, we were left to our own devices as the other two boys donned helmets, goggles and body-hugging ski suits for their first practice run.

'Aren't they simply amazing?' sighed Susannah, in a slightly irritating fashion as first Günter and then Max went howling past us. 'Oh, I wish so much that I could ski like that. What do you think, Willy, do you think I could ever ski that fast?'

(Germans always call me Willy but for some reason it does not seem to elicit the same mirth as it does in my home country.)

'Oh, I am sure that you could. I bet you're fantastic. Actually it isn't really as hard as it looks, you know.'

'Oh, are you really good too? Can you ski like that?'

'Well, I'm more into tricks and jumps, and stuff like that.'

'Really, will you show me them some time?'

Damn.

When later the other two guys skied past with the crowd yelling, clamouring and ringing their cowbells, I suddenly realised that after all I actually really rather disliked them.

Of course the day finally came when I could no longer avoid demonstrating my skiing skills to Susannah. Most days she had set off early and skied with her parents, and I had spent much of my time roaming the mountains hoping to come across them. On occasion I had spotted them at a distance but had, at the last minute, never liked to make my presence known for fear that I would be invited to ski with them. The moment that they saw my performance, my claims to be a trick skier of international stature would be undone.

Although I was only staying with the Sumanns for a month, at that age it felt like six times that. Finally, though, my trip neared its end, and at some moment that I did not care to think about, Susannah would be returning to her school in Düsseldorf and I would be returning to mine. Somehow, some time soon, I desperately wanted something to happen. Quite what and how, I had next to no idea. Günter, I had discovered, already had a girlfriend, which, in light of Susannah's undoubted attractiveness, came as no little relief to me. Given his greater maturity, I confided in him. After I had poured my heart out he sat and scratched his head thoughtfully like a renowned psychiatrist – which he has subsequently become – then he stood up and grabbed his jacket.

'What are you doing?' My voice squeaked with alarm but on this occasion I didn't care.

'I am going to tell her how you feel. It is the best way. Then everything is out in the open.'

As insecure as I was, I was not at all sure I wanted everything out in the open. I think he was a little surprised when I executed a textbook rugby tackle – my first and last – on him, and then sat on him to prevent him leaving, but he agreed that, if I thought it best, he would let me do it my own way.

Whatever that was.

When I set out on my last day skiing with Günter in Austria, I was feeling, to say the least, confused. This had been one of the most wonderful holidays I had ever had but however perfect it had been somehow it felt incomplete. Still, I shrugged, in a fairly stoic fashion, you can't have everything, and boarded the chair-lift with my friend. Günter, no doubt sensing that I was in turmoil, spent the morning congratulating me on how my skiing and my German had improved, and by midday I was feeling quite cheerful in an oh well, there you go sort of way. Eventually we stopped for lunch, which consisted, in my case, of rather squashed *Semmelbrötchen*, delicious Austrian bread buns filled with a variety of ham, salami and cheeses, along with chocolate bars and bottles of orange juice. After eating my fill, I lay back on my jacket and let the sun warm my face.

'Yoohoo!'

I sat up immediately, recognising the beautiful Germanic tones, and blinked a few times, temporarily blinded by the sun on the snow. As I looked up, there she was, her one-piece suit open to the waist, smiling down at me.

'Come on,' she said. 'Let's go.'

I didn't say anything.

For once in my life I didn't think I needed to.

Somehow, as I remember it, Günter as well as Susannah's parents simply disappeared. I didn't know where and I didn't care. What was more, I had even forgotten that I was supposed to be a skier of international standing. It didn't matter any more.

We skied together, she and I, all that wonderful afternoon.

Eventually, of course, the sun dipped away and we were drawn gradually further and further down the mountain. Skiing behind her down a reasonably wide and shallow piste, I was admiring the view, when suddenly by some neat trick, she flipped her skis around in a semicircle until she was facing me. Still moving backward she spread her arms out wide and slowly my skis slid neatly between hers, and I felt my arms wrap around her waist.

We were goggle to goggle.

As the ground dropped away, we were mouth to mouth.

Her lips were very cold but then, a second later, they were very warm.

By the time we slewed, by now quite out of control,

behind a snowdrift, her kiss was so hot it could have melted a mountain.

'Reckon we're going to head straight for the ski park,' announced Guy earnestly, jolting me back to the reality of the swinging chair-lift. 'Have to start getting some of those jumps built up if we're going to get into training for the competitions as soon as possible.'

Jimmy nodded solemnly as if they were discussing preparations for the next Olympics.

This ski park place that I had heard them talking about earnestly the night before sounded terrible – the skiing equivalent of a gymnastics hall but naturally much more dangerous. Before there was any opportunity for an invitation to be proffered for me to join them, I hurriedly made my excuses.

'Look, what I think I will do is . . . with all this new equipment, it would probably be better if I spend a bit of time just testing it out, like, check out it's the kind of gear that suits me – you know. Just check it out, see, like, it's up to it. Probably just hang around here for a while . . . maybe join you later?'

'Yeah, well, if you're sure, dude.'

'Yeah, no worries.'

Rather pathetically, I hoped that by copying some of their speech mannerisms I might make what was clearly a feeble excuse a bit more acceptable. I wished I had managed to say 'like' a few more times for that extra authenticity. In some ways of course I didn't really mind if they saw through my explanation. I was much more concerned about the eager attention that I could sense like a breaking wave behind me.

The eagerly chattering kids to the rear of me as well as the prospect of having to get off the chair-lift in a recognised manner had put me in a state of some nervous excitement. Concentrating hard, I gripped tightly on the safety bar and remembered only too well the anxiety this particular piece of equipment had always caused to bubble up inside me. Naturally you didn't want to leave it too late to lift it up and over your head or you ran the risk of finding yourself trapped 'on board' and swung round the great, big, gear wheel at the top before heading back down towards the village, to the fury of fellow passengers on your seat and the derision of countless onlookers. Nor, obviously, did you want to open it too early for fear that you might suddenly slide off the shiny plastic seat into the void below which, as I could see now, was studded with a number of rather sharp-looking rocks.

After a brief grapple with Guy, who was trying to lift the bar up and out of the way far, far too early – up it goes, no it doesn't, yes it does, no it doesn't – I gave in, mainly because Jimmy interceded and lent a little extra muscle. My skis hit the small slope that ran down from the lift and I pushed myself off and away. All in all, it wasn't too bad an effort. Flailing backward slightly, I was perhaps a little dangerous with my ski sticks but, apart from a slight grab of the arm of the woman who had been sitting next to me, I slid away quite comfortably and came to rest, still vertical, some fifty yards away.

With no time to waste, Jimmy, Aubrey and Guy pulled on hats, goggles and gloves with all the intensity of Fighter Command. Gesturing 'chocks away!' in my direction, they disappeared over the back of the nearest ridge, which I was quite sure was not part of the piste. My goggles in place, I looked around for my young pursuers. Initially, I thought that they must have gone on ahead, fed up with waiting for me as I fiddled around with my kit. I began to relax and lifted up my skis one by one, wiggling them to check that they were still firmly attached to my feet. Remembering the solid, satisfactory clunk of the bindings when I had first stepped into them down at the bottom, I felt strangely, dangerously, confident. Just as I was about to push off again I suddenly caught sight of them, ranked on the crest of the hill a hundred yards above me. Leaning forward on their ski sticks they were glaring at me intently through their dark, rather sinister-looking goggles. Tensed, poised, they were watching my every move. How long could I keep bluffing that I couldn't get the top button done up on my jacket. One little girl with blonde pigtails, turquoise sunscreen on her lips and a Mickey Mouse hat with unfeasibly large ears on her head, had idly raised one of her ski sticks in the air as if, like a diminutive Chief Sitting Bull, she was about to give the order to charge. As the General Custer of this unhappy scenario, I considered my tactical options and realised that there was nothing for it but to get going. One possibility was to try and outstrip them by skiing so fast that they were unable to keep up. My experience of nine-year-olds on skis made me abandon this option almost immediately. Plan B was to ski a little way down the hill and stop abruptly – if I still could – in the hope that they would overshoot me, get bored of waiting and clear off never to be seen again – or at least for the rest of the ski season.

Taking a deep breath as though about to take a plunge from the top of Victoria Falls, I stepped my skis around until gravity took over and I began to move. Just out of the corner of my eye I could see the massed ranks above me start to move – a horde bearing down upon me, all fluorescent pinks and dripping noses. Picking up speed, I thought that I ought to put in a turn or two before things got too out of hand. Even now I am a little uncertain as to how this happened, but at one moment I was facing down the hill and at the next I was looking up at my pursuers. The turned-up tips at the back of my skis had now taken over with enthusiasm. At least the gang of children looked mildly impressed by this sudden turnaround, I thought grimly. But any mild sense of satisfaction came to an abrupt end when, due to an unfortunate and only very slight shift of weight on my part, I suddenly swung wildly to my left and rammed backward at some speed into a snow-bank at the side of the piste.

Unfortunately, Mickey Mouse and her friends, having altogether better control over their skis, stopped some ten yards away. They stared at me silently and intensely as only children can when they feel they have been really badly let down by an adult. I nearly apologised.

Slowly, sadly, most of the youngsters skied off, yet another illusion shattered. I liked to think they were already looking out for the next excitement and would forget my existence in seconds, but one boy, seemingly rather older than the rest, wearing a Christmas-tree bobble hat, halted at the next turn in the piste and turned uphill to watch me as I rearranged myself. I half-expected him to wave, but instead, unsmilingly, he gave me what the French call the *bras d'honneur* – a flexing of the right arm upward to meet a downward movement of the left arm, the left hand meeting the inside of the right elbow with a slap of glove on cloth as the middle finger of the right hand rose abruptly skyward. As he scuttled sideways and away, I could not help musing that the gesture in this case had been more sad and angry than childish and cheeky. Shrugging, I reassembled myself. At that moment, staying upright was a much more pressing concern.

Not normally too self-conscious, I was, however, somewhat disconcerted by this first outing, and realised that it was only going to be through extensive practice that I would ever get myself to a rather more presentable level. Suddenly, I was deeply aware of the fact that the skiers zooming past me as I attempted to dislodge myself from the wall of snow were possibly people who would be, like me, here for the duration of the season. Pulling my hat further down over my ears, I made sure that most of my face was covered by my enormous goggles and that the rest was hidden behind a scarf that I wrapped around my mouth and chin. As I set off downhill again, I wondered how difficult it would be to dye my new suit.

Little by little, as the morning wore on, my confidence returned. It was certainly true that these new-style skis were a vast improvement on the old planks – much easier to turn with, much lighter and whippier. There were moments, on the other hand, when I did wonder whether they might not be a bit too quick. Yet when half past twelve came around – the time that I had arranged to meet up with the others for a ski before returning to the village – I was feeling quite pleased by the speed of my progress. Consulting my *plan des pistes* I realised that it would be an awful lot easier just to ask somebody how to get to *Les Ciboulettes*, our agreed meeting place. Some people have their brains arranged in such a fashion that they are able to make head or tail of the weird squiggles and array of strange symbols on the piste map, and are able to use these diagrams to get themselves from one place to another. However, the rest of us, certainly a large majority, find them totally baffling, but perversely never seem to give up trying to work out where on earth we are.

From the instructions given to me by an extremely cool but quite friendly lift attendant, *un remonteur*, I discovered that I need only take one more *tire-fesses* lift, which in French means very accurately a 'bottom puller' – what we know in England as a T-bar – the more sociable, but vastly more stressful, version of the old button lift. As I queued to grab hold of it and settle one side of the anchor-shaped bar underneath my backside, I remembered from years before how these contraptions varied in their nature. Some of them allowed you to slide gracefully from the gate, waving at your friends, pulling on your hat and having a cup of hot chocolate. Others, pulling you off the ground, were more reminiscent of trying to lasso a tractor going at full tilt. When the gearing of the wheel engaged with the line attached to your bar, you were lifted bodily from the ground and your arm sockets subjected to the severest of tests. Generally speaking, if you bend your knees at the moment of departure it seems to soften the jerk and, whilst not necessarily allowing you to look as if you are a model in a photo shoot, it at least minimises the risk of all your teeth shattering. Such past experience came to my rescue, and I was quietly pleased with the poise with which I set off up the hill. Of course, this was literally my downfall. Believing now that I could relax and tuck my hands behind my back as all the ski instructors did, I took advantage of the moment to admire the view over my left shoulder. It was just as I had always remembered the mountain land-scape: idyllic. From here I could see right across the top of the village and over to the other side of the valley to Mont Thierry, which was where, according to the young-sters, all the cool guys went. As a result I had already made a mental note to avoid wandering over to that part of the skiing terrain. Still, it was undeniably beautiful and looking south as it did had the best views of Mont Blanc. Further down the valley the snow line was visible, where as the elevation dropped away the temperature rose until, at a particular altitude, the snow that fell had turned to rain before it touched the ground. In normal circumstances, as the winter wore on that level would drop further and further until all the mountains as far as the eye could see were covered in snow.

Fabulous.

Smiling, I looked back down at my skis in the tracks that were following and just had time to watch their tips cross over. Then I fell over. All I had to do now was to wait for the attendant snapping, crashing and jolting that all were part of losing my skis, my brand new hat (caught on a twig), and one of my ski sticks that got stuck between the legs of the first person I skittled over. Under these circumstances, how many people you do actually end up knocking over and turning into enemies for life depends almost entirely on how high up the lift you have got before you fall off. Of course, once you have taken a tumble you are no longer responsible for your actions and should not really be held to blame. All you hope, like the other people you bowl over, is that your vertiginous descent, quite often head first, will be stopped by something not too solid, and that you may be able to retrieve at least some of the more expensive items of your equipment that you shed as they become detached from you in the course of your accident. In this case, I had not travelled particularly far on the lift and the other people affected by my unfortunate mishap barely reached into double figures.

Eventually, I came to rest at the feet of the aforementioned lift attendant who looked no less cool than he had done earlier as he gazed unblinkingly down at me. Hardly moving a muscle, he managed to stop my ski stick as it whizzed past him without even losing the ash on the end of the hand-rolled cigarette that had been glued into the corner of his mouth. He tossed it back to me, but my thanks were somewhat muffled by my goggles which had been dislodged from their more normal position in the course of my fall. Realising that without my hat and my goggles in place I was fully recognisable, I hastily rearranged my scarf over my head in the style of a Russian peasant and made my way off in a hurried and rather ungainly fashion, muttering about what a beautiful day it was in German.

By the time I actually teamed up with the others, I was some half an hour late but as they were ensconced on the terrace of a wide, attractive, restaurant chalet they hardly seemed to notice. Nor, indeed, did they seem to notice the ever-growing bruise on my chin. This I had unfortunately inflicted upon myself when, on my second departure up the drag lift, I had waved my ski sticks in a rather too cheerful fashion whilst hollering '*Auf Wiedersehen*' to the lift attendant and his mate, who were still trying to disentangle two of my victims.

The restaurant was already very busy as it was now five past twelve, and all French passport holders had quit the slopes. Aubrey, who seemed to be on friendly relations with the owner of the restaurant, perhaps because they were in the same line of business, had a table booked, and I slid onto one of the smooth wooden benches. The table was piled with hundreds of pounds' worth of ski paraphernalia, and I wondered how on earth the waiter would ever manage to fit one of the huge dishes of fried potatoes and steamed ham that I had already decided upon for my lunch, in front of me. I had forgotten how hungry the mountain air could make you and I was now starving. Although I am of an age now that requires me to give some thought to my figure, on this first day I definitely deserved a good lunch. After all, I hadn't done too badly. Picking up my new goggles, I tried to see the extent of the injury to my chin in the mirrored lenses. Nobody to date had mentioned anything and so perhaps I had got away with it. Surreptitiously, I slid two fingers over my jaw in what I hoped was a pensive fashion. So caught up was I in my own appearance that I failed to notice the arrival of two new people in our party. Squeezing up a little and trying to account for all my various accoutrements it was quite a few moments before I looked down the table to see who had joined us. To my astonishment, sitting diagonally opposite me was the little boy who had aimed such an eloquent hand gesture in my direction earlier that morning. His woolly beanie was pulled down low over his forehead and his sunglasses were seated firmly on the bridge of his nose. He was sucking nonchalantly on the drinking straw of a vast ice-filled glass of lemonade.

Next to him sat a blonde-haired woman, who flashed me a smile as she pulled off her gloves. Before the boy could react she pulled off his hat and sunglasses, sliding the zip of his ski jacket open from the neck with maternal affection. Without being able to help myself, I shot a broad grin in his direction, but he remained so impressively insouciant that I began to wonder whether I might be mistaken. Only when I looked down at the red Christmas tree on his hat did I know I was right. Just then a large glass of beer and my food arrived simultaneously and I found myself strangely distracted. After I'd finished and was slowly stirring a sugar lump into a small but sturdy coffee, Aubrey introduced me to the pair.

'Will, dude, these are my friends, Mireille and Olivier. Talk French to them, dude!' Aubrey, like many of my other friends, seemed to take a great deal more pleasure out of hearing me converse in French than he did in making an attempt to speak it for himself.

Smiling, the woman slipped her hand across the table and shook me by the fingertips.

'Bonjour, Williams. Ça vous plaît Mont St Bernard? Vous skiez souvent?'

All French people call me 'Williams'. Apparently it is the

name of a make of French shaving foam. Everyone thinks it's terribly funny.

Swallowing with some difficulty my natural temptation to overstate my skiing capabilities, I explained that I had not been in the mountains for some years but that it was a pleasure to be back, particularly here.

'Mais c'est très bien!' she replied as she ruffled her son's hair, looked at me and smiled again.

'Allez, mon chéri, on y va?' she asked the boy. He nodded slowly and glanced in my direction, his deep brown eyes quizzical.

Secretly, I was rather hoping that I would see the boy squirming, a little at least, with embarrassment. Instead, and here I suddenly felt rather guilty, he just looked a little sad. In fact, they both did, mother and son, as they waved, clipped on their skis and set off back towards the village. As they disappeared behind the trees, I wondered about them and tried to slurp up the last of my coffee. This was in the hope that the last microgrammes of caffeine might do something to revive my flagging self. How do the French go back to work after lunch, let alone ski?

Naturally, I didn't like to say anything when Aubrey proposed that we should all head up to the ski park for a few 'quick tricks', but all I was really interested in doing was installing myself in one of the many deckchairs set out in front of the terrace and having a snooze before catching the lift back down to the Café de la Poste. Puffing along after them, I eventually collapsed on a large pile of snow and leaned my back against my skis that I had planted in a rather professional X behind me.

Several hundred man-hours must have gone into making the various different types of jumps that made up Mont St Bernard's ski park. Tons of snow had been shaped and carved to allow sufficient lips and curves, and drops and lifts on which the freestylers could perform their acrobatics. Aubrey, sucking from a bottle of electric-turquoise power drink, gave me a potted history of this relatively new sport.

'Started out in Canada, mate. Way back in the 70s. Some gnarly dudes, you know, they got all the moves worked out. Moguls got, like, full medal status in the Olympics in '92 with Aerials in '94. Should be getting Half Pipes, Full Pipes, Double Moguls and maybe even Big Air in there soon.'

'Oh, right! That's good . . . yeah, very good . . .' I tailed off.

'We can get you doing some basic stuff, if you're interested? Start off with some turns, get you up to a 320°. After that it's whatever you want really.'

'320°? What's one of those then?' I asked absentmindedly. From up here the view of the village was majestic.

'Oh, you know, just when you do a full turn in the air. Start with uprights, probably don't want to get into inverteds too quick.'

'Inverteds?'

'Yeah, that's where you do the full turn in the air but you're, like, upside down. Maybe get onto that later.'

Later!

Just at that moment, a girl dressed in battle fatigues and Davy Crockett hat shot into the sky, turned twice in the air, hit the ground, fell over with a terrible life-threatening crash and disappeared over the lip of the slope in a blur of skis, khaki and raccoon tails.

'Nice 720°. Shame about the landing,' Aubrey commented, from his semi-professional perspective.

Realising that he was probably about to lose me as a future member of the British Olympic Freestyle Team, he reached inside his jacket and pulled out a pair of binoculars. 'Use these. You'll get a much better idea about technique. Give you something to go on.'

Squinting up at him silhouetted in the sun that was soon to dip over the back of Mont Thierry, I wondered whether he was, in fact, insane.

Small and light, the binoculars were also amazingly powerful and with them I picked out various of the main buildings of the village. Fluttering with red, white and blue *'tricolore'* French flags, the neoclassical lines of the town hall were difficult to miss not least because they were so incongruous alongside the softer shapes of the wooden chalet. On the wall of the church I could read the time displayed by the sundial, and below it I could see the priest in his black cassock unlocking the large wooden front doors. In the distance, a funeral cortège was crawling its way up the mountain from the lake – so that was the sad reason why the priest was opening up. It was strange to see this mournful sight in this resort where so many people came for fun and relaxation. Not wishing to intrude even from afar, I concentrated on the figures skiing down the mountains on the other side of the valley. Curiosity, not prurience, found me retraining the binoculars back down on the line of slowly moving black cars. It was obviously the funeral of someone much respected as there seemed to be at least a dozen vehicles. Looking again with the naked eye, something seemed not quite right. I stared at the magnified image once more. What was wrong?

The shape of the vehicles grated, that was it. Instead of long sleek lines, these were too chunky, too hard. Nor were they heading towards the church. At the intersection in the middle of the village the convoy turned left and started to head up the hill. Before long they were turning into the large, white car park of the Hotel de l'Aigle Brun. I peered again. 'Hummers! They're Hummers!' I shouted at nobody in particular, but suddenly I was surrounded by a crowd of excited youngsters.

'Let's have those,' yelled Aubrey, none too gently snatching the binoculars from my hands. Taking another deep suck of blue liquid, he clapped them to his sunglasses with a painful whack.

Suddenly there was silence on the mountainside as we waited for his pronouncement.

'It's them,' he whispered.

Silence.

'Er . . . sorry . . . who is it?' I looked around at the awestruck faces.

'It's them,' they said in unison. 'It's the Russians. The Russians have come!'

5

A Home of My Own

Tradition apparently stated that for the last run of the day we should all ride up to the top of the mountain and then ski all the way down without stopping. Due to the excitement caused by the new arrivals this was accomplished in double quick time, and it was in the course of this descent that I learnt two important things. First, never attempt to keep up with people fifteen years younger than you who are incredibly fit and ski all the time, particularly when it has been eight years since you have been up a mountain let alone tried to get down it again. Secondly, even though you are totally convinced that they will, and however much they feel like they are burning, your thighs will not actually explode and will in time make a full recovery.

When eventually we all screeched to a halt at the bottom of the slope, several thousand pounds' worth of skis were thrown into a pile. Although I would have done practically anything to be able to remove my boots that very instant, my curiosity got the better of me and I stumbled after the rest of my rather more agile group. Chipping our toes into the frozen surface of the pavement, we proceeded up the slope to the Hotel de l'Aigle Brun like a chorus line of demented tap dancers, arms held out from our sides to keep our balance. So swiftly had we made it down the mountain that the new arrivals had hardly had time to get out of their enormous vehicles. As we peered over the top of the frosty hedge in the company of fifty or more curious villagers, we saw half a dozen tall, square-shouldered men with shaven heads, wraparound sunglasses and long leather coats, climb out of the first and third Hummers and surround the second on all sides. On the order of the most senior of their number, one of the bodyguards, for that was surely what they were, opened the rear passenger door of what seemed to be a deluxe stretch model. As he did so, the men crowded round almost obscuring our view of the passengers as they climbed out. Just as the first foot stepped out, wearing an elegant calf-length boot made of an exotic fur, the manager of the Hotel de l'Aigle Brun, dressed in an ill-fitting suit, appeared at the entrance with his arms stretched out in welcome. What he saw as he looked down made him stop in his tracks. Fascinated, he absentmindedly pasted down his combed-over hair. He was certainly not the only one to stare in blatant astonishment. From inside the truck appeared half a dozen tall, elegant young women dressed from head to toe in furs. Lining up beside the men they waited expectantly. A few moments later an elderly man dressed in a long black heavy overcoat and a Homburg hat was helped down by a young, nervous-looking man, perhaps a secretary, and another smartly-dressed woman. Although he was quickly surrounded by tall leather coats, I just glimpsed his face, which, to my surprise, was round, ruddy and quite amiable. He wore his clothes like a poor disguise, and I fancied then that he would be much more comfortable digging a vegetable patch in vest and braces in the springtime. Here, now, he only looked cold and strangely out of place.

Just at that moment it struck me that the whole scene was almost entirely monochrome. Everyone was dressed in blacks and greys against the white snow. This impression was reinforced by the appearance from the other vehicles of another dozen or so individuals whose uniforms of black skirts and white blouses, dinner suits and bow ties, and in one case a tailcoat, denoted them as domestic staff. Clearly the boss was used to travelling with his whole entourage. From the last of the vehicles there even appeared a chef already dressed in black and white chequered trousers under his heavy overcoat.

With almost military precision, the bodyguards scanning the area authoritatively, the group moved towards the reception of the hotel. In the midst of them however was a sudden flash of colour. Vermilion red trousers and an electric-blue jacket glared bright against the snow as a small boy of perhaps eight or nine years old stepped out last from the middle Hummer. Pale and blond, he made his way up the steps in a trance, shrugging the hand of one of the young women from his shoulder. His feet finding their way without him needing to look up from the handheld computer game which he was playing with furious intensity, he floated along in a little bubble of solitude and seemed as out of place as the old man. Finally, with a quick glance around, one of the guards pulled the smoked-glass front door closed and they were gone.

Installed once again in the Café de la Poste, my spirits revived rather more quickly than my thighs. With our skis piled up outside, we had clomped through the door in our boots and shortly after had been joined by a great crowd of ecstatic skiers, all full of excitement, thrilled by the superb conditions they had found up on the mountain.

Although I felt utterly exhausted by my day, I was energised by the happy atmosphere and ensconced myself in the window seat. Of course, as far as we were all concerned, there was only one topic of conversation. I listened cheerfully to a variety of theories, more or less believable, that swirled around like the mini cyclones of snow in the street outside, about who these new arrivals were, where they had come from, why they were here and above all where they had managed to find such fantastic wealth that allowed them to take over the whole of L'Hotel de l'Aigle Brun, which was after all the best and certainly the most expensive establishment in Mont St Bernard.

Once the news of the Russians' arrival had leaked out and down the few streets of Mont St Bernard, rumours abounded. Aubrey, who had once been on a Soviet-controlled Intourist trip to Moscow in the then USSR with his Socialist Worker parents, considered himself to be something of an expert.

'You see, after the Communist State was undermined by the capitalist plot, all these bloodsuckers crawled out of their sewers.'

Most of the youngsters, who would not have recognised a Communist if he had hit them over the head with a hammer and sickle but hero-worshipped the militant Aubrey, nodded in agreement and secretly thrilled at the thought of vampires roaming the streets of the village at night.

'Of course,' Aubrey continued, 'you'll see that they'll want to take the whole place over. Have things their way. That's your oligarch for you.'

Jimmy nodded wisely, stroked his goatee, checked his appearance in the reflection of the window and mused that Ollie didn't sound like a very Russian kind of name.

'Mafia' was suddenly the word that began to be bandied about as regularly as 'powder snow', 'freestyle' or 'après-ski'. Everybody – apart from me – seemed to have their own theory about where the wealth of these Russians had come from. Drugs was in poll position, followed with a certain frisson by prostitution, but after that theories became considerably more fanciful: counterfeit vodka, fake medicines, gun-running – hence the armoured Hummers, first cousins of the American army Humvees – all these were pondered over. Guy thought it might be to do with caviar, and Jimmy, his mind racing, wondered whether they might be Cossacks although the relevance of this was lost on the rest of us.

Whoever they were, what was certain was that they were here to stay for the season, and it was rumoured to be costing them at least 25,000 Euros a day to rent the Hotel de l'Aigle Brun. We attempted to multiply that by two months, but became a bit muddled over our aperitifs, although someone finally suggested that it would cost somewhere in the region of one and a half million Euros for the whole stay.

Aubrey, incensed, did a calculation on a beer mat which I think was only distantly related to current mathematical thinking, and announced that on his current wages it would take one hundred years of toil to earn an equivalent sum.

'Once again the poor suffer while the bosses crunch the bones of the working class and spit them out.'

Several pairs of eyes shimmered, almost tearful with admiration, as Aubrey steered his already rather unsteady self back to the bar. Perhaps it was just the thick cigarette smoke that everyone was inhaling after a day of so much fresh air.

When Jimmy brought the next round over and the conversation drifted to other more mundane subjects I remembered, with a feeling of guilt, how keen I was to find myself alternative accommodation to that which I had experienced the night before. It had been a slightly more colourful version of sleeping in a New York side street, although if

anything rather more malodorous. To my surprise, it was
Jimmy himself who brought the subject up. 'Will, Will,
you've got to talk to Aubrey about your accommo.'

'My accommo . . . ?'

'Yeah, yeah, yeah. He's just gone over there. Hang on,
let me get him back. He's well cool.' Jimmy disappeared
into the bulging crowd and reappeared with the man who
I was fairly certain had appeared in *Easy Rider*. With all the
rushing about and all the new people I had met recently I
had hardly had the chance to take in his undeniable style,
but after his passionate discourse on the Russians I now
focused my attention on him rather more closely. About
five foot eight, with a permanent bandanna and sunglasses,
Aubrey had a lined, deeply tanned face covered on either
side by wide sideburns. His ski outfit was, I thought initially,
made out of leather, but on closer inspection I realised that
in fact a great deal of wear and tear had created a shiny
patina on the surface of his waterproof jacket and trousers.
On his feet he was now wearing a pair of hiking-cum-
biking boots. He grabbed my hand and shook it from side
to side as he leaned slightly toward me and then back again.

'How are you doing, man? What's occurring here? Will,
man? Yeah, yeah,' he deliberated in a neutral drawl that
suggested that the effects of the après-ski had already begun
to kick in – like a mule.

'Hello, Aubrey,' I replied. 'Again . . .'

I had after all spent most of the day with him.

Jimmy looked rather nervously from me to him and back
again with divided loyalties, but Aubrey was already
making his way somewhat unsteadily to the bar where he
was automatically handed another little round bowl-like
glass of pastis by an expressionless Gaston. Lifting it high
and kissing the glass he then proceeded to swallow half the
contents in a single gulp. Jimmy hurried over to him.

Bringing him back, I could hear him say: 'You know, it's about your little chalet place. Will is going to be here all season and he's looking for a place to stay and er . . . you haven't got it sorted yet . . . remember . . . so I thought he might be interested. You know where I'm coming from, right?'

Aubrey nodded rather slowly but, I suspected, had it not been for his sunglasses, his eyes might have been expressing some confusion. Suddenly, with a slap to his head, everything appeared to come back to him and he came back over to me quickly, or at least as quickly as a man moving through a rough sea of Ricard could.

'Sorry, man, I've been a bit messed up, you know, with these Russians and getting our brothers and sisters together again for some meetings and that, but yeah, yeah. Will, yeah that's right. Listen, man, Jimmy was saying you're looking for a place to stay. I might have just the place for you if you're interested.'

'Yes, well, you did mention something about it earlier . . .'

There was a lengthy pause while Aubrey considered this possibility further.

'Where are you staying, man?' he finally asked.

'Just with Jimmy right now, but I'm definitely, yes, definitely, definitely looking for a place for the rest of the season.'

Trying not to sound too over-enthusiastic was difficult but I didn't want to offend Jimmy's feelings. What was more, in this strange relaxed skiworld, appearing too keen about anything was distinctly 'uncool'.

'Is that right, dude? Cool, cool, cool.' Aubrey again headed very slowly, but impressively smoothly, toward the bar. I followed.

'Oh, yeah, man. That's right.' He nodded.

Just as I was beginning to get very muddled, he finished his glass and waved it by way of thanks under the marvellous moustaches of *le patron*, who managed majestically to completely ignore him.

'Right, come on then, let's go,' he said, picking up his keys from the counter. 'Wheels are just outside.'

'Go where, Aubrey?' But he was already grooving his way to the door.

Throwing a look of consternation at Jimmy, who smiled and shrugged, I clomped my way back outside fully expecting to see Aubrey swinging his leg over a Harley Davidson that had been presented to him by Dennis Hopper. Instead, he was already sitting in the cab of a small white van of the type much favoured by French plumbers – and was revving at the diesel engine.

'Okay, man, chuck your skis in the back.'

Slipping slightly on the icy road, I walked round to the back of the van and pulled the doors open. Seeing in there what I believed to be an old bit of carpet and a pile of clothes, I did as instructed and threw my skis into the back. As I did so there was a loud squeal, and a face surrounded by wild black hair appeared out of the middle of the bundle of clothing. It groaned again briefly before slumping back and burying itself once more.

'Oops, sorry about that!' I muttered, and closed the doors as quietly as I could.

'Oh, that's where he got to. Don't worry about him,' Aubrey announced rather vaguely. 'He had a bit of a wild night last night. That's to say the least, ha, ha! So he's probably just having a little rest. Anyway, in you jump, man. Let's hit the road, Jack. Haven't got my chains on yet but it should be all right. Yeah, probably all right.'

And with that we set off in the dusk and at high speed out of the village. Just at the point where the red, white and black sign announced arrival in Mont St Bernard, we took a slithering turn to the left and started to wind our way up Mont Thierry. As the incline increased, so our speed slowed. Aubrey was now able to sit back in the driver's seat, take a large draught of beer from a can in the driver's door and explain the situation to me. This was his sixth season in the village, he told me proudly. Though he said so himself, he was much admired locally. This was partly because a number of winters spent in one place conferred some sort of senior position in the *saisonnier* hierarchy. Also, he was recognised to be an excellent skier and snowboarder, and was now a fairly highly reputed chef in one of the half-dozen smartest chalets. He was also particularly pleased with life because he had just moved in with the daughter of the local butcher. Everything was looking good, Jack, he told me. By this stage, I was a little uncertain whether he had suddenly decided that my name was Jack, or whether this was simply a term of address that was so cool that I had not yet encountered it. Probably any attempt to clarify the matter was not going to be worth the effort.

Before he had met Emilie, his girlfriend, he had put a down payment on a small chalet on the extremity of a new development. Although it was a much older building it had initially been considered as the home for the caretaker of these new flats. The new incumbent of the job had actually preferred to house himself in the basement of one of the blocks of the new complex, and so the little chalet had been put up for sale. Aubrey's plan had been that he would advertise the place as a holiday let on the Internet, thereby making a tidy sum over the winter and the equally busy summer months. Soon, he hoped to set up an outdoor catering business with Emilie and the money would come in handy as he got it off the ground. It was all very interesting and I was just surprised that a man who looked as totally laid-back as Aubrey – to say nothing of his socialist credentials

– fancied himself as something of an entrepreneur. It had certainly taken an awfully long time to get any of this information out of him. What made it even more astounding that he should have achieved all this was that he seemed to be semi-permanently 'on the road' – not that that was any form of criticism on my part. It was precisely because he had been so busy 'hanging out in Thailand' that he hadn't quite got round to letting the accommodation, apart, he thought, from one week in January, but that hadn't yet been confirmed.

His van skittered on the ice as we carried on upward, and on a couple of occasions the back end swung worryingly close to the edge of the mountain road. After a rather wild attempt to get the vehicle around a hairpin bend in one loose movement, we found ourselves spinning into a 180-degree turn.

'Sod it!' muttered Aubrey, and we drove the rest of the way up the hill in reverse.

About ten minutes later, just as the stars were beginning to appear, we pulled up outside a dolls' house – quite a big dolls' house but a dolls' house nevertheless. A perfect mini-chalet.

'Here it is,' he said. 'Do you like it?'

'Yes, yes, I do. It's great.' It really was.

'Oh, I'm so pleased,' said Aubrey in a very un-'Born to be Wild' fashion. 'Come and have a look inside. I think you'll really love some of the features.'

Laughing, I went inside. I really did love some of the features. The large sitting-room was equipped at the back with a bar and kitchen, and to the front of the room was a table and chairs alongside a sofa and armchair. These last two were positioned in front of an old-fashioned, wood-burning stove that stood in an ancient-looking fireplace. Above all this, up a steepish ladder but still open to the downstairs, was a comfortable mezzanine bedroom with a large bed and a goose-down duvet with an Alpine motif. Bouncing up and down, I could not help but picture images of Heidi and lonely goatherds.

Unhealthy, no doubt.

Beside the bed was a book – an illustrated history of the Winter Olympics. I flicked through it. Perhaps it would prove to be an inspiration.

'I'll take it.'

'How much do you want to pay?'

'How much do you want to get?'

He told me.

It seemed pretty reasonable.

I agreed.

I paid.

Aubrey gave me the keys.

He showed me where everything was.

We shook hands.

'So shall we go and get your stuff now?'

'Sounds good. Thanks.'

If only everything was that easy.

6

Lazy Days at Mon Repos

'Radio 'Armonie!' sang a nameless jingles band for the sixteenth time since I had got out of my long, therapeutic bath on that first morning in my new home. It had been a mistake not to take it the night before, but by the time I had gone back down the hill with Aubrey, picked up all my stuff from Jimmy's garage, thrown it in the back of the van, made a quick detour via the Café de la Poste for what Aubrey described as a 'sharpener' to seal the deal and headed back up the hill to deposit my belongings, I was completely exhausted. This was all before we had gone back to the Café de la Poste again to have a few drinks after all our endeavours. Even Gaston nearly did a double-take as we swaggered back through the doors.

Trudging back up the hill through ever-thickening snow, I had yawned expansively. By the time I reached the wooden front door of my new home – which I had discovered to my great pleasure was called 'Mon Repos' – I was so tired that I could barely make it up the ladder to bed.

When I woke up the sun was streaming through the small rectangular panes of the attic window high in the roof. Rolling out of bed, I recognised that what I had feared might happen during the night had indeed taken place. At some stage during the early hours of the morning, a large butcher with a meat tenderiser had attacked me. Not content with mashing up my legs, he had proceeded to my arms, back, chest and neck. I made it down the ladder and into the bathroom groaning and at a pace that would have earned Aubrey's admiration.

Whilst I waited for the hot water to run, I pulled back the curtains of the sitting-room and gasped with surprise at what I saw. Sunlight shone over the entire valley and from where the chalet was situated I had a view across the whole of the village below me, the gilt bell tower of the church glinting in the morning light. Further, much further away, beyond the peaks that I had skied yesterday, and still vast despite the distance, was the summit of Mont Blanc. For a second, as I pulled the windows open wide, I could understand why somebody might be interested in mountaineering.

Although I had realised the night before that the twenty-minute hike up the hill from the village meant that I ran every risk over the course of the ski season of becoming alarmingly fit, I was delighted by the isolation of this spot. Stepping out onto the balcony, quite warm in the sunshine, it was great to think that when I got tired of the hurly-burly of the social scene in Mont St Bernard, I could escape back up here and relax, read or write in complete peace, without any fear of interruption. Apart, of course, from the rather tubby middle-aged skier in a deeply unfashionable green and purple one-piece suit who had just skied past my front door only inches away. I am not sure who was more surprised: I at the realisation that my front door gave out onto the main run down from Mont Thierry or the man as he sped by. One moment he had just been trying to enjoy a normal morning's skiing, the next he was being ambushed

by a lunatic naturist. To give the impression that I had
nothing to be ashamed of, I gave him a cheerful wave. His
shock at this was such that he momentarily appeared to
lose his balance and lurched worryingly in the direction of
some of the more mature pine trees. Correcting his course,
he skied off looking faintly appalled.

Stepping back inside and blushing, I closed the French
windows again and as I turned the curved metal handle
to lock them, four or five other skiers whooshed past me
and the noise that they made was to become my wake-
up call whilst I lived at Mon Repos. Yes, either the hiss
of ski on snow, or the cheerful banalities of 'Radio
Harmonie', the valley's local radio station and its
indomitably cheerful DJ who was called, depending on
whether he was talking in English or French, either Jay-
Pee (J-P in English) or Jee-Pay (J-P in French). Actually, I
think his mother had christened him Jean-Pierre, but this
did not seem to have the star quality required to befit his
profession. Nor, probably more importantly, did it rhyme
nearly as well – for there was nothing more that Jay-Pee
loved to do early of a morning than to regale his listeners
with his latest piece of popular verse. This first morning
it ran something like:

> 'Radio 'Armon-ieeeee,
> Eeetz with me your friend,
> from around ze bend,
> Jaaaay-Pee.'

Little did he realise that if his listening public had to deal
with many more of these impromptu rhymes, he would not
be the only person around the bend. Sadly his efforts in his
mother tongue were no better:

'Radio 'Armon-ieeeee,
Bonjour les amis,
Ici Jee-Pay,
C'est tout OK.'

Almost more irritating than his overbearing style was the choice of music that we were allowed to listen to in the brief moments before he came on to talk again. All his records had at some stage won an award for being the most irritating song of the year, but what was even more frustrating was that there were only approximately twenty of them. What in hindsight I really resent about Jay-Pee are not his limitations as a radio presenter, his ridiculous rhymes and his terrible pretensions, but the fact that I can remember practically every single word of each of those songs.

In terms of public service broadcasting, I suppose that Radio Harmonie did serve some purpose. For a start, there was always a detailed weather forecast which, in this part of the world, was often as important as it might be in the middle of the Atlantic. This was always read, in French and English, by Jay-Pee's delightful assistant (or so I imagined her), Sophie. The dastardly disc jockey, it became clear whenever it came time for him to talk of her, had less than professional intentions as far as she was concerned. How he annoyed me. How shameless he was. Of course, as the employee she couldn't answer back – it was so unfair. I had half a mind to get my militant landlord, Aubrey, on the case. Many were the mornings when I snapped on my skis in a fury at how he could treat her so poorly, at how there was no justice.

Jay-Pee, when I could stomach his appalling smugness, was also the purveyor of information about the various events that were taking place in the resort over the course of the winter season. These were surprising in their variety, and that first morning I heard him announce that in the near future there would be an iceskating dance competition for children on the small rink in the middle of the village, and later that same day there would be an adult competition in the only village nightclub, L'icebox. Naturally, both these events would be compèred by the great man himself, who would be bringing along his own collection of 'discs'.

Later in the season would come the major features of the competitive calendar: an ice-hockey match against the village of Issy, which would take place at the big ice-hockey stadium, *le stade municipal*, in the nearby town; a downhill ski competition, including a slalom and superslalom (the difference between the two being, at that time and still to this day, something of a mystery to me); and in late March there would be the inaugural freestyle competition that I knew from my brief visits to the Café de la Poste was already the talk of the valley.

Indeed, it seemed that the freestyle contest was a source of some serious friction in the area. Anyone under thirty, although as enthusiastic about the downhill racing as anyone else, wanted a competition to claim as their own. Snowboards and trick skis, which had appeared over the last twenty or so years, afforded them their perfect platform. Anyone over fifty, however, had had trouble enough accepting the razzmatazz of competitive skiing – particularly of women's downhill racing – and for them freestyle was one jump too far. However, as an advertising possibility, particularly in attracting the interest of the younger generation, it was unmissable, and a battle had broken out between the two banks in the village about who should sponsor the event. The local savings bank was already, in time-honoured tradition, funding the downhill, but a new upstart operation from Paris was keen to compete with them by putting up money for the freestyle day. They had rapidly found themselves involved in a bidding war that had taken them both to the limits of their possible offers. Now it looked as if they were both likely to pull out causing the competition to be cancelled. Tensions had risen further when a message in spray-on snow had been left on the front door of the Paris branch, suggesting where the manager might best like to invest his sponsorship money. Although in the greater scheme of things the event was of minor importance, in this little snowbound world it had assumed giant proportions. Blood had been shed for less over the years, and of course for the young male and female snowboarders and trick skiers, most of whom were barely out of their teenage years, it was a matter of life and death. After all, it was for this that they would have spent the entire season training – or 'working' as the practitioners preferred to describe it.

I had no interest in heading out onto the slopes that first morning at Mon Repos, aching and tired as I was, but before long Jimmy, Guy and a collection of other shaggy individuals were ranked up on the piste outside my window. Grumbling, I set off after them and it was late that afternoon after my sudden halt for a pee that I had got lost.

After I had dabbed at my bleeding nose a few times with a paper handkerchief and finally plugged each nostril, I had caught out of the corner of my eye an incongruous shape amongst the haphazard muddle of the natural landscape. Just above the line of trees over to my left stood – and I checked and I double-checked – pointing sharply at the sky, the bell tower of a church or perhaps a small chapel. For a moment my heart leapt, as I believed, quite ridiculously, that I had stumbled by some back route upon Notre Dame de la Montagne, the parish church of our village.

Disappointment pinched me as sharply as the cold when

I realised that of course our church was surrounded by chalets, shops, restaurants and innumerable ski-hire outlets, and that if this really was the right one I would now be surrounded by cheerful crowds, freshly bathed and changed, chattering cheerfully as they headed off for their aperitifs.

The only chattering to be heard at that given moment came from my teeth, however hard I tried to grit them behind my woolly scarf. Not that I was really that frightened. Nonetheless, the bell tower was certainly the most promising sign of life that I had seen since first I had been abandoned. Achingly, because I was now quite exhausted, I sidestepped my way up the shallow slope through the ever thickening snow until I reached the front of the small chapel. Sanctuary!

I made my way up the path, skis in an open V, more like a geriatric penguin than who I really was – the returning hero.

Not a light, not even a flicker of a votive candle, was to be seen through the keyhole of the heavy, oak, firmly locked front door. Clapping my hands together for circulatory rather than congratulatory reasons, I skied around the downhill side of the building. Suddenly this small adventure was beginning to turn into a large pain in what was now becoming a rather numb backside.

Then there it was.

Four walls, a roof, a chimney, wood smoke drifting down towards me – a real house with windows, and lights in the windows.

Saved!

A miracle!

Tearing off my gloves I reached down to open my bindings, which this time were only too happy to come undone, leaving me sprawling on all fours in the soft snow. Bouncing back up, I grabbed my skis, the cold edges sharp on my fingers, and threw the offending articles into a nearby snowdrift where they landed upright and bent away from me like two naughty schoolboys only too aware of the trouble they had caused.

Turning from them with a sigh, I hammered on the door and waited some nervous minutes before it opened and warm, almost divine, light shone out into the dark. When my eyes were finally accustomed to the brightness, I saw standing in front of me a man about my age dressed in jeans and a fleece top.

'*Bonsoir, je peux vous aider?*'

'*Bof* . . . Well, it is a rather complicated story, but I was skiing with my friends . . .' I stumbled, feeling suddenly rather moved.

'Come in, come in. Everyone is welcome here.' He stuck out his hand and shook mine firmly drawing me into the cosy interior. 'Come in here. It is nice and warm. How is your nose? You're limping. Take a seat, what can I offer you? A coffee, a glass of wine, what about a beer? Something stronger?'

'Whisky? Do you have any whisky?' I asked apologetically, feeling in need of some medicinal restorative. Discreetly, I removed my nose plugs.

'Of course, one moment. Take off your stuff. Take a seat.'

Only once I had managed to remove my clobber did I take in my surroundings. We were sitting in a comfortable farmhouse kitchen. Against the back wall a wood-burning stove, which doubled as a cooker, was pumping out a most welcome warmth. A large aluminium saucepan was bubbling away on the hob and producing an appetising smell.

'So where do you live, my friend?' asked the man, as he filled a tumbler three fingers full with malt whisky. He smiled at me cheerfully as he handed it over.

'Er, near Mont Thierry on the other side, just up the hill a little bit.'

'Well, you will probably need a lift home.'

'Oh, yes, please,' I replied, this idea warming me as much as the Scotch. 'But, do you think we will make it down the mountain. You know it has been snowing pretty hard. Maybe the road won't be passable.'

My concerns were those of a man who had seen his own country come to a grinding halt at the simple forecast of bad weather.

'Oh, yes, of course we will be able to get down. They cleared the road at lunchtime, and anyway I've got my chains on now. I was just wondering, you know, my soup here is almost ready. Maybe you would like to have some with me before we head off. Sorry, would that be okay?' His kindly face tinged pink with the thought that he might be putting me out.

'Oh, yes, fantastic,' I replied, embarrassed at his embarrassment. 'Thank you, thank you very much. By the way I am William. William*mmm*.'

'Oh, good, pleased to meet you, Williams.' We shook hands of course. 'Forgive me. My name is Jean. Père Jean. In fact, I am the village priest. I don't think I have seen you at . . .'

'No, no, no I didn't, don't . . . er . . . so is this your home? Or do you live in a monastery or something?' Oh dear. I was not very used to talking to members of the clergy. It suddenly crossed my mind that he really ought to be wearing some sort of robe, but I kept that thought to myself.

'Yes,' he laughed, but not as if to suggest I was an idiot. 'Yes, this is where I live. It is a little way out of the village but I like it. It gives me the chance to study – a sort of one-man monastery. The chapel here is only ever open on special Saints' days but my parish covers the three villages of the valley.'

'Oh,' I said, for once slightly floundering for something

to say, particularly as this was an unfamiliar subject. 'So do they behave themselves, your parishioners?' This was supposed to be a rather jokey question but he appeared to take it quite seriously. Accordingly I straightened my face and sat up.

'Well, you know,' he sighed. 'The people of the mountains have not always been the easiest sheep in our flock to manage.' Something amusing about sheep, goats and farmers flickered through my mind but, I think probably fortunately, it did not come to anything so I kept quiet and let him continue.

It transpired that Père Jean's, or Jean, as he insisted that I should call him, special interest was the Christian history of the area. Sadly, it all seemed to have been a bit of a struggle. Although religious orders had travelled here from the Holy Roman Empire in the first century AD and had constructed mountain monasteries and nunneries, initially at least, contact with the local population had been minimal. It appeared that the people of the area relied mainly on travelling storytellers for their historical and moral education. Fantastic tales were told that amazed the children and moved the parents.

Had I heard the legend of the lake of Aiguebelette?

Umm, no I hadn't, I confirmed, as I sipped the steaming vegetable and ham soup and broke off a piece of the *couronne*, a ring of crusty bread in the shape of a crown.

Well, said the priest, who proved to be something of a natural raconteur, there once was a beautiful town where we now find the lake at Aiguebelette. One night, when the inhabitants were holding a huge party, a beggar came asking for alms. Full of suspicion, they chased him out of town and it was only an old lady who lived some way out who opened her door to him. The following morning, when she woke, the old lady could see that a lake had flooded the

entire town. Just out of the corner of her eyes she caught
sight of a shadow walking away across the water. Only her
house and that of her daughter were saved. And these are
the two little islands that are still to be seen in the middle
of Lac d'Aiguebelette. 'Well, what do you think of that story
then?' asked Jean as he produced a board of local cheeses
and a bottle of wine.

'Well, I suppose it's full of Christian symbolism?' I
hazarded. Sometimes I have absolutely no idea what I'm
talking about. Does that happen to everyone?

'Yes, *tout à fait*,' he replied to my delight. 'But even some
stories that you hear today have their roots in a pagan past.'

He went on to describe the *sarvan*, a little imp who lives
in the mountains and who is the protector of hearth and
home. In order to keep him sweet, householders are
expected to occasionally leave a bowl of milk on a window-
sill lest he become grumpy and something terrible befalls
them. Many of the fairies who lived in the mountains were
the offspring of pagan gods. The grottoes and caves were
the homes of devils and sorcerers. At Sassenage, the elf
Melusine is said to have bathed in the hot water that bubbled
in the strange basins carved into the rock. The lords of that
particular manor claimed to be directly descended from
him. No doubt the fiery Fontaine de l'Arzelier, the fountain where flammable gases seeping from the rocks
occasionally burst into fire, was one of the numerous residences of the devil.

'All very interesting,' mused Jean, and despite my exhaustion, I agreed with him. 'Now let me get you back home.
You never know, if we drive slow enough we might even
see one of these little mountain people.'

7

Going On 'Une Datte'

Deciding that another day's skiing so soon after my disastrous outing would be a mistake, I decided instead to head down the hill to buy some provisions with which to equip my new kitchen. It was a splendid morning for a walk and despite the fact that my nose was throbbing and bulging like a bullfrog and I was hobbling, it was with a whistle that I slung over my shoulder an old knapsack which had been hanging on the back of the front door and grabbed a stout stick that leant against the porch. 'I love to go a-wandering along the mountain track, and as I go I love to sing,' I sang lustily to a collection of rather bewildered looking goats whose small stable I passed on my way down the hill. Across the valley I could see the small ant-like figures of skiers weaving their way downwards in tighter or wider curves depending on their ability. Watching them reminded me how strange it was that human beings would spend the best part of an hour getting to the top of a mountain in order to get back down it again – accidents notwithstanding – in a matter of minutes.

Following the road that cut across the piste I noticed that, although it was now past 10 o'clock, as yet no car had attempted to make its way either up or down, and this only served to underline my very pleasant feeling of isolation. So it was to my great surprise that, when I rounded the next corner, I found myself face-to-face with a very large and very shaggy horse. Attached to the horse was a cart with sleds instead of wheels and on it was piled high an enormous mountain of firewood. Only when I attempted to step around the horse did I encounter its owner, a tiny man with pinched features dressed in a *bleu de travail* workman's boiler suit, rubber boots, a leather jerkin and a rather greasy-looking flat cap under which was sandwiched what was unmistakably an extraordinarily poor quality toupee. Trying not to look hard at this last accessory, I greeted the man with a cheerful '*Bonjour, monsieur*', but received no more than the most grudging grunt in return. In fact, I got a jollier response from the horse, who shook its head up and down and neighed in a most winsome fashion. For such politeness it received a smack on the backside from its owner and the two of them trudged slowly on up the hill. Rude sod, I thought, as I continued on my way stepping in the horse's hoof-prints. Still, nothing on this fantastic morning was going to dim my spirits, particularly in light of the fact that I was still alive after the previous day's mishap, and I was still just as cheerful when I arrived in the main square.

After a quick breakfast in my *salon de thé*, I had a wander down the main strip. Although most of the shops were all more or less directly connected with the skiing industry – offering for hire just about everything imaginable from snowboards, *raquettes* and miniskis to strap to your feet, to any size of accommodation, hot air balloons and helicopters – others were more general in nature, servicing not only the tourist population but also, I presumed, the needs of the local inhabitants. On the right, halfway down the street was the village butcher. A huge rotisserie, fully stocked with chickens and guinea fowl plucked and dressed for the occasion, was already performing its dual task of cooking the contents and attracting extra custom with the delicious smells it emitted.

Inside, the counters were divided into two separate halves; on the left were laid out any number of different sausages, pâtés, terrines, hams and other prepared meats and salads, and on the other side were endless confusing but nonetheless appetising cuts of meat. The owner leant over the glass top and wished me a good day. What would I like? I could not help noticing, as I pointed out a variety of things, how he resembled a chalk picture of a jolly pink pig on a blackboard just behind him. All the more surprising then was it when I noticed a photograph of him in distinctly younger years dressed in ski attire and clutching the inevitable silver cup. It seemed that pretty much everyone in Mont St Bernard had at some stage earned some kind of award.

Next stop was the ski shop that I had visited the day before. I just needed to pop in to replace my lost woolly hat. Enjoying the holiday atmosphere I made my way down the high street through the crowds of tourists that thronged outside the numerous boutiques. They were studiously engaged in *la léche-vitrine* – window-licking – as the French would have it. As I approached the little parade of shops set back from the main strip I was surprised to discover that their façades were obscured by one of the enormous Hummers belonging to the Russians. It was the cause of considerable interest amongst many of the other local shop owners, who seemed unable to decide whether to take a photograph of it or report it to the police. Skirting around it, I made for the front door but my path was blocked by a large man in a black leather coat and sunglasses, his arms folded across his chest in an almost laughable fashion. This did not, on the other hand, mean that getting around him was going to be any kind of a joke. When I made to slip past him, he shifted his weight slightly making my entry impossible. Just for fun, I tried on the other side but he only swung back in my way and shook his head, fiddling as he did so with a small earpiece attached to a curly piece of wire that disappeared down the back of his jacket. Thinking of Aubrey, I managed to summon up reserves of sangfroid and with as much cool as I could muster made my way to a café on the corner of a side street. From the front window I scowled at the man with little effect, and then sat back with a cup of hot chocolate and waited to see what would happen next.

About twenty minutes later the front door of the ski shop opened and the old man that I had seen arrive at the Hotel de l'Aigle Brun appeared with his arm around the shoulders of the small boy, who was now dressed in bright-green ski clothes, with a matching bobble hat on his head. Behind them followed two or three young women now also dressed in ski suits – in their case, figure-hugging one-piece numbers that I was forced to admit suited them very well – and then the grey-faced secretary. His suit, however, remained of a business variety. Behind them appeared some more of the bodyguards, and despite their undoubted physical prowess they were almost staggering underneath the weight of skiing equipment that, it appeared, had just been purchased. In silence the group loaded themselves back into their tank, which roared into life with a spinning of wheels that spat muddy snow all over a little girl and the waffle that she was eating. Ignoring her wails of anguish, they drove off again in the direction of their hotel.

If the young Nicolas behind the counter of the ski shop was in any way surprised by his most recent customers, he most certainly showed it. When I made a slightly over-excited enquiry about what had happened he rubbed his thumb and forefingers together. He smiled and whistled before explaining what had happened.

'You wouldn't believe how much *fric* – dough – they have got. They only wanted all the most expensive things. That is the first thing that secretary man said.'

'Does he speak French then?'

'No, just English. I have never made so much effort ever in *mon anglais*. I was nearly *bilingue!*' he laughed, before rushing on. 'They paid for everything *en liquide* – cash – but there was nearly a problem because they wanted to pay in American dollars and I said, *Non!* They were angry – they said it was the best kind of money but I said, No, only Euros, so they opened up a different briefcase. Only five hundred Euro notes! Look!' He held up wads of purple notes.

Apparently, the old man, whose name Nicolas had worked out was Dimitri, and his son Alexei, the boy that I had seen, had told Sergei the head bodyguard and the young women that they could choose whatever they wanted from the shop and as much as they liked. They had, it appeared, taken their boss at his word.

So astonishing had his morning been that when I asked for exactly the same kind of hat that I had bought the day before, Nicolas showed no particular consternation. Instead, he took my money and then rather gallantly opened the door for me as I left.

I was just pulling on my new purchase outside when, to my surprise, I ran into young Guy. Expecting close questioning as to why I was not up there on the slopes getting down to it, I had prepared a number of excuses, most of which were mysterious enough to suggest that I might be involved in high finance or possibly some type of espionage. Now, though, it was Guy who appeared to be apologising, muttering about having to 'get some more gear'.

'Oh, okay, have a good time. I'll see you later on I expect.'

Whistling, I made my way in the general direction of the little supermarket. A couple of minutes later, I discovered that Guy had caught up with me again. Surprised, I stopped and smiled at him.

'Oh, sorry, dude. Can I just ask you a quick question – well more of a favour actually, man? You speak, like, French, yeah?'

I agreed that he could and that I did.

'Okay, groovy. I wonder if you could just come to the shop with me and ask them something for me.'

I didn't see why not.

Guy told me I was cool and we headed back down the street.

When we arrived in the shop, Nicolas did look more than surprised to see me return but instead of approaching him, Guy took me round the corner into the clothing section where, seated behind the counter, was the blonde-haired girl whom we had seen the day before. As we approached, I recognised that her red, white and blue outfit was in fact that of a ski instructor from the *Ecole de Ski Française* – France's self-proclaimed finest ski school. She smiled at us and stood up when we reached the counter.

'Je peux vous aider, messieurs?'

Standing next to him, I could sense how nervous Guy suddenly appeared to be; for a guy who liked to give the impression of being completely, as he might put it, 'sorted', he was now practically physically shaking.

'Well, my friend wanted to ask you something . . . I think . . .' I told her in French.

'Oh, really, okay.' She laughed and shot me a quizzical look.

'Well, Guy,' I whispered to him. 'What do you want to ask her?'

'Well, it's a bit embarrassing . . .'

For some reason we had both ducked almost below the level of the counter and were talking out of the backs of our hands.

'Well, for goodness' sake, what is it?'

'Well . . . what I really want to know is if she will go out with me.'

'Go out with you?' I asked slowly and rather stupidly.

'Yes, go out with me – you know, like on a date.'

'I can't ask her that.'

'Yes, you can. Go on. You can do it!'

'No, I can't!' I could feel myself blushing.

'Yes, you can. Just be brave.'

'Okay, but what happens if she says no?'

'Just get on with it!'

'All right, here goes.'

Slowly we both reappeared above the surface of the counter, and smiled nonchalantly at her.

She looked even more mystified.

'Well, we just wondered whether you would like to go out on a date with me – I mean him.'

'A date?'

'Yes, why?'

Only in the nick of time did I remember that *une datte* was actually the French for the fruit of a certain type of palm tree.

'No, no, I mean a *rendezvous*.'

'What has she said?' asked Guy nervously as we ducked down again. 'Yes, no, what?'

'Well, we haven't got quite that far yet,' I explained, without going into any of the finer points of vocabulary.

The girl shook her head.

Looking back up at her, Guy and I flushed. Then she laughed.

'Why not? I have never been out with *un anglais* before.'

'She says yes!'

'Oh, wicked.'

Guy and I slapped each other enthusiastically on the back and executed a neat 'high five'.

'Ask her what her name is. Go on, please, Will.'

'Amandine,' she replied.

'How do you say, "that is a very pretty name"?'

I told him and he repeated it back to her – after a fashion. Heaven only knows how she managed to decipher what it was that he had said, but she smiled, blushed and thanked him.

With a little help from his translator, Guy managed to arrange to come and pick up Amandine from the shop at seven o'clock the following evening. As we trooped through the snow he hurriedly sent text messages to all his friends telling them, perhaps a little prematurely, I thought, world-wearily, about his great success, before asking me what I thought the two of them should do on their date. As ever, I decided not to fall into the trap of providing advice. Experience told me that if the whole thing went horribly wrong, I would much prefer not to be held in any way responsible. Guy came up with a few ideas, some more feasible than others, and I grunted intermittently as we trooped round the small supermarket. This experience was about as interesting as trooping round any small supermarket anywhere else in the world and so therefore is not worthy of further elaboration.

Soon it was twelve o'clock – time for lunch and a consideration of the morning's work. Sitting in the sun on the terrace of Chez Gaston, Gaston's daytime enterprise, we watched the skiers descend like so many birds coming in to roost. A quarter of an hour later, the restaurant was filled to bursting. Now the only birds still swooping down the slopes were from a strange breed that lived most of the year round on the other side of the English Channel. When they migrated here for a week or two every winter they brought with them some of their more peculiar habits. Perhaps the weirdest of these was the tendency to make sandwiches in the morning and then take them with them to consume whilst they skied. With a number of excellent restaurants both up and down the mountain this seemed to the French almost masochistic. Shrugging, sipping their aperitifs and flicking open their menus, all the customers at Chez Gaston realised that they would never really fully understand their *cousins anglo-saxons*. Aubrey and Jimmy stumbled by a bit later on, and sat down at our table to find out whether I was getting on all right at Mon Repos and whether I had recovered from my mountain adventure of the night before. Word seemed to spread fast in this small village. Perhaps I had been mentioned and prayed for at Mass that morning. I assured them that everything was fine and showed off some of my purchases.

'Is the only way to get up to the chalet by foot?' I asked nervously. 'There isn't a bus that goes that way at all, is there?' Remembering the deep snow, I thought I already knew the answer to this question.

'Yeah . . . well . . . of course, you could ski there, dude . . .' Jimmy had, I noticed, begun to adopt Aubrey's leisurely style of delivery, and like all disciples was taking his master's teachings to extremes, even sporting a bandanna that was very similar in design and shape to that of his idol. In addition, he had also decided that the real world was altogether much too bright, and half his face was obscured by great saucers of sunglasses.

'Well, I don't think I could manage that with a whole load of shopping!' I laughed. The others didn't seem to think it would be too much of a problem.

'You would just get the *télécabine* up to the middle station and then there's a track that takes you through the woods. Stick to that and you'll find yourself coming out just behind the house. Wouldn't take you more than about five minutes.'

Well, I might give it a go, I supposed, when I didn't have all the shopping and I did have my skis.

No rush.

Towards the end of lunch Aubrey's girlfriend, the remarkably sane Emilie, and her friend Sophie, both ski instructors and it transpired friends of Amandine, stopped by for a cup of coffee. They were just off to meet their respective classes but had a few minutes to spare. It was only when everyone was introduced and there was a whole lot of kissing going on that I clicked, the pieces all suddenly falling into place.

Sophie!

It was *the* Sophie!

Sophie from the radio who was also Sophie the ski instructress. It could not get better.

Du calme, Will, *du calme*!

How beautiful she was! How poised! How perfect! How could that absolute fool Jay-Pee have been so horrible, so sexist about her? Boldly, I batted Jimmy out of the way when he tried to insinuate himself between her and me. I pondered our future together as I recovered from the playful elbow that Jimmy placed perfectly in my solar plexus. My eyes watered as rather blunderingly I struck up conversation with her.

'Oh, that's really what I should be doing I think, taking a few lessons.' I smiled at Sophie in what I hoped was a winning fashion. 'Any room in your class?'

'Maybe, it depends if you are very good.' Sophie smiled back as she readjusted her blonde ponytail, pulling her hair back from her bronzed face.

'Oh, I can be very good if you want, or I can be very

bad! Ha, ha!' A couple of glasses of red wine with my lunch had put me in a good, if rather embarrassingly frolicsome, frame of mind.

'No, I mean it depends if you are a very good skier or not.' She could look quite severe when she tried – probably because she had to deal with Jay-Pee on a regular basis.

'Oh, yes, I see what you mean, yes. Right sorry, yes. Hmm, well, I don't know that I would say I was very . . .'

'Just come along to the school sometime soon or something. Then we can give you a little test to check out your standard. It's okay?'

'Oh, yes, it's definitely okay. When would be *un bon moment*?' I said, and stumbled out of my seat as they stood up to leave.

'Well, now it will be after *les fêtes*.'

I had completely forgotten that Christmas was just round the corner.

'Yes, that will be great! *Joyeux Noël!*' I cried, and was just about to come out with another stunningly fatuous remark when the two instructresses left to meet their lucky, lucky ski classes.

Certainly the prospect of joining Sophie's ski group had put me in a remarkably positive mood. It also seemed to have provided me with a more than healthy appetite. From the restaurant, Guy, Jimmy and I – none of us seeming to have a great deal to do other than eating, drinking, skiing and sleeping – moved not very swiftly to a crêperie, and from there to the Café de la Poste for a few hot chocolates to prepare me for the route back up the hill.

How easy it was too crook your arms on a table, swill the contents of a near empty cup around and around, and chew the cud. I fear that, yet again, I overly exaggerated my past exploits on skis but I was fairly confident that I was not alone in that regard.

Yet again, rumours about the Russians were rife and it was Jimmy, who had friends all over the Alps, who presented us with his personal theory.

'Yeah, yeah, yeah, man.' He paused. 'I think they wanna buy Mont St Bernard.'

We laughed. Jimmy was a wag.

'You mean buy a chalet here or something, man?'

'No, no, no, serious, man. Look at that guy, you know, the guy who owns that football club. He tried to buy that huge resort you know. The whole of it!'

A certain quiet settled over our table. It was true that the papers had been full of the billionaire's antics. One hundred and fifty million Euros they said he had offered. It was just gossip and probably rubbish, but . . .

'Yeah, but this guy here is not in the same league.'

'Yeah, and this place is not a big resort, ha ha!'

But no one laughed.

We ordered some fanciful cocktails to cheer ourselves up. In silence we sucked our straws and then our teeth.

It was only as I was walking past the bottom stop of the *télécabine*, musing on our beautiful future – Sophie and me, the children, the house – that my mind turned to more practical matters, and I struck on an excellent energy-saving idea. Instead of taking the bubble up and skiing down to Mon Repos, I would just take the lift up and walk down a track that the others had told me about and that I had seen marked on the blown-up piste map on the front of the *télécabine* building. It had to be less exhausting than dragging all these bags up the hill through the thick snow. I couldn't think why the others hadn't suggested it as an idea.

There was only a small queue of skiers taking their last trip up the hill before the lift closed and I managed to get one of the small cabins to myself, thereby avoiding being injured by a piece of somebody else's ski equipment – usually wielded by a child under the age of six with fogged-up goggles. The view from the bubble was almost as good as the view from my front window, I thought rather smugly.

Once I'd got to the top and had avoided being sent round and back to the bottom by bashing my way through a kerfuffle of skis, sticks and small children, I went over for a quick chat with the ski-lift attendant. Dominique, a tall, broadly-smiling African from Djibouti, turned out to be not quite so ice cool as some of his colleagues and, after an exchange of brief potted biographies, he expressed great interest in what purchases I had made. This took some time as by now I had a full rucksack and two plastic carrier bags. After a rather complicated explanation of what he thought I should do to a chicken that I had bought, which seemed to involve a very delicious combination of tropical fruit, chilli peppers and spices, I managed to ask directions down to Les Hauteurs du Mont, the name, I had learnt at lunch, for the little hamlet where I lived.

'Why do you need to know that then?' he asked.

'Well,' I said, rather proudly. 'That is where I live now.'

'Ah, good, very nice. Well, I suppose you can get there on foot from here, but it is quite a long way and you know it's also pretty steep.' He pointed his fingers down at a very sharp angle to underline his point.

'Oh,' I said, with nothing-can-go-too-badly-wrong-can-it enthusiasm. 'I'm sure it'll be okay. Just point me in the right direction.'

In hindsight, I must admit that he looked a bit doubtful. Anyway, he did his best to describe the way and waved me off rather nervously as I set out across a relatively flat stretch of snow to the trees where I hoped to find the mountain path.

There was no path.

Whatever anybody else liked to claim there was definitely no path.

The long and gently winding road that was supposed to lead to my front door was nowhere to be seen. Instead, all I could make out was dense forest and untended snowdrifts. Without turning round, I considered my options, the most obvious of which was to get back in the bubble and go back down to the bottom with all the old grannies who had been having their tea at the Beauvoir Restaurant beside the cabin lift. I might at least get some more suggestions about how to best cook my chicken. There is a part of me, however, that is always very resistant to going back over the same old ground again unless it is strictly necessary. In this case though, I supposed there was no alternative, and with heavy heart I turned to head back to my attendant friend, who was still looking rather puzzled in my direction. Then, of course, I struck upon much the most obvious solution. As the piste ran past my balcony, it stood to reason that if I walked down the side of it I would eventually arrive home.

Some things are so straightforward.

Probably the first five yards of the piste were relatively easygoing. There I was just tramping along, admiring the view and whistling a jolly tune, but just as I was congratulating myself on the simplicity of my plan my feet disappeared from beneath me. Now, in a split second, I found myself lying on my back, my rucksack operating as a small sledge, my arms stretched out wide, a plastic carrier bag in each hand, heading feet first down the mountain. After a few moments I was travelling very fast indeed. Passing a number of rather surprised-looking skiers, I attempted to raise a wave, more out of panic than any attempt to be polite.

I could see between my widespread legs that I was approaching a very sharp bend in the piste and, as I

was almost totally incapable of navigating my way, I feared
that there was every chance that I would disappear straight
off the side of the track and into the trees where I would
not be found again until the following spring by a wood-
cutter in the woods. Somehow, miraculously, I hit a patch
of thicker snow which caused me very rapidly to come to
a halt. I stood up and brushed myself down. My purchases
and I all seemed to be in one piece, and I was able to smile
quite convincingly at those same skiers who now passed
me again heading for home. I started to walk. On this occasion I covered perhaps twenty yards before I went over
again. This time there was no stopping me, although I did
attempt a rudimentary steering system which involved
digging my heels into the snow, but apart from that I was
as close to being in freefall as it is possible to be whilst lying
on the ground. At one moment I considered relaxing and
just allowing myself to enjoy the sensation of hurtling down
the hill, much in the same way as some people seem to get
pleasure from descending the Cresta Run. Then I hit a large
bump and took off.

When I landed again, all the air from my lungs and all
my momentary enthusiasm for bobsleighing was expelled.
My chicken had made a break for freedom and was speeding
away from me. My deeply-buried competitive streak resur-
faced and stream-lining myself as much as was possible, I
did my utmost to overtake it. It was surprisingly skilful,
slipping and bobbing, finding the tightest, shortest route
around corners but I was fast gaining on it. As my mental
speedometer needle pointed into the red zone I suddenly
started to get scared. Digging in my heels again, I slowed
down – slightly.

After what felt like more than an hour I sensed some
movement above me, and peering up over the top of my
head, I spotted the outfit of a ski instructor. Not Sophie I

hoped – how embarrassing that would be. Actually, I did not really care who it was so long as they somehow brought me to a halt and got me home in one piece.

To my total consternation, the ski instructor, hiding behind a pair of mirrored glasses and a rather professional-looking hat, shot straight past me as if he had not seen me.

Not seen me!

He had practically skied over my head.

Just as I was summoning up a few of my choicer French swear words, I realised, my heart leaping with joy, that I was just about to cross the road that ran along the side of my house. I was only a few metres from home. For a second I worried about being squashed by a horse and cart on the road, but then realised I was already across and slowing down to a natural stop.

Relief flooded over me as I lay with my limbs spread out, gasping for air to reassure myself I was truly alive. I was. What was more I was unhurt and my chicken, which I had beaten quite comfortably, spun to a stop a couple of yards away.

It was a miracle.

However, unbeknownst to me, a fairly good bottle of red wine that I had bought at the supermarket had unfortunately come loose from one of the plastic bags that I was holding, and had been following me closely in my descent. Just as I was humming the second verse of 'I Will Survive', lying spread-eagled and relaxed on the snow in the last rays of the afternoon sun, it smacked me very hard on the back of the head.

I had a bruise for weeks, but at least the bloody thing didn't break. That would have been too much to bear.

8

Mireille and Olivier

If Aubrey moved in slow motion in his cowboy hiking boots, he went into fast forward the moment he clipped a pair of skis or a snowboard to his feet. His seniority and his undoubted ability meant that he was much admired by young French and English snowboarders and skiers alike. When he made his appearance on the slopes he became a cult figure. A snow guru, wherever he went we attempted to follow. Much travelled outside the winter months, he had more than one good tale to tell, and as long as I concentrated on slowing my heart-beat and banishing any impatience from my mind, I much enjoyed listening to his languid stories on the *terrasses* of many a mountain café.

Recognising a kindred spirit in me, or so he believed, he was assiduous in his efforts to show me the area. Although occasionally I took his name in vain, often quite volubly, as he led me down tortuously narrow, winding paths and steep snowfields that were the next closest thing to vertical, he certainly opened my horizons. More than once I felt quite intrepid. If it had not been for his kindly guidance, I would probably, paralysed by my own timidity, never have strayed far from the comfortable and rather sociable main blue run that weaved its gentle, well-maintained way from the Col du Pic down to the village.

One morning, early, surprisingly early, considering all that Aubrey had imbibed the evening before and that dawn had been breaking before he had eventually 'crashed out', we were clipping on our skis at the bottom of the main chair-lift. Jimmy, his faithful and rather shaggy side-kick, was of course in attendance. We had arranged a rendezvous with Guy and Amandine at the Iceman, a mountain café, for an early brunch. By now chair-lifts presented no concern for me and we queued up for the six-seater chatting happily. As was the case when things were busy, which they were now, we found ourselves funnelled into a queuing system with other skiers who were all coping more or less satis-factorily with the task of shuffling toward the lift whilst making as few enemies as possible. As we arrived at the automatic traps, a woman about my age, heavily disguised in hat and goggles, slid between me and Aubrey. To my right, although initially I hardly paid him any attention at all, a small boy lurched to a halt. Soon we were all on our way upward and the sun caught our faces as we rose above the frozen Lac de la Fontaine just behind the small village primary school. Keen to make the most of this unexpected and fleeting warmth, we removed our goggles, hats and gloves which we then gripped on our laps. The woman, it turned out, was Mireille, who we had met for lunch on my first morning on the slopes, and we exchanged *les bises* – kisses on either cheek – in the cramped confines of our seats.

'*Vous connaissez mon fils, Olivier, n'est-ce-pas?*' She pointed past me at the boy sitting at the end of the seat. He had been peering over the side with the definite intention of spitting on somebody's head – I knew, I recognised the type. Turning in his seat as he was introduced, he looked up into my face proffering his cheek to be kissed. For about three quarters of a second both of our brains whirred. Sitting next to me, his round, tanned features suddenly flushing a ruby red, was the boy who on my first outing had, from a safe distance, given me what Americans for some fathomless reason call the 'bird', and had then tried to hide his crime behind his sunglasses when we had last met over lunch. His brown, slightly mournful eyes flicked away for a second in embarrassment before he looked back at me. Was I going to say anything?

'*Salut, Olivier. Ça va?*' I grinned only very slightly.

'*Bonjour, m'sieur,*' he muttered, in not much more than a whisper, and suddenly interested himself in one of the toggles of his jacket.

Mireille, Aubrey and I chatted quite cheerfully during the twenty-minute ride. Aubrey, who had no formal qualification in French beyond GCSE, was well enough travelled to know that even the smallest effort pays great dividends. Now that he had spent some seven years on and off in France, he communicated, regardless of thumping mistakes and an accent more likely to be heard in a London record store, with a certain fluency, and we chatted away happily about the weather, the snow conditions and, of course, the Russians. (Apparently they had spent 50,000 Euros on champagne and oysters in the bar of the Hotel de l'Aigle Brun the previous day, and that was before lunch.) It transpired that the two of them knew one another because Aubrey, before he had gone into catering, had been employed by Mireille as an odd-job man, chopping logs and clearing snow, whilst she went out to work at the mayor's office. Olivier's mother had soft features, a gentle smile and a quiet way of talking that was entirely *sympathique*. What had brought me to Mont St Bernard? she wondered. I wondered too. How long was I staying? As long as the snow, I replied. Where was I staying? I pointed at Aubrey, who eventually explained about Mon Repos.

'So where are you living in the United Kingdom?' she asked.

'Well, to be honest, I haven't really lived there for a fair few years now.'

'Oh really, where have you been?'

'Well, it's a bit of a long story . . .' Carefully, I tried to give her a version of events that was short enough not to be boring but long enough to clarify that I had not been on the streets or in an institution for any significant part of that time. 'I'm a teacher really,' I finished. In England this last remark always seemed to be a bit of a conversation-stopper but, here, now, and in fact everywhere else, it elicited genuine interest.

'What do you teach?'

'By now, pretty much everything,' I laughed. 'In Africa, I was even teaching maths!'

As I had been telling my tale I sensed Olivier's renewed interest in the grown-up chat. When I turned round to glance at him I found him staring quite intently at me. Very quickly he looked away and mimed firing a catapult at a very fat lady in a fur hat who was snowploughing her way down the mountain behind a bronzed instructor.

When his mother spoke again I thought he might try to lift up the safety bar and throw himself into the void.

'Perhaps you would be interested in helping Olivier with his English?'

'Well . . . You know I am not sure how long I am going to be around for. It might not be worth it . . .' I could feel waves of support emanating from the little boy as I wriggled my way out of any commitment.

'Please think about it?' She paused and smiled. 'He does so need some help . . . Anyway, perhaps you will come to our Christmas party. On the twenty-fifth at lunchtime?'

'Party? Sounds great! Thanks very much.' The higher

than normal levels of hedonism inspired by the mountain air meant that I accepted without hesitation. So much was I looking forward to it that I hardly gave my departure from the chair-lift any thought at all. Only when I came to a halt a few yards away did I realise, with no small amount of surprise, that the whole exercise had been performed without incident.

We bid farewell to the mother and son, who skied off in the direction of Trappes where they were meeting some friends for lunch. They were both impressive, confident skiers, but I was surprised by the way Olivier dawdled and trailed behind Mireille rather than shooting at snow-melting speed, like his numerous peers, straight down the mountain. This, in my experience so far, certainly seemed to be the approach taken by anybody else his age.

Aubrey, who was quite used to making unilateral decisions for his troops, decreed that we were heading straight for the Penguin Bar. According to him, we needed to wait for about thirty to forty minutes until the snow was at its best; there was no point in our wasting our time with it before then. We just had time to fit in a couple of *demis*, those golden, frothy, but rather disappointing half pints of French lager. Beer drinking in France is as unimaginative as cheese eating is inspired: watery ale from a tap or bottles of Belgian beer that had all the effects of a pre-med – whichever the choice, the most exciting part of the whole experience is watching the bar person squirting a spray of water into the bottom of each glass from the pump set into the counter.

Feeling rather smug and not a little hungover I sipped a Coke as Aubrey and Jimmy swallowed their first drinks almost *coup sec* – down in one.

'Sad old job about that Mireille and her boy,' muttered Aubrey, as he played with his skull and cross-bones earring and checked out his bandanna in the bar-room mirror. He shook his head and said nothing more for a minute or two. Jimmy and I knew there was no point rushing him. Eventually he told us their story.

Sad old job it certainly was. From Aubrey's halting explanations and later versions of events the story of the mother and son became clear.

Mireille, who originally came from just outside Grenoble, had, as a French *fonctionnaire*, or civil servant, been sent up to Mont St Bernard in her mid-twenties. It had been a flattering promotion. Although she had missed home at the beginning and initially had made the trip home for the weekend on the cramped Friday night bus, she soon settled into the life of the village. She was a keen skier and had even represented her village in the regional Super slalom whilst she was still at the *lycée*. Her knowledge of all things skiing proved useful because part of her job responsibilities was the organisation of the various winter sport activities. At the men's downhill of 1991 she had met the regional champion Jacques-François Gilbert. It had been a *coup de foudre* – a lightning strike – love at first sight. Initially, he had temporarily been living in the Isère for training purposes and had had to travel a great deal for his sponsors. But soon after the end of that season he had come back to Mont St Bernard, his home, to be with her. The following year they had married at the small church in the village – an event that had even been featured on the local television news – and with his prize money and sponsorship earnings he had built them a large family chalet just down the hill from where I was staying at Mon Repos. Before long their first child Philippe was born, and a year later Olivier made his appearance.

Jacques-François had found himself a profitable career as a sports commentator and Mireille continued to enjoy her job at the *mairie*. Her mother, a widow, had moved from Grenoble to be with them and to look after her grandchildren. They had buried her back in her hometown just a few years ago. The boys, who had been deeply fond of her, had been shattered, but as winter moved into spring and that spring into summer, their memories of *Mamy* became less painfully sharp.

As Jacques-François's work was mainly concentrated in the months of the ski season he had had all of the summer to spend with his boys, swimming in the lake, mountain biking, hiking and bivouacking. He had taught them to play tennis on the municipal courts and teased them with a basketball under the hoop that hung over the garage door at home. For the whole of last summer Mireille had been driven to distraction as the three boys – as she termed them – taught each other to play the mouth organ. More than once she had told them to take themselves off up the mountain where there were only the goats to drive to distraction. Returning to the house, tanned by the fierce mountain sun, the two boys, having devoured every last crumb of their packed lunch hours earlier, would demand *tartines*, crunchy bread spread with butter and chocolate, and glasses of milk. Smiling, their father, sipping from a bottle of Kronenbourg, would watch them lovingly as they sat on the balcony eating as the sun slipped behind Mont Blanc.

The older of the two boys, Philippe, had begun to take a great interest in ice-skating and being strong and powerful was showing serious promise. Twice a week after the schools had gone back in September, his father would drive him to the municipal rink at Cluses in the early evening. For a couple of hours Philippe would be trained by a redoubtable Latvian lady, whilst his dad chatted with other parents who were waiting in the cosy café at the side of the rink to take their offspring home again. One night, on their way back home, Jacques-François and Philippe had collided with a beer lorry that had lost control as it came back down the mountain. When finally the *SAMU* – the paramedics – arrived, they found the the boy ejected from the car, a poppy bruise on his forehead, floating side by side with his father in a sea of broken, green glass. They had both been killed outright.

'Just like that, gone, yeah,' muttered Aubrey. 'Buried 'em both down there in the valley, in the village graveyard.'

Jimmy and I shook our heads, stroked our jaws vigorously and breathed out slowly. As I clipped my skis back in place later, I gazed down at the small, white church with its coppery-hued roof. Even this most innocent, peaceful corner of the world, where people came to forget their worries and just have fun, was touched by tragedy.

As we headed out toward *Le Domaine du Mystère*, in search of Guy and Amandine, my heart twisted and hurt, and I suddenly felt terrible to have accepted Mireille's offer of hospitality without a second thought, having moments before squirmed out of her request for help with Olivier's English. How much of an effort would that be? A few hours a week was the least I could do as a little gesture. At one stage, as we zoomed down to the next lift, I nearly lost my balance in a thick cloud of self-loathing, but emerged into the sunshine when I resolved to contact them as soon as possible and offer them any assistance that I could.

9

Money Matters

First dates can be a nightmare.

    Having had a quick flick through my own back catalogue I now realise that I do not wish to dwell on mine any further.

Perhaps it was the very fact that neither Guy nor Amandine spoke more than a few mispronounced words of the other's language that had made their first rendezvous such a success. Removed from the equation were the infinite possibilities for misinterpretation, gaffes, faux pas and occasional downright, even if unintended, rudeness. Instead, they had just sat in the corner of the bar at the comfortable but 'sodding expensive' Hotel Chamonix and grinned at each other over chemically volatile cocktails.

When Aubrey, Jimmy and I now caught up with them they had been going out with one another for several weeks. Today, in a state of bliss, they were sitting in two canvas deckchairs, hand in hand on the sunny terrace of the Iceman. They still grinned at each other pretty much all the time but now, at least, their soppy smiles were not quite so nauseating. They even managed to wave at us in a reasonably focused fashion. Guy regularly and cheerfully held me responsible for getting them 'sorted', and I had become firm friends with the vivacious Amandine.

When they eventually fully reappeared from their personal bubble of joy, they were pleased to see us, and we swapped bits of chit chat and gossip which seemed to mainly revolve around late-night shenanigans behind L'icebox.

'By the way,' remembered Guy, 'there's some bad news, guys.' He thought he had understood from Amandine, who had heard from her father the mayor, that both the banks had removed their sponsorship from the freestyle competition.

'Typical,' muttered Aubrey. 'Bloody capitalist pigs. Just an attempt to beat down the common man. Well, that's that. We'll have to cancel it. Have you told Nicolas yet?'

Guy and Amandine shook their heads sadly.

'He's going to be gutted,' Jimmy added.

He was absolutely right. For just at that moment, having executed a faultless 720° turn at the bottom of the piste, the young ski instructor stamped off his skis and came jogging over to us, waving and kicking up the snow in great good humour. When Aubrey told him, an avuncular arm round his shoulder, Nicolas was doubly devastated because he had just received the team lists from the other two competing villages. Now they had no advertising hoardings, no safety barriers, no expense budget and, most importantly, no prize money. Nicolas took the news particularly badly because he had been the leading light in trying to organise the event. Perhaps in some ways he had not been the best choice as spokesperson because, although he was affable, friendly and bright, he was also the village's best hope in the men's ski race. The older generation, who now acted as team selectors and trainers, could probably only imagine that the time Nicolas spent fiddling around with these stupid jumps and tricks was time that he could much more profitably have spent honing his technique on the downhill course.

Whilst the three others went into a conclave, Amandine showed me some of the pictures on her digital camera that Guy and she had taken on a trip to Thonon-les-Bains on the shores of Lake Geneva. She had invested a great deal of time making sure that Guy developed a better under-standing of the region. Ever inquisitive, I rather envied the youngster his various tours of La Savoie, and Amandine was certainly the most charming of guides.

When eventually the others reappeared, punching their fists together in an 'all for one and one for all' Three Muske-teers fashion, they looked distinctly more cheerful. Although it went much against the grain of these thoroughly modern men, who liked to feel that they were forever up-to-date with changing fashions, they would have to use some of the old equipment that had been used for the downhill the year before. Entertainment would have to be provided by Jay-Pee rather than the DJ they were hoping to get from Lyon. Aubrey would do the catering and they would see what booze they could scrounge from Gaston and the parents of various friends. Clubbing together they would try and raise sufficient prize money. They were back on track.

That afternoon the weather was unbeatable. Bright sunshine shone down on the perfectly manicured pistes of Mont St Bernard and, much cheered, Nicolas skied with me, giving me the odd useful tip. Although I would have to have been a pretty early starter to have been his father, there was still, nonetheless, quite an age difference between us, and perhaps I should have been embarrassed about being instructed by this youngster, but such is the nature of winter sports and the common purpose of its practitioners that I was just grateful for his help. Progress unfortunately was infinitesimally slow.

Christmas was nearly upon us, and this year, perhaps more than any other year, its approach was all but imperceptible. This I decided, as I wondered vaguely how I would otherwise have been celebrating it were I still in London, was because life in Mont St Bernard had about it a semi-permanent festive feel. Celebratory lights had shone over the two main streets from the very first evening I had arrived, and all around us were Christmas trees dark against the permanent snow. With only a few days to go, I enquired that evening, at the bar of the Café de la Poste, what everyone else intended to do. Apart from Mireille's party to which most people had been invited, it seemed that nobody else had given it much thought either.

Gaston, along with most of the other bars and shops, had decided to close up over this busiest of holiday periods, confirming in my mind that before long even the restaurants in France will close at lunchtime. Initially Aubrey had considered holding a 'gathering' at the chalet where he worked, but he had discovered a few days earlier that a late booking had been made and that the place would be unavailable. Instead, he suggested that we should have a Christmas Eve picnic high up on top of the glacier which would involve having to leave on foot at five in the morning. The combination of the time of departure, the method of transport and the fact that it had been dipping just below minus ten degrees at night for the last week made me a less than enthusiastic volunteer. Pretty much as usual, we parted company without reaching a conclusion. Nobody seemed to mind.

As I swung my skis over my shoulder and was about to head off in the direction of Mont Thierry for the last lift home, Aubrey hailed me with the well recognised 'Hey, dude!' Dropping my skis to the ground, I narrowly avoided squashing a rather nasty, slush-coloured dog belonging to a woman in a fur coat – the terrible woman from the ticket office. Fortunately she did not notice as she was heading off rather inelegantly in the opposite direction holding a daintily wrapped box of exquisite patisseries by a piece of golden ribbon. Aubrey offered me a lift back up the hill, which I gratefully accepted as I had been suffering from near-terminal thigh burn and toe cramp. When we pulled up outside the wooden house I invited him in for a drink as was the custom. Some three hours later, having consumed everything liquid in Mon Repos apart from the contents of the washing-up bottle, he made his still fairly steady way back to his van.

'By the way, dude,' he said, as he searched in vain for the door handle. It was of little surprise to me that he was having trouble locating it: it was now dark and cloudy, and he was still wearing sunglasses the black of a welder's mask. 'Yeah, dude. That was what I meant to ask you. I knew there was something. Some of us guys, we're going to head down to Geneva for a spot of Christmas shopping tomorrow, if you want to come. We'll ski in the morning then head on down. Could be a bit of a change.'

A bit of a change, strangely, was a really attractive idea.

Not that I didn't enjoy life in Mont St Bernard – indeed I had begun to consider it home. Wherever I lay my bobble hat, I suppose. It was just that living in the village was a surprisingly isolating experience. Gazing at the view from the window of Mon Repos, I had often found myself wondering what was happening in the rest of the world.

So once I had been offered the front seat of the van the following afternoon, due no doubt to my advanced age, and had waved at an assorted jumble of ski bums sitting on the floor in the back, I found myself in a state of genuine excitement. With great skill, Aubrey negotiated the twists

and turns of the mountain road that finally brought us to
the valley bottom. Geneva was barely an hour away, but it
was a pleasure to find myself on a road that was positively
Roman in its straightness and to be able to gaze out at flat
fields full of green grass.

'By the way, Williams,' Aubrey laughed and winked – or
at least I imagined he did, 'I saw Mireille at the *mairie* this
morning and she said she's looking forward to seeing us
on Christmas day.'

Pleased though I was by the news, I also felt rather odd
about the mother and son. It all suddenly seemed rather
intrusive on our part. Aubrey seemed to read my mind.

'Yeah, I know it's going to be kind of weird for them
but I guess they'll just be pleased to have the company.
You know, it's like the first Christmas that they've been
on their own, the two of them. I told her that you would
definitely be coming because you didn't have anything
else to do.'

'Right, er . . . thanks . . .' Piqued by his suggestion that
I was a layabout, I resolved that I would make the offer of
private lessons at the party.

It was only when we pulled up and parked in one of the
immaculate squares in downtown Geneva that I realised
quite how strange this new world was. Apart from the
obvious lack of snow, I was impressed by the extraordinary
tidiness, the spotlessness of the streets and buildings. With
a fresh breeze blowing in from the lake the place even
smelled clean.

Guy, who had emerged as one of the figures in the back
of the van, and who I hoped had been taking a lesson or
two in how to drive in the mountains, announced that he
needed to change some money. Would I help? He wanted
to buy a Christmas present for Amandine.

'Sure, well, there shouldn't be any shortage of banks!' I

laughed, and was met with a variety of blank stares. 'Oh, never mind, come on!'

Making for the first *Banque/Sparkasse* sign, I walked expectantly up to the automatic, glass sliding doors and narrowly avoided concussing myself when they failed to open. Guy pointed out an intercom button but let me do the buzzing. A red light turned green and the doors opened, and we bundled in to what turned out to be a time-lock, the doors closing and locking behind us. The next set of doors must have been made of one-way glass as we had to stand there for a few minutes, no doubt being inspected before they opened. Like new arrivals in the Land of Oz, we took a few steps and then found ourselves dumbstruck in front of the most extraordinary palace of glass and shining metal, with acres of marble, tumbling fountains and enough greenery to restock the Amazon rainforest. At the far end of the room, which was some four or five storeys high and lined with glass elevators, was a reception desk at which sat a distant figure. Tentatively, staring about us, we approached. As we made our way toward it, people wearing suits sitting in glass offices observed our progression with consternation and I thought in a couple of cases some alarm. Only once we reached the counter and I caught sight of our reflection in the massive mirror behind it, did I realise why our appearance might be cause for concern. In contrast to the pale, smooth and somewhat owlish countenance of the effete male receptionist dressed in a black jacket, tie and pinstripe trousers sitting in a leather-bound office chair, we were a distinctly rougher crowd. Pirates from a foreign land, we were all deeply tanned, some of us with great panda-eye goggle marks. We were anything but closely shaven. A number of our band sported rings around fingers and through ears, to say nothing of the metal studs that pierced any part of the human anatomy that was thought to be medically sensible. Aubrey, for a reason best known to himself, was wearing the helmet that he normally wore to go snowboarding. Our very own Tin Man, he had bought it in a German army surplus shop. Guy, proffering a number of rather grubby pound notes, would have done a reasonable audition for the part of the Scarecrow, with his blond hair sticking out in all directions and his bristly stubble sparkling in the high-tech downlights. If presumably I was the Dorothy and not the Cowardly Lion of this strange scenario then I was not going to be overawed by the situation. I leant nonchalantly on the counter, realising at a last glance that I looked more like a farm labourer than a high financier, and explained in German that we wanted to change some money.

'Yes, that will be quite in order,' replied the man, in English that was faultless but which was spoken in an accent that was inexplicably intensely irritating. 'What is the currency that you will be requiring?'

'Euros, please.'

'And the amount that you want to change?'

I sorted through the notes that Guy had handed me. 'Umm, sixty-five pounds sterling, please.'

Looking up at me suddenly, the man seemed about to laugh. Luckily for him, he managed to compose himself.

'Very sorry, sir. Our minimum sum for currency transactions is twenty thousand Euros. Perhaps you will find a bureau de change on the Main Street. That will be more suitable for, er . . . tourist exchange.'

Aubrey, who had been following the conversation over my shoulder, tipped back his helmet and with the leather strap dangling leant over the counter.

'What's your problem? Isn't his money good enough for you? You are looking at the proceeds of the labours of the working man. Not good enough for you? You know why? You're a capitalist, fascist, greedy, total twat! Yeah!'

'Yeah!' we all agreed.

Unbelievably, the receptionist slid his hand under the top of the table and pressed an emergency button. From nowhere a uniformed guard appeared. Now, my past encounters with uniformed guards have rarely ended to my benefit, so with as much self-respect as I could manage, I suggested to the others that we should take our, or rather Guy's, custom elsewhere and as a group we headed back towards the sliding doors. Silently the security man followed us. As we were backing away across the marble floor, the frosted-glass door of one of the offices that lined the massive hall opened. Over my shoulder I could hear two voices speaking in English, one with a Swiss accent bidding an emollient farewell; the other replied with an intonation that was indubitably Russian. It couldn't be, could it?

The others clearly thought the same and we turned simultaneously to discover Dimitri and Alexei emerging from the little room holding matching leather briefcases. They were followed by the harried-looking secretary. Alexei was dressed in a smaller, perfect copy of the three-piece suit that his father was wearing. The three bodyguards who appeared behind them were dressed as before in their regulation uniforms of black rollneck sweaters, black trousers and shoes, black leather jackets and black sunglasses.

The banker who had been dealing with them took one look at the situation and decided with innate discretion that he would wave away the security guard and retreat behind a closed door.

Our groups stood stock still and stared at one another.

'Hello. You are Williams, the teacher, yes?'

My companions and I took a little time to register that the old man, Dimitri, was talking to me. I could feel my friends staring at me as if I had just been unmasked as a double agent. About to plead my innocence with them, I looked at Dimitri instead and replied simply that I was. 'But how did you know my name and what I . . .'

'I make it my business to know everything.' The first 'e' of this last word was stretched out no doubt to impress upon us his thoroughness, but sadly its effect was more that of a pantomime villain. Snorting a little, I looked down to recover my composure and, as I did so, I was quite sure that I caught the little boy rolling his eyes and allowing a small sigh to escape his lips.

'Tell your men to stand back,' he said, as he waved away his bodyguards with a gesture of a gloved hand. Grinning, I waved my posse away, who to my surprise entered into the spirit of things and moved slowly backward staring darkly at the black-clad men. 'I have business proposal for you, Williams. You are living in this village Mont St Bernard, I think?' His accent was strong but he spoke clearly and deliberately.

'Yes, I do, but I'm not really a businessman.'

'We are all businessman,' he assured me.

'Oh, right.' I smiled and looked down at the boy, who was gazing at me curiously.

'This is my son, Alexei. He is learning English to work in UK and US. You will teach him. He will speak very good English . . .'

'Well, now listen, I'm not really here to . . .'

'And you must find nice friends for him so that he can speak with them and, how you say, have fun.' In his mouth this last concept sounded more like some minor surgical intervention.

'Now, look here . . .'

But it was too late – the man had already turned away, his arm over his son's shoulders. As they moved off and the bodyguards resumed their position, the child looked back at me rather blankly.

Little boy lost.

Of course, 'my men' were incensed by the way that Dimitri had spoken to me and were all for throwing down the gauntlet, or at least a thick-leather skiing glove. Laughing, as we toured the treasure trove of Geneva's shops, I suggested that they didn't take themselves or the Russians too seriously. But they were all quite young and so they did.

As we drove back up the hill, the only thing that really stood out in my mind was the image of the boy Alexei, so obviously uncomfortable and out of place. As we motored up into the snow line, I was reminded of the number of times that I had found myself out of my comfort zone. Although travelling was now an exciting challenge and something that I looked forward to, I could remember times when I would have done anything to have been back at home. So had it been when I had found myself in that deserted train station in Austria, or the time that I had found myself floating adrift in the Pacific or on the wrong end of eleven Zambian machine guns. Oh, home, sweet home, I thought, as I finally kicked the snow off my boots in the porch of the Café de la Poste.

10

A Merry Mountain Christmas

Christmas Day in Mont St Bernard turned out to be one of the best days' skiing to date, and so Mireille had rung around her various guests and suggested that they only come over once they had finished on the mountain. Feeling sun-scorched and extraordinarily hungry, I climbed the wooden staircase to the first-floor balcony of the handsome new chalet clutching my Christmas presents. Although I am by no means antisocial, I always have a feeling of vague nervousness prior to any social gathering, and on this particular occasion, given the sad events of that year, I perhaps felt more apprehensive than normal.

I need not have worried. Mireille, who greeted me at the doors of a large sitting-room open to the eaves and pressed a glass of *vin chaud* into my hand, had made great efforts to put her guests at ease. No doubt to lend her moral support, her cousin had come up from Grenoble and they had spent the day before getting the house ready and preparing the food. Through the lattice partition was a dining area, and the long table was laden with the finest produce that France has to offer. As a centrepiece, a long silver dish bearing a roast suckling pig, or more precisely

a *marcassin* – a baby wild boar – was flanked by a beautifully decorated goose and two roast duck. Terrines and
pâtés, foie gras, smoked hams and sausages overflowed
from wickerwork baskets alongside trays of oysters, crabs
and langoustines. Over on another table nearby were iced
bottles of champagne, fine red and white wines, and a
variety of home-bottled *digestifs*.

The preparation of such a feast, even with the assistance
of another pair of hands, would have required me to book
into a sanatorium for a week even before the arrival of the
guests, but Mireille and her cousin looked, as so many
French women manage effortlessly to do, as if they were
guests at their own party.

I was the first person to arrive apart from Aubrey, who
was looking surprisingly debonair in an American-style
tuxedo and had even eschewed his normal bandanna. Of
course, he was still wearing his sunglasses as he attempted
to repair a meat-slicing machine in the kitchen under the
watchful but silent gaze of Olivier. Aubrey waved a screwdriver in my general direction with a quick 'Yo, dude', and
the boy summoned up a weak smile of recognition.

Although I was itching to load my plate from the delicious array of food, good manners suggested that I should
wait until others had arrived. To pass the time Mireille
offered to show me the house.

Like many chalets built into the side of the mountain,
the living accommodation was spread out over the first
floor, the 'ground' floor being given over to garage space,
ski lockers and storage areas. This being a fairly spacious
example, there were four bedrooms all with their own
bathrooms, an office that had belonged to Jacques-
François and now appeared to be out of use, a large kitchen
and a mezzanine area that was given over to a children's
playroom. When we took the spiral staircase up to this

level I was taken aback by its extraordinary spotlessness.

'You must have the tidiest son in France!' I laughed, and then immediately regretted it as I saw Mireille's face fall.

'This room doesn't get used as much as it used to. Olivier doesn't seem to like coming up here any more. He used to play up here with his brother. Now he seems to spend most of his time in his room. Maybe there are just too many ghosts up here for him.' She paused.

'You know about my husband and Philippe . . .'

Glumly, I nodded. There did not seem to be much else to do.

As we walked back down into the living room Mireille confided to me in a low voice her various problems. Although we were relative strangers she was happy to reveal private information without embarrassment. Perhaps I have the face or the body language of someone quite approachable but this does not in any way mean that I then know how to respond. She said she had considered moving back to Grenoble where she still had family. Her cousin had been urging her to sell the chalet.

'But you know, Williams, some part of me says that I cannot, that it would be somehow unfaithful to my husband's memory.' She leant against the mantelpiece and gently rested her chin on her clenched hand, gazing into the fire.

On either side of an emblem carved into the middle of the ledge were the initials of the married couple and below it the date of their wedding. I could see her dilemma.

'Well, perhaps it is better for Olivier if you stay here. At least he has his friends around to distract him. At least he knows people here, rather than having to go off to start a new life somewhere else.'

'No, that is the worst thing. Since his father and his brother died . . . since the accident, you know, Olivier doesn't seem to have any more friends. It is not that they have been *méchant*, you know, nasty to him. It is just that I think they do not really know how to cope. They are perhaps a little frightened of the whole story. And also he has become much shyer, much more *introverti*, you know? He used to be such a popular little boy and he had so many friends, always laughing, always playing. Now it is like he is a shadow, almost like he is a ghost himself.' She looked up at me and my heart tightened painfully for a moment.

'Well, my experience of children is that if they were on a reasonably even keel before this kind of family tragedy, then, in time, and it's true it may be some quite long time, they will recover their lost selves,' I said, feeling, perhaps wrongly, rather pompous but still hoping to go some way to reassuring her.

'What worries me more than anything else is that he has begun to refuse to go to school. Next year he is supposed to be going into *sixième* down at the *collège* in Thonon-les-Bains with his fellow classmates, but at this rate he will have to repeat the year.'

My knowledge of the French education system meant that I understood her concerns. The move from primary to secondary school here was a significant rite of passage and having to delay this move by a year, something that happened in French schools with much more regularity than in England, could have a profound effect on youngsters.

'What is more his present school is what we call *une école Européenne*, partly because we are living in a tourist area, and so the pupils start to learn English from the age of six. With all the time that he is missing, even if he does move schools he will find himself seriously behind.'

'Well, if you think it would help, I would be happy to give him a few extra lessons. Only if you think he would be ready for that.' Far too often I make offers that I seriously regret afterward, but I knew that here this would not be the case. Their plight had moved me a great deal.

'Well, yes, I am sure that would be fantastic.' Her face lit up. 'He seems to be rather shy of men recently and I am sure that it would do him good to have the chance to talk about what is on his mind with someone else apart from his *maman*. Shall I ask him what he thinks?'

'Yes, but perhaps not right at the moment.' I certainly did not want to run the risk of once more being the cause of a family dispute over Christmas.

Mireille nodded as we wandered back into the living room where now a number of guests had appeared. Before long, after a celebratory round of champagne, the atmosphere became quite lively and I passed the rest of the afternoon engaged in pleasant but quite inconsequential conversation about snow, skis, wine and, of course, food.

Nicolas and Amandine arrived towards teatime having spent the earlier part of the day with their father, Norbert, the mayor, and the rest of their extended family. Guy until then had appeared quite disorientated, not least because he understood next to nothing of what was being said. He had been invited to go to Amandine's house but had, as he described it, 'bottled it'. When his girlfriend appeared he was transformed, and they slipped off into the furthest corner of the living room where they disappeared into their own private world. Nicolas had been told something of my recent travels by Guy, and as he was proposing *les voyages* himself over the course of the summer he was keen to pick my brains. Fuelled by good food and drink I trotted out a few anecdotes, not, I hope, because I was showing off but because I am genuinely enthusiastic about things that I have seen and enjoy discussing them with other people, particularly those who have an equal desire to discover some of the magical places that the world still has to offer.

Only when I was accepting another cup of coffee from Mireille did I notice that Aubrey and Olivier were sitting cross-legged on the floor next to us. They had been silently showing each other magic tricks but broke off to listen to my theories about the most dangerous animal in Africa.

Finally, I drew breath, and we were all a little surprised when Olivier, who had remained all but speechless during the course of the party, looked up at me quite sharply and spoke.

'The hippopotamus – the hippopotamus is known to be the most dangerous animal in Africa.'

'Yes, I have heard that too but can that be true? They seemed so slow and fat.'

'I think that their acceleration isn't that quick,' said the young boy solemnly. 'But I think when they are up to top speed, then they are very fast. You must never go between a mother and its baby, or between one and a river, or even between one in shallow water and deep water.'

'Excellent!' I exclaimed, pleased to discover some of these facts for myself. 'How do you know all this? It's amazing!'

Speaking softly, his lips hardly moving, he began to shuffle the cards in front of him, carefully and thoughtfully. 'My *papa* told me. He told us lots of things, *Philippe et moi.*'

11
Back To School

According to Sophie, our wonderful weather-announcer and my soon-to-be ski instructress, the forecast was good for early January. Sunshine all day and then further snowfall over 1100 metres overnight. She really had a very charming accent when she spoke English and made a delightful break from Jay-Pee, who this morning had taken to calling her *ma petite caille* – my little quail – which I could have told him for nothing she most certainly was not. At least by joining her ski class I would be able to provide her with some moral support.

Luckily, I was ready to go before I had to listen for the third time that morning to the song that makes people dance around like chickens. In fact, by my standards, it was really quite an early start, but I was spurred on by the prospect of being able to join Sophie's class before lunch. Despite my improvements I knew I still needed lessons. There is nothing worse than holding people up when you are skiing with them. Well, there is one thing worse and that is being held up by other people.

Sitting on the wooden boards of the porch I snapped my boots into my skis on the edge of the piste, reached back to give the front door a final rattle and launched off down the hill. Without further incident I soon found myself on the threshold of the ski school. So keen was I that it was not yet quite open and I had a few minutes to kill. At least I did not feel lonely because waiting with me were several hundred small children. Although they were of slightly different hues, they were all dressed pretty much identically in one-piece suits, helmets, goggles, and mittens attached to one another by a piece of elastic that ran inside their sleeves. None of the children, it appeared, were capable of carrying their skis more than about three yards before dropping them or jabbing them into someone else. At least a third of the youngsters were in tears before the teachers had even turned up.

Eventually Amandine opened the front door, waved at me and soon, with admirable organisation, had ranked the children into their various different classes. For half a dozen little boys and girls, and me – for some years at least – this was the first day at ski school. Kneeling down in the snow, Amandine explained to us how they were going to assess our ability. It was quite difficult to hear what she was saying so I decided it would be altogether simpler if I knelt down in the snow too. One little boy looked at me rather strangely but the others did not seem to mind. We were to take the shallow button lift up to the first brow of the hill and ski down slowly negotiating a number of fairly wide-set slalom flags. Despite a brief flashback when I grabbed hold of the button lift it all went relatively easily, and I even received a small round of applause from the other boys and girls when I reached the bottom. I had only snagged one of the flags, and I handed it over to an assistant instructor before snapping off my skis and wandering over to have a chat with my instructor Sophie. She was looking particularly fetching in a tricolour headband.

'Oh, Williams, good morning.'

'We were watching you skiing just now,' said Nicolas, who I now understood was still a trainee ski instructor, although with only just a couple of months of practical work to go before he qualified.

'Oh, yes, I'm a bit rusty I'm afraid.'

'Oh, no, but you are quite good,' said Sophie flatteringly. 'Unfortunately, you are not *very* good so you will not be able to join my group. You will end up being very tired and that is when accidents can happen.'

'Oh, yes,' I replied crestfallen, unable to cover up my disappointment. 'Maybe if I make some improvements perhaps it will be possible to move up a class?'

'Yes, perhaps. *Venez les enfants.*' And with that she swept gracefully away. I scowled at her oh-so-brilliant charges as they followed her.

'Oh, Williams, here comes your teacher now – Madame Brassard,' Amandine announced, with what I thought for a second might be a hint of humour in her voice. Nicolas was definitely smirking as I looked past him to where Madame Brassard was busily making her way up the hill, her skis balanced on her shoulder like two strips of balsa wood. For some reason the word Visigoth sprung to mind, although apart from her girth there was nothing in her appearance to remind me of invading barbarians. No helmet with horns – instead a headscarf printed with horses' bridles was tied neatly under her chin – and instead of a warrior's armour she wore a tight-fitting, very tight-fitting, gold ski suit which matched her not inconsiderable jewellery collection.

'She lives very high up in the valley,' Amandine told me, by way of an explanation for Madame Brassard's slight lateness. I bet she does, I thought, along with Bigfoot, Sasquatch and the Yeti. No, that was very unfair. I was sure that she was very charming and an excellent teacher until, that was, she lined us up and explained in no uncertain terms the dos and don'ts of the Brassard method of ski instruction. There seemed to be considerably more don'ts than dos, and the military approach which she clearly intended to take to our self-improvement left all the children looking slightly shell-shocked, and in a couple of cases glancing nervously over their shoulders to see whether in fact their mothers had already left.

'Okay, Nicolas, today you will be joining . . . let's see which group.' Amandine ran her finger down the list on her clipboard before looking up and saying with a completely straight face to her brother: 'Oh, yes, that's right, today you will be accompanying Madame Brassard.'

That had absolutely the desired effect of wiping the smug grin off his face, and I gave him a complicit wink to which he replied with a weak smile and a slight shake of his head.

Actually, despite or perhaps because of the fact that Madame Brassard was extremely demanding, we made astonishing progress. Things were probably slightly more difficult for me than the little ones because nearly all the equipment that we used was designed for human beings who were somewhere between four foot and four foot three tall. Not since a particularly torrid evening in a Madrid nightclub have I wiggled my hips as much as I did trying to get down the children's slalom track.

On the several occasions on which I fell over I had the rather curious experience of being surrounded by little people who grabbed at my clothing and pulled until I was upright again. It was the reverse of Gulliver being pinned down by the Lilliputians.

'*Allez, venez, Williams! Plus vite! Plus vite!*'

Blimey, six-year-olds can be demanding.

Still, by the end of the first day I felt distinctly more confident than I had the day before last. Skiing back down from the top of Mont Thierry passing the scene of my impromptu luging performance, I did very much wonder whether I would be able to walk in the morning. Back in Mont St Bernard, just as I was arriving back at my front door after my lesson, I spotted, not for the first time, a few yards up the little lane, a small low chalet, the ends of its roof touching the snowdrifts. Outside it stood the sleigh that I had seen towed by the horse that had plodded up the hill a couple of days before. There was, on the other hand, no sign of either the horse or its owner. Overcome all of a sudden by neighbourly enthusiasm, I unclipped my skis, planted them outside the front door of my house and trotted up the slope to the front door digging the toes of my ski boots into the snow to create my own little set of steps. Pulling my new bobble hat from my head, I knocked on the front door and then rang a small brass bell that I found next to it with some energy. The clean sweet notes it gave out through the fresh light air must have been audible down in the village.

Initially there was no response, but then I noticed some movement coming from a chicken coop; a few minutes later a monolithic woman appeared dressed in an apron that had once had a floral pattern but was now almost uniformly the same grey as her hair and her moustache. From behind her, like a suspicious fox, appeared the head and wonky toupee of the man I had seen on the lane shortly after my arrival at Mon Repos. Neither of them looked particularly pleased to see me, but convinced as I am, however corny it might be, that a smile has been my most useful piece of equipment on my travels to date, I beamed at them. Staring at me closely, the husband whispered something into his wife's ear and she nodded and seemed to grip the long-handled pitchfork that she was holding a little more firmly. The old man took a step forward waving his hand at me – shooing me away.

'*Vous, vous êtes Russe? No Ruski, vous comprenez? No Ruski ici!*'

No, I explained hurriedly, I was not Russian. I was English. I was their neighbour!

They looked mildly less unimpressed.

I tried to get our relationship back on course with a cheery '*Bonjour, monsieur'dame.*' '*Bonjour, monsieur,*' they rather grudgingly replied.

As is my habit, perhaps rather too often, I launched into a quick breakdown of who I was, why I was there and what I thought of most of the world's problems. This normally works very well with French people, who often seem to be rather more interested in what is happening on our planet than my fellow countrymen.

In this particular case my theory did not appear to be proving true. Nonetheless, I pressed on.

'My name is William. William and not Williams! What is your name?'

The little man wiggled his cap, thereby scratching his head with his hairpiece, and thought for a minute.

'Job,' he replied.

'My job? Oh, well . . . *Bof* . . . *Bof* . . .'

'*Non, non!*' The man tutted and his wife put her hands on where her hips would normally have been. 'Our name is Job.'

'Oh, I see. *Enchanté.*' And then suddenly thinking that perhaps this last remark was perhaps more normally reserved for empresses and heads of state I added, '*C'est cool.*'

'Would you like some eggs?' Madame Job asked, smiling slightly.

'Yes, yes I would. *Merci,*' I replied, much flattered by this gesture of friendly neighbourliness. I knew it. A smile worked every time.

'How many would you like, er . . . Williams?'

'Actually, it's Will . . . oh, never mind. *Une demi-douzaine?* Six?'

With a bit of a bustle, which slightly dislodged her husband and had him reaching instinctively for his cap, Madame Job disappeared back inside the chicken house. Before long she reappeared with the eggs held in the front of her apron.

'*Tenez.*' She proffered them with not very clean fingers. I took them three in each hand.

'That will be two Euros, please,' she requested politely.

Later that evening I headed down through the snow to the village where I had arranged to meet the 'gang'. The stars, rarely seen in big cities, filled the night sky and the moon lit my way as brightly as the street-lighting that was yet to reach Les Hauteurs du Mont. A solid base of ice had formed under the twenty or so centimetres of powdered snow, the surface of which swirled slightly in the cold breeze that blew down the mountainside. Now, though, I had adapted to the vagaries of Alpine temperatures. It had taken some time to remember the trick of wearing a number of thin layers which, when the sun shone as hot as a summer's day on the restaurants at lunchtime, could be stripped off and then replaced at that sudden moment when the temperatures plummeted as light went to shade and the rays of the sun disappeared behind the tips of the mountains.

This evening, though, I was well insulated, not least by the comforting effects of the omelette I had prepared from Madame Job's eggs. It had taken me some time to pay her the two Euros as my hands were full of the six eggs. Having considered momentarily resolving this problem by juggling them as I reached for my change as clever party entertainers can do, I decided instead to put the eggs into various of

my numerous pockets. Strangely, I only ever found five of
them again. Just as I was wishing them a good evening and
heading back down the hill to Mon Repos, Madame Job
called me back. Perhaps she was feeling slightly uncharit-
able because after digging around for a while in the wide
pocket at the front of her apron she pulled out a dirty
handful of something.

'*Tenez, c'est très bon pour les omelettes.*'

'Oh, yes,' said the old man, suddenly interested and
smiling slightly. 'Yes, *les cèpes*, just soak them a little, fry
them in good butter for a few minutes with a little parsley.
Then you can just sprinkle them on your omelette and *voilà*!'

Sniffing the contents of my cupped hands, crisp, dark-
brown chips of mushroom, my head was suddenly filled
with the rich, damp smell of the humus of the forest. Stoking
up my little wood stove, which had the thoughtful habit of
quietly smouldering throughout the day before bursting
back into life on my return when I opened the small vent
on the front, I cooked the omelette with butter and cream.
Along with the mushrooms, two feathery slices of *jambon
de Savoie*, some crispy bread and a glass of the local, light
red wine *La Mondeuse* had the effect of making me want to
head straight for my bed, but I had promised the others
that I would meet them 'for a few beers', (although this I
had discovered was a euphemistic phrase loaded with
understatement).

Nicolas and I had shared quite a few surreptitious laughs
through the course of the day, and I was looking forward
to meeting up with him to have a few more – sadly probably at the expense of the good Madame Brassard.

When I reached the café it was already late and a last
few weary punters were making their way unsteadily
towards the door, leaving only the *saisonniers* crowded
round the fire. It did strike me then that of course it should

really have been them leaving first because, as most of them worked in the various chalets, they would have to be up and about quite a lot earlier than the guests, clearing up from the night before and getting all the breakfasts ready. Somehow, this logic did not seem to apply to the lifestyle of a chalet boy or girl, and instead of yawns and farewells conversation was lively.

More news had filtered down the valleys from a local, larger resort. At the Office de Tourisme they had been doing some market research. Over a two week period in December, it was reported, fifteen thousand Russians had shelled out exactly ten times the amount of money spent by forty thousand French.

'Here's one for you,' Jimmy called from the chair behind the bar on which he was standing. Frowning slightly he fiddled with the buttons of his mobile until he found the text message sent from our spy in the other camp. 'Here you go: new record set at the Babylon Hotel. Vladimir Dumorov sprayed his guests with two hundred and sixty magnums of champagne in one evening. Estimated cost of each bottle four hundred and forty Euros, so total bill of one hundred and fourteen thousand, four hundred Euros.' We shook our heads in disbelief over a last bottle of rough red wine.

After we had finished gasping Aubrey started to chunter and do his own calculations, but sometime later Jimmy threw a white dish-cloth over the top of the brass beer handles, pulled a large bundle of old-fashioned-looking keys out of the back of the drawer where the used coffee grains were usually dumped, and pronounced the words that ever since I hit thirty have filled me with a leaden sinking feeling.

'Right, guys, let's go clubbing!'

Before long we were queuing outside what looked like a large woodshed, and I pondered on the fact that the

'Licebox' – the apostrophe had sadly gone missing some seasons earlier – was no exception from the couple of dozen or so other nightspots that I had visited in various ski resorts over the years. It was a complete dump.

Common to all these establishments were a number of equally depressing features: astonishingly, outrageously expensive drinks – often marked up by some fifty times their true value – appalling decor that was normally in a very poor state of disrepair, seating that was without fail and for a variety of reasons best not considered either wet or sticky and, above all, dismal music. This did though, in the case of the Licebox, have an upside because it meant that this evening, for the first time, I was actually to encounter Jay-Pee in the flesh. As we walked in I recognised his braying but somehow also rather plaintive tones before I actually clapped eyes on him. As a puff of dry ice cleared away from the turntables there he was in all his disc jockey glory. Surely even by his standards the shirt open to his midriff, the body hair and the long, looping gold chain were a massive mistake. His jeans were of such a tightness that they made movement difficult and, I would have imagined, procreation a biological impossibility. So astonishingly tight were they that it was almost impossible to take in the true dreadfulness of his white socks and black latticed slip-on shoes. Hawk-nosed and eagle-browed, he was keeping an eye out for prey as he held a pair of headphones to one ear, fiddled with one of his records, combed his hair, which was long, blond and remarkably well-kempt, smoked and bopped around. Next to him, a study in narcoleptic boredom, was his assistant Sophie, who was looking just as splendid as she had on the slopes earlier in the day. Occasionally she would have to jab Jay-Pee with one of his free giveaway Licebox pens or swat him none too delicately over the back of the head with a record when he overstepped the mark. All of this he found remarkably amusing and responded with an exhibition of crotch-pumping that would have made the King wilt with embarrassment. Sophie, sophistication incarnate, managed, for the main part, to stand aloof smoking cigarettes with a style that French girls must be taught at school.

Jimmy and I admired her from a distance. Up there on her podium she looked quite unattainable.

There were quite a few familiar faces in the crowd. Gaston, who owned the Licebox as part of his portfolio of local businesses, played the role of a near motionless Mine Host at one end of the bar; occasionally people would come up to him to pay their respects and if he liked them well enough, he would wave a drink in their direction from the busy barman. Jimmy was soon giggling away with a number of girls who looked as if they had just returned from auditions for the Addams family and whose makeup guaranteed that their skin would never be affected by the ravages of the mountain sun. Aubrey and his *plongeur*, his washer-upper at the chalet, Jerome, an old friend, were reliving experiences in Mexico over a bottle of French tequila, and Nicolas was charming all and sundry on the dance floor. Only Guy appeared not to be enjoying himself, and was peering rather dismally into a glass of flat beer at the other end of the bar from the expressionless Gaston. I asked him how he was.

'Oh, okay, I suppose. Amandine has had to go to Chamonix for a week because she's got some training course.'

'Oh, okay, I see. So how is that going anyway?' I asked. A lifetime of teaching youngsters had taught me that asking questions was the very worst way of trying to find out what was going on, but Guy didn't seem to mind.

'Oh, it's going absolutely great. She's such a nice girl.

The only thing is, I'm a bit worried because I don't think she can understand a single word that I say to her.'

'Oh, I see what you mean. That probably is a bit of a problem.'

'You know I learnt French for five years at school and I can't speak a single word of it. That's so bad, you know. I wish I could do some lessons or something. Hey, Will, you used to teach French? You could give us all some lessons, you know, just maybe for a couple of hours. Cool.'

'Well . . . er . . .'

'Totally awesome!' He looked so pleased I could hardly bring myself to disappoint him, and he charged off to tell the others.

Despite the fact that on every occasion that I have been to a nightclub I make a promise to myself on arrival that I will not dance, I always do. Something happens. It's terrible. On this particular evening, however, I mistakenly believed that it might be a sensible tactical manoeuvre. Jimmy, in a blatant play for Sophie's attention, had taken to the middle of the dance floor and was hurling himself around in a fashion that would suggest that he was receiving a number of particularly nasty electric shocks through the soles of his feet. So powerful were they that on occasion he was knocked to the ground in order to bounce up seconds later. When the object of his affections appeared more interested in sending a text message, he took desperate measures and was soon to be found spinning on his back, and on one occasion on his head. Although I had no intention of behaving in any way so foolishly, I took it upon myself to enter into competition with him. Over the years I have adopted a number of dancing styles – each as inept and certainly as embarrassing as the last. That night I tested out each in turn but none, from my electronic robot moves to my cowboy hoe-down through rock-a-billy knee-wobbling and a one man tango, seemed to elicit remotely the right reaction. Despite our every attempt to attract Sophie's attention she hardly seemed to notice our presence, preferring to chat to a few of her girlfriends and sip, rather elegantly, from a glass of mineral water. Eventually the two of us gave up and staggered to the bar. Our rivalry, of course, was unspoken, and Jimmy and I chatted, as much as was possible whilst shouting at the top of our voices, about everything under the mirror ball it was possible to imagine – except Sophie.

Soon I was experiencing the craving that besets me every time I go nightclubbing – the desperate desire to leave and go home. It was as I was concocting excuses for my departure that I noticed the party of new arrivals.

One corner of the Licebox had been entirely colonised by the Russian party. Dimitri sat in their centre, a long slim glass of champagne bubbling gently next to a magnum of Krug resting in an ice bucket. Before long, Sergei, the head bodyguard, came wandering slowly over to me, cool as you like, or as nonchalantly as it is possible to do when everyone in the place is staring at you, convinced that you have a machine gun hanging down under your leather coat.

'Mr Dimitri would like to offer you a glass of champagne.'

Shrugging in the knowledge that more often than not in life resistance is useless, I followed him over and Dimitri made space for me to sit next to him. The conversation was brief. Alexei would be beginning lessons with me the following week. What days should he appear and where would the classes take place? Knowing that the chances were that I would come across the Russians again, I had given this particular question some thought. I explained to my oligarch host that the boy could join me and Olivier. It would probably be nice for both of them to have some company.

'Excellent, and now we can have some toasts to celebrate this.' If Dimitri was surprised at my acquiescence he did not show it and gestured at his secretary, who in turn waved at one of the bodyguards who spoke to Gaston at the bar. Within a moment a most authentic-looking frozen bottle of vodka was produced and oily shots poured into a number of small glasses. It was pretty authentic tasting too I discovered.

Looking reclusive and almost invisible behind his dark glasses and shrunken in a huge black cashmere overcoat, Dimitri was an off-putting sight but, perhaps because of the enlivening effects of the champagne, he was nothing less than chatty. Fortunate, really, that the Krug was having some influence. The Licebox price was 3,500 Euros a bottle. Conversation was complicated not only by the pounding music provided by the pumping Jay-Pee but also by the fact that Dimitri's English was limited. His secretary, looking even more exhausted than the last time I had seen him, did his best to fill in the gaps.

'So,' Dimitri asked. 'You are an educated man? And you have been to high school, university?'

My face flushing not from any false modesty but from the fire that had just broken out in my belly, I nodded.

'Pah!' replied Dimitri in a not very comforting way. 'I am man of the people – a working man – not intelligentsia like you. All my life I have working, working. Look, this is the sign of my work.'

Holding out his hands, palms upward, he shook them in front of me. I looked down and was surprised by the contrast between the calloused scarred skin and the soft silk of the cuff of his shirt and its large diamond cufflinks.

'Show me yours,' he demanded.

Imagining a quick game of 'paper scissors rock', I held out my hands, which trembled slightly, not from trepidation but from my manful attempts not to laugh.

'You see? Look,' he called over one of his bodyguards. 'Soft! You have never chopped up logs in Russian winter. You didn't ever dig vegetables in the frozen ground. I hate you people.'

Silence.

'By the way, you know France, I think? What is best? Krug or this Dom Perignon champagne?' He gestured at a number of upturned bottles in sparkling ice buckets. 'Just recently I have been reading in *Kommersant* newspaper – and this is best newspaper in Russia – it is newspaper for businessman. Yes, I think the best. But yes, I have read maybe I should try American champagne? What do you think?'

'Well . . .' Somehow, in this company, I did not think that ignorance or disinterest would cut the mustard. Bullshit seemed to be the order of the day. Feeling somewhat in my element, I tossed a mental coin and was just about to put in a vote for French champagne-makers out of some sort of misplaced patriotism when suddenly a blue glow appeared at Dimitri's ear. His hands-free headset was receiving a call. Hurriedly he stood up and headed for the main door followed by a group of black-coated men.

Fiddling with the briefcase on his knees, Dimitri's secretary smiled a watery smile.

'Have you worked for him for long then?'

'Since the beginning.'

And so it was that I heard the story of Dimitri's millions. For thirty years, Dimitri, a bachelor, had lived with his mother, a widow worker, in a tenement block in Lovino-Petrovsky, a satellite town a few hundred kilometres from Moscow. At quite a young age, he had been employed as the janitor in a state-run factory that produced gas pipes. His job had been undemanding but he had enjoyed the security of the routine and the company of his comrades at work. He was responsible for cleaning the offices of the managers and checking that the boilers provided a steady stream of warmth through the bitter winter months. Not too much news from the outside world filtered into the little office that he had been given next to the canteen, but by 1994 things were on the move in the USSR. The ice floe of the Russian Empire was cracking up and sections of it were floating off in disparate directions. So, too, the restrictive infrastructure of the state creaked and finally split. The tightly controlled economy burst apart like a mildewed money bag and everything changed. Suddenly, shockingly, the factory closed.

Most of the party-appointed managers never showed up again, but the workers, for want of anything better to do, continued to appear as usual. One day, about a week after the factory officially stopped production, Tarasov, one of the better managers, came into the factory on his way south. Rushing about, he handed each member of the workforce a sheet of paper allowing him one per cent ownership of the factory. 'Do what you can, comrades. It's up to you now. There is no one to look after you,' he called as he jumped into his Lada.

Slowly, over the next two weeks, production started again and within a few months things returned to a strange kind of normality. Over this period of time, Dimitri, who had never been a particularly dominant character, found himself being leaned on by his colleagues to hand out tens of litres of floor cleaner that he had locked in his metal cabinet. His workmates' interest in the product did not stem from any love of household chores but more from its impressive fifty-four per cent alcohol content. A one per cent share certificate could buy you two litres, which was enough to make for a fine party. By the time the spring sunshine started to warm the grey concrete of the ugly factory buildings Dimitri owned eighty-nine per cent of the company. When he sold the company a year later he was suddenly extremely rich. Many of his colleagues, less lucky than he, would pop around wondering whether they might borrow some of Dimitri's good fortune. A year later the first branch of his bank opened and, this was all that the secretary would divulge, these days he had 'many different business interests'.

His telephone call at an end, Dimitri returned demanding that now some Russian music be played. A cassette was shoved into Jay-Pee's rather unwilling hand and the Russian party took to the dance floor. I was not sure what I expected from Russian disco music, but I think that I imagined something that involved a balalaika, a degree of leg-kicking and the odd reference to Rasputin. Ruki-Vverkh, the name of the band that was played, was not at all like that. Theirs was a rather aggressive version of technopop that had the bodyguards leaping around with such energy that I feared for the safety of some of the supporting walls. It transpired that the name of the band meant 'Hands Up!' which was in some rather curious way rather apt.

'You will look after my son,' whispered Dimitri, as much as was possible in a room which was bulging from an astonishing decibel level. 'He is all that I have now. I was married very late and now his mother is dead. You know this?'

'Er, no . . .'

'She is killed by gangsters in the early days.'

'Oh, I see, right . . .'

'Yes. Alexei is just a small boy at this time. Now I don't have any women. Oh, these girls here they are just, er, how is *Raspisnye* in English?' He consulted his secretary. 'Yes, they are just models from the agency. They are just, what you say, "dawly burds".'

'Yes,' I muttered, admiring the gyrating legs on the flashing squares of the dance floor. 'Very good.'

'Yes, of course very good! These girls are from Russia. They are the best.'

When the second bottle of vodka was finally finished Dimitri leaned over to me and asked me if I was ready to leave.

'Oh, yes,' I replied with relief. I was exhausted.

'Goodnight,' he said quite politely, and gestured towards the door. 'Now it is a Russian time.' As I stood up rather unsteadily and turned around I realised that all the non-Russian customers apart from Gaston, the bar staff and the gawping Jay-Pee were being shepherded towards the door. I was relieved to see that Sophie had already made good her escape and not with Jimmy who was making his grumpy way to the door. Outside in the street, the atmosphere was nothing if not disgruntled. A mood of revolution swirled around with the snowflakes.

'Now you know what the people felt in 1917,' muttered Aubrey. Jimmy was not sure that he did and the two pottered off into the night discussing the Bolshevik uprising.

Somehow, I finally made my way back to Mon Repos. Collapsing into bed, I fell asleep to the smell of wood smoke and dreamed of skiing down the slopes of Mont St Bernard with my hands up, pursued by fur-clad Cossacks waving bottles of oily vodka and singing the *Marseillaise*.

12

The Dancing King

Fairly early the next morning I broke my leg.

Actually, to be honest, I did not break my leg. I'm just allowing myself that small degree of exaggeration that all sportsmen employ and other men use when telling you how much they earn or about their success with women. It makes you feel so much better.

When I had emerged from Mon Repos rather groggily the morning after my impromptu meeting with Dimitri, I had spent longer than usual fiddling with my skis before stepping into them. Just as I was about to take the plunge and set off down the hill to the lifts, I happened to notice a figure lying on a snow-bank some few hundred yards above the Jobs' house. He was camouflaged in a white ski suit, cleverly marked with splashes of brown and green which meant that he blended into the landscape almost perfectly. In fact, I might not have noticed him at all had the lenses of his large binoculars not caught with a white flash the reflection of the morning sun. All the rumours that were running around the village about the presence of the Russians combined with the ill effects of the night before began to stir fantastical ideas in my mind. Perhaps he was a French secret agent employed by the *Fisc*, the French Tax Office, to spy on Dimitri. He did seem to be focusing on their hotel. With the vast quantity of money that the Russians were bringing into the country there were deep suspicions of money-laundering. Although I had always been slightly confused about what this involved and thought that it was primarily a Chinese activity, I did not want to miss out on what might well turn into a police swoop. Removing my skis quietly I climbed up the bank to get a closer look.

Before long I was behind him and able to look down on his activities. With his small notebook on the snow in front of him, his careful camouflage, his high-powered binoculars and a moustache that was more than likely stuck on with spirit gum, he did look most suspicious. As I moved back slowly, keen to head down to the village to announce my discovery, I caught my toe in the root of a pine tree and fell through the air back down toward my little house. Just before my knee twisted and bent to a most unnatural angle, I spotted the man flicking through a guide to the birds of France. What a clever cover I thought as a flash of pain shot through my already aching head.

When I came to a halt I realised that my knee was in very much worse shape than it had been when I had fallen as I had tried to make my way down the mountain on my own in the dark some weeks before. On that occasion I had regained use of my leg after a few moments. Now, due to my investigation of the ornithologist, whose lectures I was later to see advertised on the Mont St Bernard entertainment programme, I discovered I had done myself enough damage to require being ferried to the bottom of the mountain in one of the infamous red 'blood wagons' – those tin stretchers on sleds that are towed by a bearded mountain rescuer at speeds that do nothing to improve the health of the accident victim. This terrifying experience did at least convince me that this was a proper injury, which cheered me up a lot.

Not that the experience had been survived without a great deal of pain. As my leg buckled I had felt a large elastic band, which I presume was my tendon, flip over on to the wrong side of my patella. (Every skiing injury victim always knows the correct anatomical terms.) Fortunately, as I released a less than manly cry, it sprung back to where it should rightfully have remained. When eventually I sat up again smiling weakly at some emotionless, heartless passers-by, I realised, without having to inspect it, that the whole joint was swelling like a balloon attached to a gas canister.

Finally I was wheeled into the clinic and I realised how lucky I was that this should have happened outside the main school-holiday periods. At peak times there seemed to be a permanent conveyor belt of skiers, young and old, passing any part of their anatomies under the expert hands of the medical staff. This being a quiet time, after the Christmas and New Year festivities, I only had to wait for ten minutes or so in the waiting room, decorated, I thought rather inappropriately, with a series of large photographs of people performing incredibly dangerous-looking stunts on skis. Jimmy greeted me cheerfully as I pulled up my wheelchair next to his. His personal skiing style meant that he was a relatively regular customer. Hardly had the physio-therapy from his last incident allowed him back on the slopes than he had bashed up another piece of himself that needed to be stretched and squeezed back into place. What a shame, I said, that the rack was now outlawed. He didn't seem to understand the joke. Either that or it wasn't really very funny. He admitted that, if he was not actually injuring himself on purpose, he did have an ulterior motive for visiting the doctor's surgery as often as possible. That motive appeared at the doorway in the dazzling form of the wonderful Sophie, Jay-Pee's assistant, ski instructor and part-time physio. My admiration for her capabilities was boundless. When she called me out first I winked rather smugly at Jimmy as if this was a sign of her preference for me.

If I had wanted to commiserate with her about the disc jockey's appalling treatment of her, she, ever businesslike and superbly professional, did not afford me the time. Within seconds I was in a state of partial undress and lying on my back. When, somewhat dazed, I looked up she was rubbing her hands together – but only to warm them rather than to signify any malicious intent.

'Right,' she said as she asked me to proffer my *membre inférieure*, my inferior member, which I was relieved to discover was the medical term for leg. 'Let me know when it hurts.'

Let her know, I most certainly did, in a variety of languages. All this when I was not rearranging a pair of rather voluminous boxer shorts in an attempt to preserve my dignity. When eventually I had been fully inspected I was rather pleased to discover that I had inflicted upon myself a stretched tendon and a torn muscle, which, admittedly, was so small that I cannot now remember its name. Still, due to the extraordinarily cautious nature of French doctors, only too acutely aware of the new craze of patients taking legal action, the injury was sufficient enough for me be barred from the slopes. I certainly had no intention of ignoring any of Sophie's instructions. What was more, this would afford me plenty of spare hours in various restaurants and bars to tell people in minute detail what it was that had happened and show them my more than professional-looking, plastic and metal knee-brace. Eventually I reappeared, limping most authentically, having thanked Sophie profusely, over-profusely. She must have walked away in her white uniform thinking she was up there with Florence Nightingale. Jimmy was not best pleased with me. Because Sophie had been attending to me he had had to undergo his treatment at the hands of a man he described as a 'bloody sadist fascist'.

'Never mind!' I said cheerfully, waving his disappointment aside. 'Come on, let's get down to the Café de la Poste.'

I had a few stories to tell.

When we hobbled in through the door I was somewhat taken aback by a barrage of popping, white camera flashes that bounced off the plain stone walls of the restaurant. Sliding my sunglasses on discreetly I made for my usual table. Once I was installed, Emilie, Aubrey's girlfriend, who worked part-time as a waitress for Gaston filled me in on the latest *événement* in Mont St Bernard.

Sitting in two chairs either side of the fireplace, with Gaston standing in between them, were two fairly unremarkable men in their early thirties. One of them had the makings of an impressive multicoloured black eye. Both of them were wrapped in bright, reflective, first-aid aluminium sheets, although it transpired that this was just for the benefit of the pictures that the local newspaper photographer was taking of them with the owner of the restaurant. This was as close as I ever got to seeing Gaston express any emotion at all.

'Those two, they are from Paris,' Emilie explained, pronouncing the name of the French capital city with a bizarre combination of mild revulsion and strange reverence.

They had only arrived in Mont St Bernard the night before last. A whole coach-load of *Parisiens* had arrived for a four-day *meeeneebrek*, which apparently was the French for a mini-break, and were staying at the Hotel Chamonix. Practised skiers, these two had all their own equipment and so were able to set out on the slopes first thing in the morning. Sharing a room they had both agreed in the morning that they would leave their *portables* – mobile phones – behind as the last thing they wanted was a call from *le patron* asking some sort of ridiculous question. Like most self-respecting Frenchmen they only pursued their careers for the cash and the time off.

They had had a wonderful morning and at lunchtime congratulated each other on having chosen to come to Mont St Bernard – it was their first visit to the little resort. As they were only there for a few days it was imperative to make the most of the skiing, and they proposed to make their way up every lift and down every piste across the whole of the *domaine skiuble*. While many of their fellow skiers were exhausted by three o'clock in the afternoon and some never made it back after lunch, these two had put in a whole fitness regime at their gym between the office and the restaurant where they regularly had lunch together. All the running on the treadmill had paid off and the two of them felt equal to the challenge of skiing every minute that was available. Hearty self-congratulation was in order as they boarded the chair-lift for the last ascent of the day.

Friends more by circumstance than natural affinity, they nonetheless got on pretty well, particularly in light of their common interest in all things Alpine. Indeed they intended to come back to Mont St Bernard some time in the summer with their mountain bikes – that was bound to be a great laugh.

Suddenly, as they chatted, the chair-lift stopped, dead.

They were left bouncing in the void, the lambs' testicles that they had had for lunch stirring uneasily in their stomachs. Mind you, this was a frequent occurrence. Normally, it was because some beginner had fallen flat on his face trying to get on or off the lift. They tutted and laughed. And what about all those idiots who couldn't handle the bottom puller – the button lift? The idiots who fell over and knocked everybody over with them. They tutted and laughed again while somewhere a long way away my ears burned.

About five minutes later it was actually getting quite cold. This they commented on with the occasional '*Merde*', which after another five minutes was extended to '*Putain de merde*', and then finally, when they had been sitting there for twenty minutes, turned into '*Putain de bordel de merde*', because now they were seriously freezing.

They were not certain at which particular juncture they had fully realised it, but before long it became clear that this lift had not simply temporarily broken down, it had been turned off for the night. There were several tell-tale signs, not least the fact that there was nobody, absolutely nobody on any of the other chairs. Nor in fact was there anyone on any of the ski pistes. They thought they had caught a glimpse of a dark figure skiing over the back in the direction of L'Abbas, and although they shouted and hollered he or she was too far away and just continued carving some last elegant curves into the snow before the piste-bashers turned up to obliterate them later in the night.

How could it be that nobody had noticed that they were left there all alone?

Merde.

In the course of the lengthy post-mortem that took place much later, the truth was eventually revealed.

All the chairs had a number and under normal circumstances it was the responsibility of the lift attendant at the bottom to note the number of the seat that was the last to be occupied. He would then radio to the top of the lift and tell his colleague the number of the last full seat, which in this case was one hundred and ninety-six, which in French is *cent-quatre-vingt-seize*. Unfortunately, the attendant at the bottom was a man named Eric, who was approaching retirement and whose principal interest in life was red wine, notably its quantity rather than its quality. Equally regrettable was the fact that the lift attendant at the top was a Dutchman called Johannes, who had a great fondness for marijuana, and who for much of the time was so far departed from reality that he believed himself to be the steward on a cruise ship greeting arriving and somewhat startled skiers with a resounding 'Welcome on board!'

The combination of the sender of the message, the receiver of the message and the method by which the message was sent – a crackly walkie-talkie – conspired for Johannes to understand 196 as 186, which in French is *cent-quatre-vingt-six*. When finally 186 appeared, Johannes gave its passengers a cheerful salute, closed down all the machinery, somehow managed to get his skis on and then float his way back down to L'Abbas. Perhaps he was the figure that the two men glimpsed before night fell.

In hindsight, dusk had been the most difficult moment because they had only a very short space of time in which to make a decision. Leaning over the safety bar they had peered down and attempted to judge the drop below them. As they were looking into a completely virgin snow-field it was almost impossible to tell. Perhaps it wasn't that far but there were various other reasons that finally dissuaded them from leaping from their perch. First, they did not know what was under the snow. Was it rock or ravine? Second, the course of the chair-lift did not follow the piste, which was out of sight on both sides, hidden by trees. Even if they survived the drop without injury they had no way of knowing how to get back on to the beaten track. Third, they would be jumping against the slope of the mountain, in a curious sort of way backwards, and the outcome of such a landing was difficult to imagine. No, they would just have to stay there the night.

Putain de merde.

It was not getting any warmer – in fact it was very, very cold. Still there were two of them, and one of them had a hip flask full of *marc de bourgogne*, the rough spirit which his cousin made from the skins of the grapes that he pressed from his own vines in Burgundy. He, the cousin, also had a small *élevage* of Charolais cattle, and so they were able to spend just over two hours discussing the bountiful variety of products to eat and drink that came from that estimable part of France. Once the robust effects of the liquor had worn off they agreed that they felt colder than ever.

'Oh, if only my wife was here. I could hold her close to me and we could share our body heat,' said the one.

'Oh, yes. I wish your wife was here too so I could share her body heat as well,' replied the other.

'And what do you mean by that? What is my wife to you! I can't believe what it is that you are saying to me!'

'No, please don't misunderstand me. It is just that I have always thought that she is such a beautiful woman. I just remember her body close to mine, feeling her beneath my hands when we were dancing at our Christmas party. Do you remember?'

'Yes, I do remember. Was that the one where they had some fantastic stuffed partridge with a Calvados sauce?'

'Ah, yes . . .'

They sat and bobbed a little as they contemplated the night sky and what had been a truly memorable meal.

'Hang on. What do you mean? Her body beneath your hands.'

'Well, you know how ticklish she is.'

Whack!

This was all too much for the husband, who could see no alternative course of action but to punch his friend, which he did hard on the side of the nose. Despite the cold the bruise under his eye immediately began to swell, but he made no attempt to retaliate. Unlike any other encounter that comes to blows, where there are normally a number of people to hold back the assailants and then drag them off to the bar where someone will slide a shot of whisky down the counter to soothe troubled brows and sore knuckles, they were stuck. Here, unfortunately, there was no escape route, and all that the two of them could do was to stare off in opposite directions at the empty mountain-side.

By three o'clock in the morning the cold was so intense that they decided there was no alternative but for them to share body heat, so unzipping their jackets they placed their arms around each other and nuzzled. It was in this close but rather grumpy embrace that the rather confused and surprised Johannes discovered them first thing the following morning.

Although they had had to go to hospital for a check-up they were soon released, but their story had already run around the small village. Gaston, never shy of promoting his numerous establishments, had offered the two heroes a free lunch and had even asked them to come on later to the Hotel Chamonix to retell their tale, although this last proposal was politely refused. The two men had already decided that a siesta should take higher priority.

Weeks pass almost imperceptibly in the mountains, even if some of them are spent stomping round the village clutching a walnut walking stick, which did nothing for my image as a young and dynamic winter-sports enthusiast. The passage from one week to the next was only really recognised on

Saturdays when the morning traffic heading down the mountain was nose to nose. After a brief break at lunchtime exactly the same thing would happen but in reverse as the new punters appeared for their week's holiday. By Thursday or Friday their faces would have become familiar both on the slopes and in the cafés, restaurants and bars that they had chosen to frequent, then suddenly they were gone and the whole process started again.

Living in the mountains is not dissimilar to living on an island. As I had no car, the limits of my world were governed by how far I could ski and still be able to get back home by nightfall. In many ways this was comforting, a world with borders, but also in some strange way it became claustrophobic – an environment that held you in its grasp. Today, the transport connections are much improved due mainly to the explosion of interest in winter sports, and most of the villagers travelled relatively regularly to either Cluses or the lakeside spa town of Thonon-les-Bains. Here they could purchase the necessities of modern life from one or other of the large hypermarkets to be found there, but Monsieur Job's parents, he later told me, had never left the valley. Born in the chalet in which their son now lived, his father had been baptised in the village church, where eighteen years later he married the girl from the chalet next door. After their brief education in the little elementary school they had lived the lives of peasant farmers, herding and cultivating through the summer and bottling and storing for the winter months, all the while bringing up their own family. Retirement, as we know it today, had not really been in vogue, and finally they returned to the church to be buried in the graveyard amongst the tombs of the five or six other extended families of the little valley.

Nowadays many teenagers travelled further afield to

Grenoble or Gap to pursue their secondary education and to go on to university. Many of them stopped in the big cities, but most returned *en saison*, re-adapting to this mountain life. One of the highlights of each week was the village reunion, a get-together of relatives and old friends to which the tourists were also rather grudgingly invited. *Le vin d'honneur*, normally a glass of piping *vin chaud* in the winter and a glass of fresh, straw-coloured, white wine in the summer, was always served up on the steps of the strangely inappropriate neoclassical *Mairie*, the official seat of Nicolas and Amandine's father, Norbert. The latter was the mayor and was known universally – even, with tongues stuck firmly in their cheeks, by his children – as '*Monsieur le Maire*'. Each week, at five o'clock on a Thursday, regardless of the state of the weather, blue skies or blizzard, he would step forward, dressed in his Republican sash of red, white and blue held together with a polished brass tassel which denoted his position, to proudly welcome all the villagers to this display of friendship and citizenship, and also, as something of an afterthought, 'our visitors'.

That particular Thursday, the first after Sophie had given me the green light to return to the slopes having made a good recovery from my fairly serious injury, there were many more guests than normal. Skiing back down to the village after having been to inspect the efforts of the 'gang' up in the snowpark to build some new jumps in preparation for the freestyle competition, I had had to drop into the Iceman Bar about four hundred yards up the mountain. A couple of Belgian beers had steadied my nerves and helped me to forget some of the irrefutably dangerous and stupid stunts that I had witnessed. Extraordinarily, despite the complexity of the twists, turns and loops, back flips, somersaults and rolls that they all performed high in the air, nobody seemed to be very seriously hurt. Of course

there were the odd cuts, bruises, torn tendons, snapped
cartilages, broken collarbones and occasional concussion but
most of them only rarely needed to visit the Starship Enterprise that was the doctor's surgery in Mont St Bernard more
than once a week.

When finally I got back into the village, I headed in the
direction of the Café de la Poste, where I had left a pair of
shoes as I was now in the habit of changing out of my ski
boots before heading home. The moment of removing ski
boots after a hard day on the mountain is, as anyone who
has ever been skiing will agree, without doubt the best
thing about the sport. Yes, there is the wind in your hair,
there is the fresh mountain air, there is the thrill of speed,
the excitement of danger, but the relief of taking off those
bloody boots makes all the rest feel strangely tame.

Now, walking as if on air, I wandered along the main
strip in the direction of the butcher to make a few purchases
for that evening. After my conversation with Guy in the
Licebox, he and a few of his friends had got into the habit
of coming up to Mon Repos for 'French conversation'. Most
of the time it involved playing games in French and practising useful set phrases. Although in nearly all their cases
their French was still execrable, their confidence levels
seemed to be very much improved, particularly when we
got to the part of the lesson in which if you gave the wrong
answer you had to down a shot of vodka.

As I approached the ice rink I could hear the tinny tones
of what could only be the travelling discotheque of the great
Jay-Pee. My first thought was to retreat and head hurriedly
back up the hill, but part of me knew that it would at any
rate be entertaining and another more chivalrous part of
me worried about the welfare of Sophie. No doubt Jimmy
would be keeping an eye out for her. As I hurried towards
the ice rink I could see a great crowd of people massed

around its wooden sides. Night was falling and Jay-Pee's three patriotically coloured disco lights – red, white and blue, thereby not causing offence to either British or French punters or, now I come to think about it, the Russians – played reasonably prettily on the surface of the ice.

Grouped around a table that had been erected next door to the turntables were hundreds of small and not so small children all dressed up in fancy costumes. Madame Brassard was enthusiastically, if not very delicately, safety-pinning entrants' numbers to their chests. Even this enrolment procedure was enough to reduce some of the competitors to convulsive sobs, such was the excitement engendered by the annual '*Dancing sur Glace*' competition. So seriously were applications taken that identity cards had to be produced and parents' sworn affidavits taken. Some years previously, it was explained to me, a diminutive, surgically enhanced forty-year-old from Brittany had taken the first prize and was back in Honfleur before it was discovered that it was the selfsame person who later that evening had done a striptease on the bar of the Magic Marmot and picked up the trophy for the quickest yard of ale.

The rules appeared to be relatively simple: all the children would be packed onto the ice rink where they would dance, such as they could in the restricted space, until they were either deselected by one of the judges lining the edges of the rink, were too exhausted to go on, or were mown down by one of the other participants and disappeared under skates only to be seen some time later appearing on all fours at the edge of the mêlée.

Afterward there would be a presentation of a number of different prizes for various categories including best individual dance, best skating trick, best fancy-dress outfit and best right hook. Then the mayor would offer all the adults the *vin d'honneur* whilst the children went off to play. This invariably involved throwing large chunks of ice at each other and then, when screams were heard, concocting horribly complicated stories which made it clear that it couldn't possibly have been me, could it, *maman*?

To start off with, it was all pretty good fun, although Jay-Pee's selection of the Serge Gainsbourg and Jane Birkin duet '*Je T'aime, Moi Non Plus*', a song that consisted of little more than an extended series of pre-, mid- and post-coital groanings, as the opening number to kick off the competition could not have been less suitable for an audience whose average age was eight. His staggering lack of what the French call '*le feeling*' was further underlined when he accompanied this first record with the habitual bump and grind of his hips and a curious rowing action of his arms.

Sophie, saint-like, took action. To Jimmy's and my delight, Jay-Pee, looking perplexed, was seen heading for the Licebox to get more suitable music, slipping and sliding in a rather curious pair of suede cowboy boots that he wore on the outside of his jeans, but which did at least match the light blue and white cowboy hat that hung down his back. Under the sensible guidance of the marvellous Sophie the music had soon changed to the French equivalent of 'The Teddy Bears' Picnic'; not that this seemed to have any effect on the hectic rate at which the remaining competitors, those who had not been knocked out of the ring like underweight sumo wrestlers within the first few seconds of the dance, continued to pelt round and around the small rink. Some of the children were surprisingly young and really very talented. Some had adopted a sort of 'elegant glide, leg in the air, slight wobble, quick spin in the air, land with a grimace' type approach but others were distinctly more up-to-date, and one little boy, who had brought what he had learnt at his after-school hip-hop classes to the whole proceedings, was spinning on the ice on practically anything but his skates.

Watching the children disporting themselves on the ice reminded me of what I had read in the illustrated *History of the Winter Olympics* that lay at my bedside back home at Mon Repos. When the very first games took place at Chamonix in 1924 there were none of the fantastic facilities available today and people had to make their own entertainment, even their own competitions. I would love to be the owner of the gold medal for fishing through ice. In the twenties, sportsmen and women were also considerably more reliant on the weather, and I grinned at the memory of a photograph of the Canada versus USA ice hockey final. It had taken place on a particularly warm day at the end of the season, and before the players could even contemplate trying to put the puck in the back of the net, they had to pay close attention to where they were going in order to avoid falling into one of the numerous holes that had appeared in the frozen surface of the lake. Some things, even in those first games, were worked out very quickly – not least that the heavier the contents of your bobsleigh, the quicker it would slide down the hill. Hence I had been impressed with photographs of Fatty Arbuckle lookalikes and their friends dressed in golfing outfits and flat caps squeezing themselves into their sleighs.

One of the cheerful barmen from the Licebox was circling the ice-skating proceedings with a tray of glass cups filled with steaming *vin chaud*. I grabbed one and drank it. *Vin chaud* is dangerous. It seems innocuous but it can make you do some ridiculous things.

In my case one of those ridiculous things was to demand from Nicolas, who was responsible for dispensing skates to those who did not possess their own, a pair of size forty-fives. One problem that I have often encountered in France is being able to find shoes to fit me. Forty-five is after all only a modest size ten in England but still remains relatively hard to find the other side of the Channel. If only that had been the case on this occasion. I think my plan had been to introduce Alexei to Olivier, as they would be meeting in a couple of days for Alexei's first lesson with us. Sadly in this aim I was thwarted. Both of them were swirling around the rink, avoiding contact with the other children, skating alone in their own little bubbles of solitude.

By the time I felt confident enough to let go of the side rail, two thirds of the children had been disqualified, leaving only the talented, the tireless and the lunatic. Most of the latter category, I suddenly realised, had been in my skiing group with Madame Brassard. Thanks to her tutelage they were the skating equivalent of the Marines. As surprised as the rest of the village to see my appearance on the ice, they came rushing over and wrapped themselves around my lower arms and legs.

'Oh, s'il te plaît, Williams. Allez, plus vite, plus vite!'

Soon, the combination of the mulled wine and the previously consumed Belgian beer was being whisked together into a fatal brew in the centrifuge that was my whirling stomach as we spun in wider and wider circles. Finally, I realised that an early exit would be the most sensible course of action. Wobbling still, I made to leave, shaking off the last of my tormentors, who out of the corner of my eye I happened to see spin away across the rink and connect rather violently with the wooden hoardings. Fortunately, the little boy, Luc, had come dressed as a police motor-cyclist and therefore was suitably protected. Equally fortunately, he seemed to have left his firearm at home.

With a couple of mighty strides I shot out of the narrow exit onto a piece of rubber matting, which brought my skates at least to a very sudden halt. All of the rest of me was cata-pulted forward and I found myself in a close embrace with the disc jockey in temporary residence: Sophie. I could not believe that Jay-Pee only that morning had had the cheek to describe her as *ma vieille poule* – 'my old hen'. Unbelievable.

In the course of my somewhat sudden exit I had involuntarily jostled the mayor, who was already standing behind the table of silverware and by way of rehearsal mouthing the words of his speech, which were written on a strip of paper in front of him. Although he knew I was friendly with his children, he shot me a somewhat less than welcoming look and muttered something about 'les Anglais' under his breath before turning away. Then, suddenly, a thought struck him and he turned back.

'You are Williams, is it not?' His English was dismal, but considering his exalted position, I decided to make no mention of it. Instead I confirmed that I was indeed Williams.

'You speak the French, is it not true?' I agreed that this was indeed true.

'Oh, it is very well. I think you will be able to render me a service.' Before I had the chance to enquire what kind of service, he had turned away again and was beaming in his best mayoral fashion at a trio, two men and a woman, making their way along the sidewalk at a distance from the skating hoi polloi. As I absentmindedly stroked Sophie's arm, I suddenly recognised the woman as the fur coat of the ticket office. On closer inspection I noticed the two men to be none other than Dimitri and his secretary. What could the three of them be cooking up together?

Today the woman was dressed up in some kind of moon suit that anyone less kindly than I might have been tempted to suggest gave her a striking resemblance to the Michelin Man in a pair of sunglasses. On a diamante collar and lead was the absurd and now increasingly familiar curly dog, the colour of melting slush. Luckily, its owner did not seem to recognise me as she was too busy giving little waves to Monsieur le Maire. Her voice like fingernails on a blackboard was screeching away: '*Monsooor Lemaire, Monsooooor Lemaire, comonttallyvoos?* Let me introduce my new friends, Dimitri and yes this is . . . yes . . . they are from Russia, you know. Dimitri is a businessman. He is a big lover of France and, you know, the French and that. Anyway . . .'

Wobbling my way back to Nicolas in his office, feeling rather chastened after my brief holiday on ice, I caught him chuckling, possibly at me.

'By the way, Nico, who is that woman over there? I keep seeing her around the place – she's a nightmare.'

'Oh, her. She is your compatriot. They call her Margie, or something like that. She has had a chalet here for years. She has lots and lots of money. Not like the Russians of course. She says that she is a great friend of the Baronne de Rothschild; you know, the daughter of the one who started up skiing in France in Megève. Bet they have never met, but she thinks she is doing the same thing in Mont St Bernard,' he laughed.

'She gives me the heebie-jeebies,' I told him in English as I unlaced my boots.

'She gives you what?'

Heaven knows what he thought she was giving me.

'You see those two who are with her, the two Russians. I've just heard that they're interested in doing some sort of property development. You know, like those guys we were talking about, you know, that have been doing stuff on the other side. They want to do a deal here in Mont St Bernard. They've come to see my father because he has to give his permission.'

Pleasantly struck by the surprising power of the village mayor in France, I asked Nicolas what he thought his father would decide. He laughed loudly.

'You know what I think? I think he will murder them.'

'What, really kill them?' He had used the verb *massacrer* with some relish.

'No, not really. But I tell you, Williams, I wouldn't like to be at their meeting that's for sure. Not if my father *explose*!' He laughed again.

'No, nor would I. Let's go to the *vin d'honneur*; that's if your dad allows this particular *Anglais* to go along.' I looked back at the skating rink with a shudder.

As it was, his father was far too busy giving away prizes, delivering speeches and kissing babies to take any notice of my presence. To our surprise, it was young Alexei who had remained on the ice the longest and he was duly awarded a small plastic, but gold-coloured, medal to warm if rather bemused applause. He allowed himself a small smile and tiptoed on his skates over to his father and sat close to him as they inspected the glittery prize that he had been awarded.

Although the English did have a certain tendency to hang around the free drinks table, something that, in the past, I have not always been entirely innocent of myself, it was pleasing to see how everybody mixed so freely, and how everybody, despite major limitations of communication, seemed to get on so well. However, the Russians, who had now been joined by their part-glamorous, part-muscle-bound entourage, seemed to be left at arm's length. *Mépris*, contempt of some sort, hung over the local population, mixing with their misting, mulled breath.

Out of the crowd appeared two familiar figures. Monsieur and Madame Job always came down the hill to this occasion, and what an effort they had made. Both now seemed to be wearing regional dress: he dressed in a forester's outfit, she as a rather outsized milkmaid. I had now encountered the couple on numerous occasions, and each time that our paths crossed I had felt their greeting to be a little warmer. Now, possibly as a result of a few glasses too many of the *vin chaud*, Monsieur Job was positively chummy. I was now it appeared his *ami*, which is only one step behind being someone's *pote* – best mate. We exchanged polite chit-chat for a little while before he looked up at me and asked me whether I thought I would like to have a day out with him *en montagne*. This invitation of an outing was to be in exchange for rendering him some *service*. Unfortunately, at that moment his false teeth seemed to come rather dramatically adrift, and I was a bit unsure what kind of assistance he required. Nonetheless, I agreed cheerfully, and he suggested that I should be at his front door at half past seven the following morning.

'Half past seven? But isn't it dark then?' I asked, appalled at the prospect.

'*Mon cher – mon cher!*'

My dear fellow!

We really were friends.

'It is the very best time of the day,' he enthused. 'So, you will be there?'

'Then you will stay with us in the evening to eat?' asked his wife sweetly.

'Oh yes, I'll definitely be there. Are you staying for the dancing tonight?'

'No, no, that is for the young people.' And with that they wandered slowly back to their horse and sled, and before long were clinking their way cheerfully back up the hill.

As one of the young people, before long I was making my way to the Licebox. Sadly, Dimitri, who now obviously considered me to be onside, insisted on more magnums of champagne and the obligatory vodka.

By the time I made it back up the hill to Mon Repos, I knew two Russian marching songs word perfectly.

In all, I think I got two hours and forty minutes' sleep.

13

Over the Hill

Goose-down really does have the most amazing qualities. Not only is it light, warm and soft, but it also
appears to possess some sort of anaesthetic capacity that
makes crawling out from underneath a duvet filled with
the stuff a massive challenge. Now that I was accustomed
to the *sshing* of skiers outside my window, it was not enough
to rouse me, and I had laid out a whole minefield of devices
to disrupt my snooze, which otherwise would have carried
me along quite comfortably to midday. Two mobile tele-
phones and a brass alarm clock with bells, which I had
found in a cupboard, were lined up on my bedside table
each set to maximum volume; should these not be powerful
enough I had tuned an electronic alarm clock, with confus-
ingly few buttons, to start up every morning with Radio
'Armonie, confident that Jay-Pee would annoy me enough
to force me into action. My plans were occasionally thwarted
if, when the radio began to play, I discovered that it was
Sophie who was speaking. Upon hearing her dulcet, but
eminently sensible tones, I would almost immediately slip
back into a charming reverie.

The morning that I was supposed to be reporting for

duty at Monsieur Job's, I was much surprised to realise that the tone of the mobile telephone that had woken me was not that of the alarm but one that signified someone was calling. It was barely six-thirty.

'Hey, dude, just thought I'd give you a call, make sure you are up okay.' By the end of the sentence I recognised the voice as belonging to Aubrey. It was slick with booze. Presumably he had remembered my outing with Monsieur Job and in his altered state had decided that he would assist my efforts in getting up. 'Yeah, me and the boys, we're just heading back to my chalet. They're going to crash there because we haven't got any punters in at the moment.'

'Really?' Despite my hardest efforts it was impossible to sum up even the faintest echo of interest in my voice.

'Actually, Will, there is a real reason that I wanted to ring you, and I thought I would do it now because then you can have some time to think about it. Do you remember that when, like, when you first moved into Mon Repos, I said that I had got the place you're in rented out for a week or so in January?'

Very vaguely I did, but only very vaguely.

'Er . . .'

My legs were resisting any attempt to get them to move but I felt my feet finally planted on the floor.

'Well, actually, I forgot to remind you about it. I am, like, really sorry about that, man.'

'Oh, are you? Okay.'

It was still pitch dark outside. I hate that.

'But I've got a brilliant idea. You know Josie? She's got to go back to England for a, like, wedding or something. She's going to be gone for about a week – so you could have her room. You can be the chalet girl!' Aubrey thought this much funnier than I did.

Josie, a sweet girl from Cornwall, who was peppered

with so many metallic studs that getting through security checks at airports must have made her deeply unpopular, worked as a chalet girl in the same lodge where Aubrey was the cook.

Now chalet girls do get a terrible amount of stick. Not only do they have just about one of the hardest and most tiring jobs in the world, they also more often than not have to put up with people who, whether they should know better or not, abuse their financial superiority. Rather than attracting the sympathy of their colleagues in the ski industry, chalet girls remain absolute favourites as the butts of every vulgar, bar-room joke. Unfortunately, generations of young women before them have embraced the party spirit of the mountains and just about any male partici-pant with such enthusiasm that they stand very little chance of being considered as anything other than 'goodtime girls'. Was this really the image I wished to adopt?

Still, it did solve my accommodation problems.

Blearily, I had been trying to put my legs into my ski jacket. I tried to remember what Aubrey was talking about.

'Sounds great. Thanks very much for the offer. How much do you want for the week?'

'Well, I just thought it would be easiest if you lend us all a hand, you know, by way of rent. You know, just do the stuff that Josie does – waitressing, cleaning up the rooms, helping me in the kitchen, bit of chatting to the punters, maybe go out skiing with them one day. Easy.'

'Well, sounds like a possibility, I suppose. Look, I really ought to get going because I've got to be up the hill fairly soon . . .'

'Yeah,' laughed Aubrey down the line. 'I've got to go back and get some stuff sorted for the owner anyway.'

With that I heard the unmistakable *pssh* of a beer can being opened and Aubrey's throaty chuckle.

'Cheers, then.'

'Okay . . . cheers . . .'

Finally, I was ready. Slip-sliding my way up the short slope, I knocked on the front door of the Job establishment not too loudly, lest I had made some ridiculous mistake, misunderstood them and they were in fact quite sensibly still tucked up in bed.

Almost immediately Madame Job opened the door dressed magnificently in a dressing gown made out of tea-cosy material with a genuine, white, night-bonnet on her head. Before long a bowl of milky white coffee was plonked in front of me along with a piece of baguette the length of my forearm, thickly buttered and loaded with Madame Job's special cherry jam. I chewed on it with genuine enjoyment, resisting with ease the temptation to dip it into my coffee – still, astonishingly, a habit much favoured by the French. Whilst he pulled on his blue overalls over an impressive set of all-in-one long johns and vest – he was already wearing his cap and wig – Monsieur Job was enthusiastically dunking his bread into his coffee.

His *tartine* was spread with pâté. I could hardly watch.

Soon we were ready. The old man picked up a bag of equipment, a box of cartridges from a kitchen cupboard and a rifle that I had not until that moment noticed, propped as it had been behind the door.

Outside it was still dark, but Monsieur Job's eyesight seemed to be rather better than mine in the gloom and he made his way unerringly past the chicken coop, and also to my surprise past the stable and the barn in which he kept his wooden sled cum cart. Instead, we walked a little further up the hill to another farm building, rather newer than the rest, which was locked with a large brass padlock. Reaching inside his padded jacket he pulled out a hefty key on a string and proudly swung back the wide double doors.

Stepping in he flicked a switch and the whole place lit up like an aircraft hangar. In the middle of the room something was hidden under a large, green-grey tarpaulin. He looked at me quizzically, like a magician. Reaching down, he took the edge of the cover and in one swift move pulled it back.

Brand spanking new, gleaming with self-satisfaction, black as the night outside and with all the pedigree of the type of vehicle that has appeared in a James Bond film, there was a magnificent snowmobile. Its exhaust pipes were sparkling with anticipation.

'*C'est ça, l'Union Européenne!*' he almost purred.

Lifting the double bench of the machine seat, Monsieur Job reached inside and pulled out two pairs of goggles. One pair were very similar to the ones that I had bought just recently in Nicolas's parents' shop and the other set had most recently been modelled by Captain Scott. These he passed to me. Snapping on the large comfortable modern pair so that they sat goonishly on his forehead with tufts of his hairpiece sticking out around it, Monsieur Job swung one short leg over the chassis of the machine and began to fiddle with the controls. Looking at my own eye protection more closely, I could see that they were confected from what looked like the ends of a couple of old tin cans, bits of an old wine bottle and some animal hide of unspecified genus. In order for them to be kept in place they appeared to have to be tied back behind the wearer's head with fraying bits of baler twine, so for the time being I stuffed them in one of my pockets. On his signal I climbed onto the machine behind Monsieur Job and was rather surprised when he reached behind him and took both my hands before linking them around his stomach.

When finally he was satisfied with the readings on the variety of dials in front of him, my neighbour turned the key fully and the snowmobile shook into life with, in the confines of its garage, a deafening roar. Monsieur Job manipulated the accelerator as if he imagined himself at the starting line of the Manx TT. When the garage had filled with a suitable amount of exhaust fumes, he jammed the foot pedal into first gear and released the clutch handle in a fashion that could only be described as abrupt. For the first, and I suspect the last, time in my life I was actually pleased to have my arms snuggled around the waist of an eighty-year-old man as we rocketed out of the door and into the night. Pulling us round in a hairpin, Monsieur Job aimed the machine at the mountain.

Experiencing something not dissimilar to G-force, I struggled to hold on, gripping Monsieur Job's waist and praying that my driver was not suffering from osteoporosis. Initially, I tried to make out where we were going, but I soon realised that because of the thick cloud cover and the spray of ice thrown up by the Bucking Bronco it was impossible to see anything at all. Groping vaguely for my goggles, I gave up and closed my eyes, hanging on as tightly as I thought advisable just in order to stay onboard.

After a journey that seemed so vertical it would take me to another planet, we levelled out, and I peeked briefly over Speedie's hunched shoulders. Over to the east, I could just see a few rays of sunshine getting ready to cast their light over the valley into which we had emerged. Only a few minutes' drive had taken us through a narrow mountain pass, and now we appeared to be following a track that had previously been traced by a similar vehicle but was dusted with fresh snow. All of a sudden the mountain terrain that I had long recognised in the ski resorts I had visited over the years seemed to have disappeared, and we found ourselves in a very much wilder place. Gone were the electric pylons, the sturdy cables of the ski lifts, the pistes prepared as carefully as greens on a golf course, the restaurants and the endless reasonably helpful signposts. Now we were in a place which the French like to describe as '*la pleine nature*', which translates approximately into English as 'the middle of bloody nowhere'. It was all at the same time awe-inspiring, fascinating and slightly unnerving. I held on, perhaps tighter than was wise, as we approached what was quite clearly a crevasse. With the most minor adjustment of the front ski of the impressively powerful machine, Monsieur Job negotiated our way over a narrow ice bridge and I stared down into a hole at the bottom of which could only have survived goblins and hobgoblins, whatever the difference between these might be.

Now the sun was fully risen and I began to relax, and to sense that feeling of selfish excitement that comes with visiting a place that next to nobody else has ever seen. As our little planet shrinks I have only had this experience perhaps half a dozen times, and at least three of these have been by complete mistake. Now, as we slowed and balanced out to follow the valley floor, the engine of the snow-mobile quietened to a gentle popping and soon became quite unnoticeable. Clusters of icicles perhaps some thirty or forty feet long hung from overarching cliffs, held in place only by the ambient temperature. Were they suddenly to come loose they would tumble down to smash into a million, tiny, sparkling shards on the flat rocks of the river bed along which the most vivid greeny-blue water thundered. Here and there, the tracks of a variety of different animals crisscrossed the otherwise virgin snow. I tried to imagine what timid creatures had been frightened into hiding by our intrusion into this secret valley.

Only when we came to a halt perhaps an hour later, having still seen no other signs of civilisation and Monsieur Job turned the ignition off, was I aware of the fact that he had been talking to me – probably for most of the journey. The only words that I heard him say as he climbed off the machine were: *'N'est-ce pas?'*

Isn't that so? – the one-size-fits-all expression that attempts to elicit someone else's opinion about all matter of things and hence the reason why tentative French speakers of English are often heard to ask 'isn't it?' at the end of their sentences. Now, I had no idea to what he was referring.

Fortunately, Monsieur Job minimised my bewilderment and embarrassment by making it clear that he wanted me to agree that this was indeed a fabulous place. This was something I was more than happy and able to do.

'Bon, une petite casse-croûte, avant de continuer?'

It was now just after half past nine but this snow-mobiling business was indeed hungry work and I heartily agreed it might be time to *casser la croûte* – break the crust – have a snack. Out of the back of the snowmobile came a wickerwork basket covered in a white cloth, and out of this basket came home-baked bread, homemade cheese, home-made garlic sausage and, *naturellement*, a bottle. Out of the bottle was poured small tumblers of light, now slightly chilled red wine, which raised the spirits, washed down the freshest of food and provided us with at least a little of the energy required for what turned out to be a fantastically long walk.

Once we were suitably fed and watered and the remains of our provisions had been packed away, I swung my leg back over the comfortable seat of the snowmobile.

'We can't go any further on that,' Monsieur Job said as he pulled the key out of the ignition. 'We have to go ahead on foot, because with this depth of snow it is too easy to forget the original paths and we don't want to find ourselves out in the middle of the lake, do we?'

No, we most certainly don't, I agreed.

Thoughtfully, he had brought along a pair of *raquettes* just for me. Although today these curious pieces of footwear can be found in a variety of vibrant plastic hues with a range of brand names stamped across their edges, the ones he held out to me dated back to some stage in prehistory and were, in common with all Monsieur Job's equipment, or at least all the equipment that he was willing to lend me, to be attached to my person with strips of leather and bits of string. Made of sturdy birch and wicker they were surprisingly light and, when I tested them, strangely effective. Now that my weight was spread over these wide strange shoes, instead of sinking knee deep in snow with each step and expending excess energy, I hardly made any indentation. As long as I remembered to avoid stepping on the inside edges of the *raquettes*, a mistake I only made three times, all was well. Fortunately, on the occasions that I did make a full face plant into the snow, Monsieur Job was ahead of me on the path we were plodding down, his back turned and talking.

For a man that had been taciturn to the extent of rudeness when I had first met him, he had opened up considerably. In fact he practically never shut up. The fact that I was clearly a pretty hopeless skier – he had seen me arrive in the village just before the ice-skating debacle – was definitely in my favour. He was convinced that the tourist industry was the ruination of his family's roots and their sense of belonging in the area. His own children had left the area because they could not afford to live in any of the villages turned resorts, let alone buy or build their own home. His son, who he had hoped would finally take over his smallholding, now worked in the chewing gum industry in Lille. Rather candidly, he admitted that some of his fellow farmers had been pretty stupid. Usually if parents died, or moved in with their children, the door of the original family home was simply closed and padlocked. More often than not the contents, apart from clothes and daily necessities, were left in a timeless dark to gather dust, disturbed only by the pawprints of various hurrying rodents. When wealthy city-dwellers from Paris and Lyons, but most notably *les Anglais*, had arrived in the 1930s and immediately post-war, excited by the prospect of getting involved in the new sporting experience of skiing, they had been more than eager to snap up these old properties so that they could convert them into sumptuous mountain residences. Too often, the local farmers, who in common with the rest of their compatriots had fairly little interest in bricks and mortar, failed to realise the true value of what was after all a relatively limited number of dwellings. Delighted to have received £150 or £200 for something that otherwise would simply have fallen down, it was with disbelief that they read in the windows of the now numerous estate agencies that the value of *grandmère*'s house had increased some ten thousandfold in less than fifty years. Anyway, as far as Monsieur Job was concerned, the people who came here once a year for a week for what he described as *la glisse* – the sliding – were the lowest of the low. I was all right, it appeared, because I could speak French and didn't shout and scream too much when I'd had too many warm, brown beers. He shuddered and turned his mind to other things.

He remembered the mountains when they were really a wild place, a terrain that you could travel for days on end on foot or on wooden skis, staying in mountain huts and tending herds of sheep, cows and goats, and never seeing another living soul.

'When we were young boys, we knew these mountains like the back of our hands. We knew every nook and cranny, every shelter and every hiding place. That was why,' – and here he puffed up his chest with pride, unlike me who was puffing up my chest with near exhaustion – 'that was why we were so useful to the Maquis. You know what that is, the Maquis? That is the *Résistance*! *Bah, oui, la Résistance!* My family were always on the side of the Resistance. Not like those *sales collaborateurs* who live across the valley.' He spat with amazing velocity into the snow and still managed to retain control of his dental apparatus.

Astonishingly, still, today, in the *commune*, for many interest groups there needed to be two associations, particularly the hunting clubs: one organised by former Resistance members or their offspring, and the other organised by people who had not been quite so demonstrative in their efforts to protect '*la patrie*' from '*les Boches*'.

'So were there that many Germans up here, you know, during the war?' I asked, looking around carefully, fancifully, as we plodded along.

Not when France was first invaded, no, they hadn't really bothered too much with this isolated corner, the old man explained. Although they had heard reports on the radio of German presence further down in the valley, for the first six months there was no sign at all of the invaders. When finally they did appear Monsieur Job had only been seventeen years old. Lorries that came trundling up a dusty road one summer from the *Kommandantur* were greeted with incredulity rather than anything else. The local population had never seen Germans before. In the last war they had all been far away up in northern France. When these new arrivals jumped out of their armoured troop carrier in the middle of the little square in Mont St Bernard, the women going about their business were less frightened by their machine guns and stick grenades than fascinated by listening to them talk in their strange guttural accents – so different from the lilting Swiss German that they had heard from occasional visitors from Geneva.

Things took a turn for the worse when it became clear
that the purpose of the first visit by the Germans was to
take into custody the primary school headmaster and one
of his assistant teachers. Later they learnt that the assistant
was in fact a Jewish intellectual who was being hidden by
his former university mate. They didn't much like the Jews
in the village but this man had seemed like a decent sort.
He had even taught Monsieur Job's eldest son who had
been killed in another hopeless conflict, 'Indochine' –
Vietnam.

The two men were never seen again – Monsieur Job had
heard that they had died in a camp called Mauthausen, shot
by the Nazis in the back of the head before their bodies fell
into a big open grave – but their disappearance was enough
to galvanise the villagers into action. Through the mountain grapevine of the Maquis, they had made it known that
they would be willing to use their Alpine knowledge to
assist anyone, Jewish or otherwise, who was being pursued
by the enemy. They would help them make their way
through the mountains and eventually to the safety of
neutral Switzerland. After a few months, a steady trickle –
sometimes as many as two or three a week – of pale,
frightened-looking men, women and children were moved
from hayloft, to stable to mountain hut, and eventually to
freedom – all in the dead of night and in the most dangerous
of freezing conditions.

When one day Monsieur Job and some of his comrades
were returning from such a mission, they noticed across the
valley on the Col de Ventoux – on the downward slopes
below the Massif de Mont Blanc – the shadows cast by a
line of carefully camouflaged skiers. This was their first
sighting of Hitler's famous *Gebirgstruppen* – the German
mountain commando. Before long Monsieur Job and his
merry men were playing hide and seek with them. Equipped

with high-powered rifles and telescopic lenses, these soldiers were crack troops. Specialists in Alpine conditions, their regimental emblem was the Edelweiss – the small, white mountain flower that nowadays is more closely associated with lonely goatherds tied up with string. Although they were in many ways a fairly autonomous fighting unit, the fact that they wore the inscription '*Gott mit uns*' – God with us – on their belts was a sure sign that their allegiance was to the Nazis and their *Führer*. Monsieur Job still had one of the tin buckles in a drawer at home. He did not explain how he had come by it. A *Gebirgsjager* was a past master at ambushes. Many were the occasions that the partisans had had to take refuge in the numerous caves, where often they had spent the night as the bullets whistled through the pine trees. Looking round at the crests that surrounded us I could imagine the sense of vulnerability the escapees had felt as they made their slow progress towards liberty. By now it was surprisingly hot and Monsieur Job was still skipping along in a way that, at his age, should simply not have been possible. Diving occasionally into snowladen bushes he reappeared somewhat crestfallen. His traps, he told me, were are all still empty. It was not yet cold enough and the animals still had plenty of food.

'So what animals are you hoping to snare?'

'*Ah, chevreuil, chamois, même marmotte, lapin, bien sûr, et lièvre de montagne de temps en temps . . .*'

Not recognising any of these species apart from rabbit and hare, I was secretly relieved at his lack of success.

'Let's hope that Madame Job will be putting together a nice little *ragoût* of rabbit for when we get home. My favourite!' He smacked his lips with relish and I had terrible fears for his dental plate.

'Oh, yes, let's hope so!' I said, as I plodded on, mopping

my brow, stripping off layers of clothing, but I was secretly sure that Madame Job had much better things to do with her time than cook up a poor little rabbit.

Eventually, as the sun was sliding off the side of the mountain, we decided that it was time to head back in the direction of the snowmobile and, turning round, we saw the paths that we had made, snaking through the snowdrifts. First steps in a foreign land.

'Some people say that I am an old *braconnier* – an old poacher – but I say, *pah*,' he exclaimed emphatically, as he blew away another small snowdrift with a well-aimed piece of spittle. 'This is my home. This belongs to me and my family more than it does to any of these goddamn *skieurs*, or *les Anglais*!'

Grinning, I waited for him to realise his faux pas. He didn't. He just carried on with his tirade.

'And now here are these Russians. What is happening here?' We climbed onto the machine. 'This is our place. Anyone tries to tell me anything different they will soon see.'

He shook his fist at the sky and, as if in answer, from high above us somewhere behind the crest of the mountain range came a low drone that quickly became a throbbing growl. As we looked up a helicopter rose into view. Tipping forward menacingly it picked up speed and swooped down into the valley. As the light fell on it we both recognised that it was not the red machine that belonged to the mountain rescue. This was a sleek black model piloted by a man that neither of us recognised. Both of us on the other hand immediately saw that sitting in the passenger seat beside him, his window open, was the wizened figure of Dimitri, his Homburg hat cocked now on the back of his head. Unmistakably, tucked tightly into his shoulder, his eye screwed to its telescopic lens, we could see a modern high-powered hunting rifle. Behind him in the cramped cabin I could just make out the huge figure of Sergei, scanning the countryside with binoculars, presumably for something for his boss to kill. At that moment the only living creatures that I was aware of were Monsieur Job and me. Fortunately, neither of them seemed to notice us, perhaps because I had slid off the snowmobile and was sitting on the ground pretending to check my shoelaces. The hovering metal bird lifted its tail and blasted off down the valley.

'*Mais ce n'est pas vrai!* It's not true!' exclaimed the old man, and I wholeheartedly agreed with him as we disappeared into a stinging ice cloud whipped up by the throbbing rotor blades. As it cleared, we watched the black machine disappear out of sight. This ignominy was too much for my neighbour who reached down and drew out his gun, which had been slung in a rabbit-skin holster that he had fashioned on the side of his machine. Holding it aloft, he manipulated it in such a way that I could hear that it was loading itself, and I just managed to restrain his arm before he took aim. As we zoomed off back down the path we heard away in the distance a couple of shots that rumbled in dire warning across the mountainside.

14

Lapin à la Moutarde

There might be many ways to skin a cat but, according to Madame Job, there is only one correct method to skin a rabbit, and she was quite insistent on showing me her technique. After we had finally returned the snow-mobile to its garage and spent an inordinately long time in the freezing cold washing it down with warm water before giving it an all-over polish, we stepped into the compara-tive boiling heat of the house. Madame Job had stoked the wood-burning cooker to a red-hot temperature, and it was with relief that we removed all our various layers of clothing and took up our positions at the kitchen table. Neither of us foragers was expected to take part in the domestic routine, it seemed, as Madame Job peeled vegetables into the deep, stained, stone sink, before scooping up the peelings and shuf-fling out to the back of the house in her industrial-strength slippers. Monsieur Job stripped down his rifle on some old newspaper, before pulling wads of tissue paper through the barrel attached to what appeared to be a section of Madame Job's tights. Whilst he did this, he instructed me to pour us a couple of pastis – 'des petits jaunes' as he fondly call them – the little yellow ones. Pastis is the generic name for all the aniseed-based aperitifs that are drunk with such gusto particularly in the South of France – it's an interesting drink, particularly if you are a chemist. Although the liquid that is poured from the bottle is light brown and clear, the moment it comes into contact with water and ice cubes, it turns a cloudy but rich, nappy yellow. In taste, it is not dissimilar to chewing slowly on a Liquorice Allsort, and in effect, it is much the same as being mugged by an angel. In the bottle's neck had been plugged a round glass *doseur*, which measured out the precise amount of liquid that should be poured into each glass. After a hard day's work such as our own, Monsieur Job instructed that the dose should be doubled. He was still fuming about the Russians and their behaviour which he thought to be *dégueulasse*.

Just after Monsieur Job had propped his now gleaming gun back up behind the door and we were settling in for another round of reminiscences, his wife walked in holding a blinking, nose-twitching rabbit upside down by its hind legs.

'*Ah oui*,' she agreed. Marceline, her niece, who worked at the Hotel de l'Aigle Brun, had endless interesting information about those Russians. Not now, not now, please, implored her husband as he sighed and sipped.

Smiling at me with almost maternal affection, she pulled open the drawer of a fine-looking dresser, brought out a wooden rolling pin and killed the rabbit with one blow to the back of the head. Before too much blood could seep from its mouth she swung it still twitching into the sink. Although much of her subsequent activity was hidden by her person, I could not help noticing – as Monsieur Job was about to embark on a description of how to set off an avalanche should you wish to block the advance of a German, or possibly a Russian, armoured column – Madame Job stripping, arms pulled wide apart, the entire skin from the animal much as you might pull a washing-up glove from your arm. Helping myself to the pastis bottle, I tried hard to concentrate on the explanation of what kind of dynamite was most appropriate at what altitude.

When finally Madame Job set about cooking the now dismembered rabbit, I found myself completely absorbed by watching how she went about it. The floured pieces of meat were lightly browned in a combination of butter and olive oil before being joined in the thick iron casserole dish by handfuls of carrots, onions, garlic, small quarters of turnip and slices of leek. A bouquet garni and the better part of a bottle of white wine only followed when everything was stewing to her satisfaction. Just before the dish was brought to the table she mixed an egg yolk and some crème fraîche with a large spoonful of mustard. Once it was smoothly bound together she stirred it slowly and with great pleasure into the stew. After an *entrée* of cured hams and sausage, the rabbit, accompanied by home-grown *'pommes de terre vapeur'*, was so delicious that I was quite able to forget its origins. By the time we had tasted some of Madame Job's rather mouldier but mightily pungent goat's cheese and finished off some of her preserved cherries, all this washed down by a couple of bottles of vin de Savoie decanted from a wooden barrel that was kept next to the dresser and protected with a muslin cloth, I had little desire even to make it back as far as my own house. The elderly couple brewed coffee for me, and finally Madame Job settled back in her rocking chair and regaled us with further stories about the strange new visitors to the village. Her niece was bursting with exciting news when they had met at the weekly market outside the town hall. Apparently, Dimitri allowed the residents of the hotel to do whatever they wished after he had taken to his suite. Gambling was a particularly popular pastime, and only the night before one of the party had lost $65,000 at a game of backgammon. He had apparently celebrated his loss by ordering a bottle of Château Petrus Hors Classe 1981, which had had to be dug out of the hotel cellars and was served up with great pomp and ceremony at a price of 4000 Euros. The two gamblers had enjoyed it mixed fifty-fifty with a can of Coca-Cola. Breakfast was always served at nine o'clock prompt, and for the past three days everyone, men, women and the child, had had caviar with their scrambled eggs. Three hundred grams each. Four thousand Euros each plus three Euros for the scrambled eggs. Fortunately, they had recently had stocks of vodka flown in direct from Moscow because there was now none of the required quality left in the entire village.

When they weren't skiing with their personal instructors, the Russians spent much of their time discussing their plans for the summer. Apparently, they hoped to head to Africa to shoot elephants and lions, and today, when we had seen them, they had just been out practising. The hotel had already made more profits out of their stay than they had over the last three seasons.

Fighting off my yawns, I attempted to focus, as much as I was able to focus on anything at all, on these extraordin-ary revelations. After a couple of shots of the local *eau-de-vie*, a sly, light-green concoction known as 'Genépi', all the figures that Madame Job was trotting out swirled into a great big, rather sickly muddle. It was definitely time to go. As I finally pulled on my ski jacket, I inspected the Genépi bottle, with one eye closed, for the sticker that read 'For External Use Only'.

Pleasingly, my knee had stood up surprisingly well during our day in the mountains, although I had been a little disappointed when Monsieur Job had cut short my explanations of the symptoms and treatment with a loud '*Bah!*' and the expulsion of spittle of his normal surprising velocity. Even so, I was not sure that it was wise of me to have accepted Guy and Amandine's invitation, a couple of days after my excursion into the mountains, to go to *le Bowling*, which is French for a bowling alley. As it turned out, the experience was greatly different from the pinging, whistleblowing, bell ringing, light flashing, clunking and crashing of the American-style alleys that I had visited in the outskirts of various English towns. Automation had not yet reached the mountains, and the game that I took part in as a partner to Nicolas's grandmother much more closely resembled the skittles that I had often played in the backrooms of various pubs in the West Country. It was nonetheless a hard-fought battle against our opposing teams: the Mayor – who on this social occasion asked me to call him Norbert – and his wife, Guy and Amandine, and Jimmy and the marvellous Sophie. As the teams had been drawn up by Norbert, there was little I could do about this unhappy situation except to watch Jimmy closely, particularly when he attempted to assist his partner with her technique.

Fortunately, Sophie was nothing if not capable and Jimmy got nothing more than a pat on the head for his efforts. The fact that the outcome of the competition was secondary to good conversation and food – in this case a variety of handmade pastries – and drink – *kir* for the women and beer or pastis for the men – made it very much my kind of sporting event. Much of the conversation was of course about the freestyle competition. The boys seemed to have got hold of some equipment that they had carefully locked into a small store around the back of the Café de la Poste. There was much good-natured banter about who it would be that would lift the cup, the funds for which still had to be found. This did not mean that every point of the bowling competition was not lengthily and volubly discussed, the losers of each argument finally giving up with a great deal of shoulder-shrugging and head-shaking. Nicolas, who was the self-appointed arbitrator, had his work cut out trying to re-establish the peace, but Gallic exuberance, often so

alarming to Anglo-Saxon onlookers, was simply a demonstration of what a good time everyone was having.

The grandmother turned out to be something of a ringer,
having played, it transpired, for Mont St Bernard during the
1950s. Soon we were streets ahead, and sadly for Norbert,
whose natural inclination was to be somewhat more competitive, there was to be no arguing with *maman*. Flushed with
elation when we won, I shook the hands of my opponents
with great gallantry, and my euphoria was only slightly diminished when I discovered that the winners had to pay for the
fondue that we shared at the Restaurant Mont Thierry. The
mix of the various mountain cheeses with white wine and
garlic was delicious, served alongside some very good *jambon
de Savoie*. Once again I was slightly befuddled by the end of
the meal. When, with a twinkle in her eye, Granny started to
count out Franc coins onto the red and white tablecloth, three
years after the introduction of the Euro, I sent up a small
prayer for my bank manager Mr Jolly's sanity, and paid the
bill. Gripping me in what I believed to be an alcohol-inspired
bear hug, Norbert the Mayor thanked me profusely before
kissing me on both cheeks.

'*Brave garçon!* Next time it is for me. You and me we will
have a big, how you say, *déjeuner*?'

'Lunch?'

'Yes, *launch*, we will 'ave very big *launch*. You are
welcome! It will be *fantastique!*'

'Yes, I'm sure it will be . . .'

'Oh yes. We will eat good French food. Not your
Engleeeesh food!'

Having suffered for years any number of insults about *la
cuisine anglaise*, I had now built up a hide like a rhino when
it came to any discussion of British gastronomy. I shrugged
and smiled as Norbert stomped off informing a total stranger
that lamb with marmalade was *de la merde parfaite*.

15

Banking and Bonding

Aubrey, despite appearances, was, it seemed, capable of effective action when the moment required it, and a few days after my outing with Monsieur Job, he appeared on my doorstep, car engine running, to give me a hand with my bags as I left Mon Repos, where I had been so very comfortable, for my week as a chalet girl. In the event, I had very nearly decided against the whole exercise. Aubrey had explained that the lodge was going to be used by an American bank in Britain as the base for a 'team-building' exercise over the course of ten days. It sounded dreadful, but then at least I was not part of the team.

'Which bank is it then?' I am not sure why I asked. For the past twenty years I have never changed bank, relying as I always do on the good advice of Mr Jolly.

'Oh, I think they're called something like London Bank of the Americas. Something like that.'

'You are joking! No, you are joking!'

'No, why?'

'Sorry, Aubrey. I really don't think I'm going to be able to help you out this time.'

'Why on earth is that?' He didn't put it quite like that.

In a whisper I told him.

Just after I had left school, my parents had already been cooking up all sorts of plans for me to fly the family nest, and I had found myself some jobs through a temporary employment agency with which to furnish me with the funds for my departure. One Friday, as I collected my, in hindsight, rather meagre pay cheque for a job just finished, I was instructed to make myself known at the reception desk of London Bank of the Americas the following Monday and offer my services as the post boy. Dutifully, I appeared. By Thursday I had been sacked. It is a long story.

'Well, if that was just after you left school and it was that long ago, there's no way that there are going to be any of the same people working there,' Aubrey replied with a smile after I had explained what had happened. His logic was good even if his tact was less so.

In twenty years I have changed in appearance considerably – for the better I like to think – and I had only been at the bank for three days, so the risk of rediscovery was, I agreed, slim. By the time Aubrey pulled up his van outside an extraordinarily luxurious chalet, I could not help but feel rather more enthusiastic about my new position. I had already cast myself in the role of an Alpine *Upstairs Downstairs* butler, dressed in the ski version of a tailcoat and serving cocktails to Roger Moore and Lauren Bacall types, before confiding to an Hercule Poirot in a one-piece crumpled linen ski suit that I had seen one of the guests slip the crystal ashtray into her handbag before the host was murdered with a blunt instrument. Thus, he was able to solve the crime, and I was subsequently honoured by the mayor with the keys to the village.

When I woke from my daydream I actually discovered the reality to be possibly even stranger. Aubrey was surely mistaken when he showed me what he announced was my room.

'Are you sure it's here?' I looked at him doubtfully, and then up and down the basement corridor of identical doorways. 'This is just a cupboard. There isn't even a window – or a bed for that matter.' This last, at least, I believed to be a prerequisite for a bedroom.

Aubrey laughed hollowly and flicked the light switch back on.

'Right here is a storage space.' He slid back a hidden panel to reveal a space in which it would have been quite possible to store a large sandwich. 'Over here is a hand basin.' He pulled open a letterbox-shaped hatch and revealed a bowl with miniature taps. After I had had a chance to admire it – which did not take more than a matter of a few seconds – he closed up the cupboard, and turning through one hundred and eighty degrees, reached high up the wall to a handle that I had not noticed and pulled. Down from the wall swung quite easily what was clearly intended to be a bed. Some cunning mechanism allowed two legs to drop out of the panel to prop up the foot of the bedstead and its micro mattress. It was not enormously long, but if I adopted the foetal position to sleep all should be well.

'Make sure you're definitely ready for bed before you pull this down,' he advised helpfully. 'Once it is out you can't get at the hand basin or the cupboard.'

After a moment of confusion as Aubrey, my bag and I tried to negotiate our way around the small space, he offered to show me the rest of the chalet. What in practically anybody else's hands could have been a magnificent place to live had been, almost as if on purpose, ruined by staggeringly bad taste. More gilt than is to be found in the average Arabian palace had been applied to every conceivable fixture and fitting from door handles to curtain draws, from the controls of the home cinema to the handle of the mock-Louis XIV pushbutton telephone.

Vying with these to instil a profound sense of malaise in the visitor were a number of pieces of artwork that could only have been produced as a joke. Perhaps the only feature of the room that did not automatically provoke a feeling of sudden nausea was a huge fireplace open on all sides in the middle of the room and raised slightly from the ground, above which hung a huge copper hood to evacuate the smoke.

My eyes shimmering, I asked Aubrey who on earth owned this place.

He winked.

'I think you're just about to find out.'

From somewhere beyond the door to the living room, I could hear a female voice warbling the tune to Ravel's 'Bolero', in a fashion which even to my untuned ear was paying the composer no homage at all. As the door swung open I half expected to see La Castafiore – Tintin's some-time bejewelled, opera-singing friend – burst through the door. If anything the figure that appeared in the doorway was even more alarming. It was the Fur Coat.

Under one arm she was carrying her slush-coloured dog, and with her spare hand she was conducting her own musical performance. She appeared to be in great good humour as she greeted Aubrey.

'Aubrey, deaaaaarest, are we quaite ready for our guests? Is everything just so?'

For a moment I thought I had made a mistake, and in fact this was quite a different woman in a fur coat. Her pronunciation now, although about as genuine as the Louis XIV pushbutton telephone, had nothing in common with the guttural bark that I had heard in the ticket office.

'Yeah, I reckon so. Oh, and Margie,' – Aubrey gestured towards me by way of introduction – 'this is Will, here. You know, I told you about him – he's going to be taking over from Josie for a week. He's a mate of mine so he said he wouldn't mind doing me a favour.'

'Hello,' I said, in what I thought to be a fairly innocuous way and stuck out my hand. From the way she avoided it, I had to momentarily check that I had not recently contracted leprosy. She contented herself with staring at me icily.

'By the way, you will make sure that everybody knows that Snowy's room is out of bounds, won't you?' She indicated the mutt as she placed it on the floor and gave it a brief scratch behind the ears with long vermilion fingernails. 'We wouldn't like Snowy to be disturbed now, would we, darling?'

Snowy responded to the idea of being disturbed in his chambers by squatting and leaving on the shiny faux-Iraqi carpet his most profound thought on the matter which, curiously, was the colour of American mustard.

Circa eight o'clock on that Saturday evening, as I sat in the kitchen topping and tailing, on the instructions of Chef Aubrey, a pile of green beans the height of one of the Ten Tors, we heard the puffing of pneumatic brakes and the rubbery unsticking of a coach door as the guests arrived. Aubrey, who had been reading the local French paper with a certain degree of mystification, leaped to his feet and grabbed for his tubular white chef's hat. He went very quiet, and I could tell that he was listening closely through the swing door to the noise of the new arrivals. I threw the bean I was holding into a colander and made for the door myself and we stood with our ears to the door like two characters out of a French farce, which is exactly what it turned out to be. Outside in the lavish sitting-room various tired voices were expressing their first opinions of the chalet, and I grinned widely when I heard a young male voice exclaim: 'Jesus, look at that phone!'

From what I could make out there was a wide range of age groups and different English accents all mixed together with a combination of false bonhomie, a certain guardedness and perhaps a scintilla of genuine excitement about what was to come.

Margie the Fur Coat had clearly taken on the role of hostess, organiser and challenge-setter. She strode to the door of the kitchen and swung it wide open, thereby only narrowly avoiding giving Aubrey a perforated eardrum.

'Come on, you two. I need to introduce you to our new group,' she ordered, and with that she strode back out again.

'Sorry about all this,' whispered Aubrey. 'Shouldn't last too long.'

'Neeeuw, let me introduce the staff who will be looking after you this week. This is Aubrey, your chef, who will respond to all your dietary needs – just let him know.' From the glint in Aubrey's eye, I suspected that he would most definitely respond, probably with a sharp and pointed instrument.

'And your chalet girl this week, well, boy, well, man, is Will!' Somehow she managed to pull off this last revelation with something of a flourish, but as I stepped through the swing door the disappointment in the room, certainly from its male population, was palpable. At least three of the men drooped and looked as if their week away had already suddenly been ruined. One of the women, however, a late-forty-something with makeup to suit the decor of the room, was sitting rather coquettishly on the arm of the chair. When I caught her gaze she winked at me and smiled in a way that made me want to go and hide under my pile of green beans.

After the punters had found their accommodation and faced the possibility of having to room with someone with whom, until now, they had shared nothing more intimate than a stapler, they reassembled in the *'grand salon'* as Margie liked to describe it. On the instructions of Aubrey I had lit a surprisingly successful fire, and was just quietly trying to remember the number for the French fire brigade when Margie stood up and began to address the twenty or thirty-odd would-be bonders.

Scarcely daring to listen to what she was saying, I cast my eye over the group from behind a thick pall of smoke. They had grouped themselves – consciously or not, I do not know – in terms of rank or certainly age, and their expressions ranged from the solemnly attentive, 'got to do the best by my company, after all they're paying all this money for us to work better as a team', to the totally bemused, to the 'this is a bit of a laugh isn't it, wonder how much free wine you get before you have to start paying for it'. On that first evening I was not at all sure that I would have put any money on a successful outcome to the week, but then at least I was not quite as dismissive as Aubrey.

'Bunch of typical capitalist tossers,' he pronounced, as he flicked through a magazine of wincingly expensive ski clothing, having just slammed twenty-five *magrets de canard* into an industrial Swiss oven.

Aubrey, our unofficial union activist, was righteously angry about the conditions under which he and his fellow seasonal employees had to work in a world that to all appearances was drifting with cash. If all the anecdotes that he recounted to me were to be believed then ski resorts have the poorest working conditions since children were shoved up chimneys. Long hours, appalling accommodation – which I could attest to – dismal pay, and non-existent contracts are all accepted by, generally speaking, very young employees who will put up with practically anything in order to have the opportunity to ski for three or four months at a stretch. More often than not most of them do find plenty of time to ski as the punters themselves are out on the piste all day. Usually a ski pass and insurance are thrown in as part of the deal, but if any of the employees injure themselves they are rapidly sent back home and their employment terminated. The fact that more often than not these youngsters do not complain was not good enough, according to Aubrey. He could cite a dozen examples of rich chalet owners holding back partial payment of salaries until the end of the season and then finding a reason, however small, to sack their employees with a week or so to go. If Aubrey had his way he would have all these employers swinging from the nearest chair-lift as soon as it was possible to get them lined up.

'*Vive la révolution!*' he bellowed, before turning on the food mixer to maximum speed to create his red berry sauce, which was rather suitably a rich blood colour. 'And I would start with that fat cow next door,' he added, in what I feared was a rather loud voice, as he gesticulated in the direction of the living room with a gory spatula.

'Margie! Margie-bloody-Antoinette, that's what I call her.' Whilst he checked on the state of his individual portions of '*pommes dauphinoise*', he muttered something about cake that I didn't quite catch, before adding very curiously, 'And she's as common as muck! Have you seen the state of her hands? There's more nine-carat crap on those fingers than you will find in your average South African gold mine. Shit!' This last epithet was partly to underline his point, and partly because he had taken the lid off the mixer before he had thought to turn it off. Suddenly he was transformed into a very bloody *révolutionnaire*.

Trying not to laugh, I peered through the crack of the swing door to see those same gold fingers being waved around with some aplomb. Margie was, as far as I knew, in no way qualified for her position as team leader and her only attribute for the role, apart from the fact that she owned the premises, was her capacity to be incredibly bossy.

'So, come on everybody, out we go!' And with that she threw open the French windows that gave out on to a wide flat lawn behind the chalet which was lit by powerful arc lights. 'Let's see how expressive you and your partner can be with all that lovely snow!'

Apparently their first task on the long and tortuous path to becoming a fully bonded band was to create an ice figure before supper. Aubrey and I observed their efforts through the side window of the kitchen. Quite naturally, everybody had chosen as their partner someone who was like-minded. Whilst a couple of men in their late middle age attempted to create the initials of the bank to denote their veneration for their employer, the woman with the winsome wink and a man dressed in beige spent a great deal of time expressing astonishment at how cold the snow was. Two likely lads on the fringes of the spotlit area contented themselves with constructing a number of phallic objects, each of which they destroyed as soon as Margie came anywhere close to them. The following morning the frozen sculpture of a naked woman who bore an uncanny resemblance to the team leader was discovered on all fours in the middle of the lawn; a snowman's traditional carrot was seen to protrude from the most untraditional of places.

It was well past two o'clock in the morning by the time I barricaded myself into my cupboard and, following Aubrey's instructions, somehow managed to find my way into bed without ending up walled in.

After the evening meal, which had been remarkably well received, particularly by those whose fingers were not so numb or chilblained that they could pick up their knives and forks, Aubrey and I had snuck out of the back door and headed down to the Café de la Poste to meet up with all the other *saisonniers* who had just finished their respective shifts.

Training for the freestyle competition was going particularly well, and Jimmy was being much fêted as the only person in their team, or posse, as they absurdly chose to describe themselves, who had, to date, achieved a full seven hundred and twenty degree turn in the air. Actually, others had achieved a seven hundred and twenty degree turn in the air, but what separated them from Jimmy was that he had managed to remain upright when he came back to earth again. He was feeling very pleased with himself not least because he was now officially going out with Sophie. Sophie must have been some few years older and surely needed a more mature, sophisticated man than he, but as he had confided to me – 'tell anybody and I'll kill you, sir . . . Will, sir, dude. Seriously. Promise, okay?' – he had been feeling rather homesick recently so perhaps he was looking for some maternal affection. Baring my teeth, I told him how pleased I was for him, convincing myself that his limited French skills meant that he had misinterpreted her intentions. She was such a kind-hearted, pleasant girl that I was sure she was simply cheering him up.

Nicolas had made it through to the last heats of the men's downhill, and was most insistent that I should be available to come and support him at the finals. As the race was taking place the day after my employment came to an end I assured him that I would be there. He was going to be a very busy guy over the next few days as he had also been selected to play for the village ice hockey team in the annual contest against their arch rivals, the village of Issy. Three days later he would also be representing his village in the freestyle snowboarding competition. Such was his success at the sports to which he turned his hand that I would have been quite understanding if the rest of the youngsters had loathed his guts, but he was so unassuming and had such an engaging way about him that the others felt delighted for him and pleased that he could be counted amongst their friends.

Guy and Amandine were sitting on almost the same bar stool under what might have been the avuncular gaze of Gaston if his face had ever betrayed any expression at all. Holding hands they gazed lovingly into one another's eyes listening to their own romantic soundtrack. I waved over at them and they both looked as if they thought that they might have met me somewhere before.

In order to wake them up a bit, Jimmy, who was sweeping peanut shells off one of the bar tables and onto the floor with abandon, hollered across to them over the sound of the music. 'Oi, Guy, have you given her one yet?'

Now, over the course of many years of teaching I had on occasion found myself bewildered by various aspects of 'teen-speak'. The expression 'getting off' with someone, for instance, seemed to cover any multitude of sins ranging from a fairly chaste kiss to what they used to describe on a sign at Putney swimming baths as 'heavy petting' (which to a six-year-old, as I was, observing the picture alongside, involved running around the side of the pool carrying a large blonde woman whilst being pursued by the lifeguard whose intentions were unclear). It could also possibly mean full sexual congress of a Kama Sutran complexity.

Unfortunately, it was very difficult to misinterpret

Jimmy's question but Amandine did not appear to understand it. 'One what?' she whispered into Guy's ear – and Guy himself was feeling so blissful that he could only react with a slight shake of his head.

Oh, the immaturity!

Everyone settled back into the rhythm of the evening. An impromptu pool competition between the ski instructors and some piste-bashers with time off was taking place in the little alcove of the main bar. The click-click of the balls could just be heard over the music that Jimmy had put on the stereo system. Something mellow, he had explained. Gaston stood at the heel of the bar, impassive as a waxwork, apart from the occasional wiggle of his wing-like moustaches. Enjoying the relaxed atmosphere, I even began to become involved in the ski racing that was showing on the television screens high up on the walls. At about midnight, just as I was beginning to think rather wearily about heading back up the hill, a blast of freezing air swept through the bar as the doors burst open.

Immediately, the atmosphere as well as the temperature chilled dramatically. In through the doors staggered a dozen or so drunken men. They all seemed to be wearing the skiing equivalent of Hell's Angels colours and they looked to be in a pretty ugly mood as they approached the zinc top of the counter.

'L'Abbas!' breathed Nicolas, as the piste-bashers abandoned their game and stepped solidly back into the bar.

As the leader of the gang from the rival village ordered a dozen beers from the sceptical-looking Jimmy, Gaston unfolded his arms, took two deliberate steps toward him and told him that the Café de la Poste was now closed.

Perhaps they will just decide to take their custom elsewhere, I pondered rather naively a millisecond before the first glass flew through the air and shattered against the dartboard. From my vantage point behind a comfortingly solid pillar, I could see that the situation had very rapidly deteriorated into an all out bar-room brawl. Now, I do not have a great deal of experience in this particular field, but it did strike me that this was going to be an especially fine example. I almost applauded when a body rolled backward over one of the low tables and crashed against the wall, only stopping myself when I realised that it was Jimmy. When I went over to pick him up I only received a shove in the chest for my pains.

'Let me at 'em, let me at 'em!' he panted, as he charged back into the fray only to reappear in a heap at my feet a few seconds later.

Just as it looked as if the invaders were about to get the better of our lads, the door burst open again and I fully expected to see the local gendarmes arrive to make arrests, restore order and see justice done. Instead, framed in the doorway were the dark outlines of Sergei and three of Dimitri's bodyguards. Initially, they seemed quite taken aback by the scene before them, but then they came into the room with clear relish. Although obviously keen to join in the fun, they thought it rather pointless to just start walloping all and sundry indiscriminately, and so they chose out of some slightly unfocused loyalty, to support the cause of Mont St Bernard. Within a few bone-crunching minutes the L'Abbas hoodlums had been expelled, to either extricate themselves from snowdrifts or to hobble back down the hill clutching bruised parts of themselves. When it was all done, Sergei and his cronies stood stolidly at the bar and stared at Gaston who stared impassively back. Finally, shrugging, he instructed Jimmy to pour them a round of vodkas and leave the bottle on the bar. Laughing, they downed them in one and to our surprise smashed the glasses on the floor. Not that it made much difference to the general state of the decor in the Café de la Poste.

Sergei turned back to Jimmy, towering over him. He reached down as our plucky barman leaned back nervously, and wrapped his great leather-bound arms around him in a crushing bear hug. Jimmy squeaked as his feet lifted from the ground.

'Nu ti krutoy! Nu ti krutoy, mi brat! You are hard man, taken no shit, my brother! *Krutoy*, yes. Vodka for *krutoy!'* bellowed Sergei.

'Yeah, yeah, yeah. Well, thanks, guys! Cheers!' Jimmy had straightened his baseball cap as he came back down to earth.

'Santé for Mont St Bernard!' toasted Sergei.

'Santé, cheers!' we chorused and grinned until it hurt.

16

High Flyers

Margie's leadership skills were sorely tested on more than one occasion. Foolishly, she rejected Aubrey's offer of assistance – and Aubrey was an extremely experienced skier – when she took the group out to ski on the first morning of their stay. By the time they called it a day shortly after lunch, two of the party were already being fitted for plaster-casts in the village clinic and two others had quite simply been lost.

Standing at the bottom of the village chair-lift, Margie was attempting to hold onto her composure behind an enormous, and frankly rather extraordinary, pair of sunglasses given to her, as she told anybody who asked and quite a few who didn't, by the Baron de Rothschild himself, who was 'a close personal friend'. If indeed this was true, by the time the rest of the group assembled he was about the only one left.

The managing director of the British branch of the London Bank of the Americas was an affable, strangely simple man called Charles, who could have only got the job, according to Aubrey, thanks to the 'greasy pole'. Initially, I had thought that this referred to another member of the great capitalist conspiracy, and even when I realised that he meant an

object rather than a nationality, I still couldn't quite understand what image he was trying to portray.

Although in manner not dissimilar to Sergeant Wilson,
Charles decided on this occasion that he must take action.
His cherished employees had to be found. Aubrey, who was
sitting on the terrace of Gaston's restaurant observing the
proceedings, suggested in a mutinous whisper that if they
were permanently lost, he, Charles, would never have to
pay them their 'billion pound bonuses'. Charles didn't
appear to hear him and was already beginning to talk about
getting hold of the police, whom he insisted on referring
to as the 'johndarmes'.

The thought of the arrival of the forces of law and order
sent Margie into paroxysms of disquiet. The way she pulled
on her headscarf and pushed her sunglasses further up her
nose made me wonder at that moment whether she might
not have criminal connections. Looking round despairingly,
she caught sight of Aubrey who was just finishing a piece
of 'wicked' *fondant de chocolat*. Casting his eyes heavenward,
he pulled his jacket back on over his shoulders and with a
cometh-the-man-cometh-the-hour shrug stepped nimbly
into his ski bindings and headed for the chair-lift, his mobile
phone strapped to his ear.

Eager not to be left out of the adventure, I hurriedly, but
possibly with rather less élan, put on my own skis and
followed. By the time we had got all the way to the top of
the Col St Croix, Jimmy, Guy and Amandine – who were by
now practically wearing the same ski suit – Aubrey, Emilie,
his girlfriend and the daughter of the butcher, and Nicolas
were all waiting for us. After a brief discussion about the
best way of sweeping the mountainside we divided into four
groups and set off to find the errant bankers. As I knew only
too well, once the sun goes off the mountain, not only does
it become immediately much colder, but the night arrives

remarkably quickly. By the time we commenced our third descent, long shadows were being cast by the pine trees across the wide pistes, highlighting the contours of the slope in a way that could not be seen in the bright sunlight of the day.

'Perhaps they have gone off piste,' suggested Guy. 'Whatever that old battleaxe is called, she said they were probably okay skiers.'

From the descriptions that Margie had given, I realised that the missing parties were none other than my friend, the woman with the wink, and her beige boyfriend.

'They're probably down in the bar right now and nobody has bothered to give us a ring.' Aubrey was quite convinced that that was the kind of people they were.

Surprisingly, I was the first person to spot the missing duo, probably because I was moving at a considerably slower speed than the rest of them. Just out of the corner of my eye I caught the flash of something through the trees, something pink, something that I am now in hindsight quite convinced was a glimpse of hurriedly concealed male buttocks. By the time we reached them, they were able to smile quite innocently and maintain that the reason that they were in such close proximity to each other and up against a tree was to preserve body heat. Jimmy's clenched fist and backwards and forwards arm movements, as we skied in triumph back down to Mont St Bernard, suggested he did not believe them for a moment.

Such were the stress levels provoked by taking the group downhill skiing, Margie handed them over to the tender mercies of Madame Brassard for the remainder of their stay. By the time this latter had finished with them they could ski with the same precision as a brass band can march. Whenever she issued instructions over her shoulder as they weaved down the slopes, I fully expected the entire group to reply as one man and woman 'Yes, Sarge!'

Having had a few days to recover from the excitements of her first day's ski guiding, Margie summoned up enough courage to suggest that she would, after all, accompany them for their last day. Despite the raised eyebrows of Charles and a number of his senior colleagues, she assured them the night before that nothing could go wrong. After all, they were not going downhill skiing this time. No, she had decided that she wished to show them the rudiments of cross-country skiing – *le ski de fond*. The forecast was good – Sophie had confirmed as much on Radio 'Armonie that morning as Aubrey and I had set about scrubbing the kitchen and laying out the breakfast. In fact she had said that it was going to be 'spectacularly sunny' and a perfect day to *se bronzer* – get a tan. Unfortunately these innocent remarks only served to tempt Jay-Pee to make some rather lurid references to what Sophie might look like were she skiing in her bikini or even, he went on, in her *'leetle monokini, eef you know what ah mean'*. If this was not enough, he followed it all up with a series of *'hein, hein'* type noises which meant that you could practically see him winking.

Disgusting old pervert.

Mind you, it did set you thinking.

Because the weather was going to be good and many of the cross-country skiing courses ran through countryside of great peace and tranquillity – one of, or in hindsight possibly the only, attraction of the sport – Margie suggested that we take a picnic. The tins of foie gras, bottles of champagne, legs of cured ham and a wide variety of cheeses would be carried in a hamper on a small sled to the front of which would be attached Aubrey. Although he did not argue the toss at the time, he did mutter something about the slaves of Egypt as he was strapped into his harness by me. Laughing uncontrollably, I was almost unable to do up the buckles.

He, on the other hand, was in no mood for mirth. That morning, Guy, who had taken on the role of organiser for the freestyle competition, had been down to the ski store with some luminous marshal's jackets that he had been lent by a road gang that were repairing the local roads. When he arrived there he had discovered that the padlock to the door had been picked and most of the equipment was missing. Yet again, the freestyle competition was in doubt. He had rung Amandine and the two of them had taken themselves to the small *Gendarmerie* in order to report the crime. The police, who were in the midst of an anti-alcohol campaign and had been arresting skiers on the slopes as they attempted to make their way home after lengthy lunches, were initially not terribly interested. When they discovered that Guy was English, one of the officers made a joke about Sherlock Holmes, and the thrusting sergeant who was hoping to go on to greater things suddenly saw this as a great opportunity. For want of a deerstalker and meerschaum pipe he managed to find a fingerprinting kit in the storeroom and set out to the scene of the crime, accompanied by a young policeman – his Watson. Have no fear, he told Guy, we will soon have your man. Aubrey was less than certain that the crime would be solved, but he was quite sure that if they didn't find the culprits and recuperate the gear then the competition would be in serious danger of being cancelled – again. What was more, he was pretty sure where to look. It was bound to be those idiots from L'Abbas. He shook his head with frustration.

'Off you go, off you go! Remember, breathe in and stride, breathe in and stride!' shrieked Margie as she grappled with the bindings of her skis, her handbag and the lead that was attached to the ridiculous Snowy.

Cross-country skiing is a strangely deceptive sport. When

you see people practising it on the television it looks as if there is not really that much to it. Just strap on a pair of endlessly long and surprisingly thin skis and, using your poles for leverage, stride off into the mountains. Nothing, of course, could be further from the truth. As I and most of the punters worked out very early on, you can stride all you like but the progress you make is rather similar to that you might expect trying to climb up a downward-moving escalator. And if there is even so much as the smallest incline to climb your task is made a hundred times more difficult. By lunchtime we were still in sight of the minibus that had delivered us to the beginning of the cross-country trail.

Nevertheless, fortified with a few glasses of Perrier-Jouet 1988 champagne – this was an American bank after all – and a few bites of fattened goose liver, everybody in the group made great efforts in the afternoon. Occasionally, these efforts were a little too great, for there is only one thing more difficult on a pair of cross-country skis than trying to go uphill and that is trying to go downhill. So narrow are the skis that you need a very low centre of gravity just to stay upright. At six foot two and bringing up the rear my job was made doubly difficult. Watching the rest of the group falling over like tin soldiers every few yards, it was extremely difficult to keep my composure which, naturally, did nothing at all for my balance.

After one particularly awkward steep slope, the winking lady, who had been placed in the front position so everybody could keep an eye on her, took a tumble and blocked the entire path. The rest of the group, entirely unable to stop themselves, careered into her with an impressive clattering and smacking until they all lay in one enormous bonfire stack of skis, poles and groaning bodies. Margie had lagged some way behind and was only not the last in line because Aubrey and I could not circumnavigate her. She had built up an impressive head of steam, Snowy yelping on his lead as he tried to keep up alongside her, before she collided with the rest of her party. Once everybody had finally disentangled themselves, it became clear that all was not well with our group leader, who had gone strangely pale under her pancake makeup. She indicated through use of language not entirely appropriate to someone in her respected position that all was not well with her arm.

Aubrey, who took all mountain matters extremely seriously, announced after a brief inspection that Margie had dislocated her shoulder. This drew an impressive array of 'oohs' and 'aahs' from the rest of the group as they huddled around her.

'Just have to pop it back in,' said Aubrey, with a very definite glint in his eye. Despite the fact that Margie, during the course of the brief surgical intervention, accused him at very high volume of having an ongoing and not entirely natural relationship with his own mother, Aubrey succeeded with a rather nasty snap and pop to get the arm back where nature had intended it to be.

You would never have thought it for all the thanks he got, but I know he was sure that it was all definitely worth it. Margie lay back in Charles's arms and took an amazingly long swig from a hip flask that was proffered to her. Just as she was about to have another slug, a two-seater sedan chair, a sort of rickshaw on skis, drawn by two of Sergei's minions in jogging tracksuits, came round the bend at a swift clip. As it passed our party a red-and-white checked curtain was pulled back, and the faces of Dimitri and a young lady in a fur hat appeared at the window. They stared and stared some more before letting the curtain fall back and gliding away. Margie's language was simply appalling.

Finally, the London Bank of the Americas group made

their way back, with the odd limp, to their smoked-glass offices somewhere near Baron's Court. Perhaps the only thing they had learnt as a group was that at all costs they should try and avoid getting into a team-building situation again.

'Thanks a million, dude. You know there's no way I could have got through this week without you. You're my main man.' Aubrey was clearly grateful. 'You know what I've done? You know, just to show you that I really appreciate what you've done?'

'No, tell me?' For some reason, but none that I could put my finger on, I was ever so slightly nervous about how his appreciation was to demonstrate itself.

He laughed with the other guys that were lining the bar at the Café de la Poste as Gaston looked down on us and wondered what on earth could be so funny – or indeed funny at all.

'Let's make it a surprise. Meet us up Mont Thierry tomorrow at ten, okay?'

'Okay,' I replied, yawning. I could quite happily have stayed under the goose-down at Mon Repos for a week, and I simply did not understand how it was that people who were only ten or so years younger than me could have so much energy. Still, I could not possibly refuse their hospitality, could I?

Since my injury, I had barely skied, preferring to sit in the safety of any number of mountain refuges and go over the circumstances of my accident with anybody who would listen. When I arrived at the top of Mont Thierry, I realised that I need not have worried about whether my knee was going to be able to cope with the rigours of the piste. As I wandered out of the bubble lift and inspected my goggle marks in the mirror window of the Beauvoir restaurant, I could see over my shoulder the reflection of numerous gaudy parachutes laid out on the sparkling snow. The weather conditions were clearly perfect for the ludicrous pursuit known in French as *la parapente*, which involves hurling yourself off the edge of a mountain attached to a sheet of material which would have been put to far better use creating various styles of lingerie. As I wandered over to the bottom of the ski lift where we had arranged to meet, I could see various of the loonies spreading out the numerous bits of string that attached the parachutist to the rest of his life.

'All right, mate?' enquired Aubrey, after he, Jimmy and Guy had hurtled down the mountainside and screeched to a halt a few fractions of an inch from where I was standing minding my own business.

'Fine, thanks,' I replied, wiping the stinging snow spray from my face. Now, I'm no cynic, but I was beginning to sense something was amiss.

'Here, Will, this is Christophe,' introduced Aubrey. I looked up and standing in front of me was a tall man wearing a helmet, mirror sunglasses and a green jumpsuit open to his midriff. The thick hairs on his chest were hardly ruffled by the stiffish breeze. He was wearing a harness to which, quite clearly, could be attached the large pink parachute that lay limply on the ground beside him.

'Aren't you cold?' was all that I thought to ask him, but before I could say anything he wiggled his huge handlebar moustaches, smiled and then instructed me to turn around.

'So, now I can just strap you against my body and we can fly away over the mountains together. Are you ready?'

'No, I'm bloody not. Anyway I can't afford to do things like that. My physiotherapist has told me that I have to train my knee.' This last bit was entirely untrue but desperate times, desperate measures.

'No, it's all cool, dude. We've got it all sorted for you. Don't worry about it. It'll be an absolute gas,' said Guy in a stupid, overly enthusiastic voice.

'Yeah, dude, go for it. You'll absolutely love it. It's amazing. You'll feel like you're flying,' the others urged me. Their enthusiasm was so immature.

'No, you don't understand. I'm not in the mood. No, seriously, you don't seem to understand. I've got a terrible head for heights. I'm not feeling very well. I've got to make a phone call.'

As I thought about suggesting to Christophe that I had a contagious ailment, I heard the clips of the harness clunking into place. Before I could come up with the name of a mysterious disease, I could feel my legs running in front of me and the parachutist's body hair itching the back of my neck.

Two seconds later we were aloft. I felt not a little like a rabbit that has been scooped up in the beak of an all-powerful eagle and knows that before long it is about to meet its certain death. Helplessly, I thought of one of my teaching colleagues who had been hung up by his trousers on a coat hook. It had caused a bit of a scandal at the time particularly as his pupils were only eleven and all girls. Christophe yanked on one of the very thin-looking bits of string to which we were attached and we began to spiral in a sickening, not to say completely out-of-control fashion.

So this was how it was all going to end.

I squeezed my eyes closed and tried to think about . . . well about anything. Miraculously, the terrible swinging nauseous sensation came to an abrupt halt and we were soaring, soaring like a graceful bird across this beautiful valley. Suddenly I became aware of how much I was enjoying it, floating free. Then I realised that it was probably because I was dead. Although if this was the kingdom of heaven or the Elysium Fields or wherever it was that I had ended up, how strange it was that it was made up of a little wooden village and endless ski lifts, hotels, shops and the smell of wood smoke. How odd too that the Russians should be there as well, disporting themselves, as they were, in the steaming outdoor pool of the Hotel de l'Aigle Brun. We zoomed in low over them but they took little notice of us, occupied as they were shooting the tropical fish, that they had had shipped up from Geneva, with spear guns.

Yes, I thought, as we drifted over chimney tops looking down at the red specks of fires, I was definitely dead.

17

Living at Windsor Castle

Despite the fact that I would have quite happily spent the next few days in the safety of Mon Repos after my aerial exploits, I had to make my way down to the village to give my lesson to Olivier. Mireille and I had arranged that I would spend an hour with him on Wednesdays, which was a day off from school, on Saturday afternoons, and on Thursday evenings when she went to her badminton club. Today, Alexei was going to be joining us for the first time.

Progress had been a little slow in gaining Olivier's confidence. Just as I had been leaving the Christmas party those weeks before, I had remembered that in the pocket of my jacket was the present that I had bought in Geneva for the young boy. When I had handed him the small packet he had looked embarrassed and confused so I thought it better to leave without further ado. In any case it was all I could do to negotiate the wooden steps down to the road and make my way back up the hill. Although I had given it little further thought, I was pleased that he had produced my gift, a nice but not overly complicated Swiss Army Knife from his trouser pocket at our first meeting. I was less delighted when, during the course of the lesson, he decided to practise with the corkscrew on the surface of the dining-room table, but not willing to upset him I had tried to push various pieces of paper and ends of books under his fervent efforts. On this first occasion the conversation had been very one-sided. When I had explained what I hoped we would be able to achieve, he replied with grunts and the occasional '*Oui, monsieur*', but otherwise kept his eyes downcast and scuttled away when his mother reappeared.

Thankfully, as time went on, he appeared to open up considerably, and now we discussed any matter of things, sometimes in English, in which he seemed surprisingly confident, and sometimes when things became more complicated, in French. When he had arrived, Alexei, starved of any conversation in the strange world in which he lived, was more than happy to grab this opportunity to join in with our chat. Pleasingly, Olivier, who I had primed about the Russian boy's arrival, seemed more than happy to let him take part.

After I hurriedly explained to them the horrors of *para-pente* and made them promise me that they would never attempt anything so absurdly dangerous, I asked Alexei if he would tell us a little bit about himself, his home and his way of life back in Russia. Olivier and I sat in gawping silence able only to gasp occasionally as Alexei gave us a thumb-nail sketch of his world.

'My name is Alexei. I am nine years old and I live with my father because my mother is dead, but I love her very much and I pray for her every day.' He paused and looked at us solemnly with his clear blue eyes and his cheeks flushed a little. Olivier stared, stunned, at the other boy and then at me. The silence was heavy for long moments before Alexie, taking a deep breath, started again. 'I am very lucky because I live in Moscow in Russian Federation and we live in former KGB district. Our house has very many rooms and swimming pools.'

'A swimming pool,' I corrected gently.

'No, swimming pools.'

'Right . . . sorry. Go on.'

'In my garden we have many animals like deer and some bears, and lots of birds like ostrich. It's right, ostrich? Yes, okay, and every morning before my tutor comes I drive around and feed them in my car. We have just taken some Mercedes car. Big one for my father and sport model for me. For my next birthday I hope I will have elephant.'

'Elephant?' Olivier and I gasped.

'Yes, African elephant. They are better than India elephant – they are much bigger.'

'Yes, but not so easy to train, I think,' Olivier added quite seriously.

'Yes, maybe that is true.' We pondered this point for a few moments.

'So what kind of things do you do on your birthday?'

'Well this last year we had pirate party.'

'Oh, great. That must have been fun.' I remembered that I too had had a pirate party as a child. Cardboard cutlasses covered in silver foil, paper tricorn hats, burnt cork moustaches, eye patches and painted on tattoos, that sort of thing.

Alexei's pirate party appeared to have been a rather grander affair. His father had hired a three-masted schooner that had recently featured in a blockbuster movie. The crew comprised all of Alexei's favourite Russian movie actors and television personalities – rather more poorly paid than their American counterparts. They had been hired in for the day and suitably costumed. Together they had sailed down the Moscow River in search of boats to board. In fact, the party organiser had prepared a boat, various casks of treasure, barrels of rum and a crew of stuntmen who fully expected to be tied up and asked to walk the plank.

Unfortunately, in the excitement of setting off the real cannons, confusion had settled over the proceedings like the big cloud of cordite smoke. The intended victims found themselves free to sun themselves on their decks as Alexei and his crew boarded an entirely different boat – a sand dredger from the Gulf of Finland. Imagine the surprise of the captain of this vessel when he found himself being tied up by a well-known TV weather presenter.

'Well, your friends must have loved it.'

'Actually, I didn't have so many of my friends there because I don't have so many friends. I do know one boy who lives at Windsor Castle, but I don't see him very often, only when my father goes for business meetings with his father.'

'You mean Windsor Castle in England?' I wondered which minor Royal this could be.

'No, Windsor Castle in Moscow. They have built a copy of it in my district. It is the one that is next to the palace of Fontainebleau.'

'Near the Taj Mahal, I suppose,' Olivier said, and I laughed.

'Not far,' Alexei replied without expression, before carrying on his train of thought. 'You see, my father is a very kind man. Very kind. But always very busy man. So sometimes I just stay with our cook – her name is Ludmila and some-times she makes cakes for me. That makes me very happy. I love her very much. You know, sometimes when my father takes me to do things, I ask if Ludmila can come. She came with us the time that we hired some army tanks and had a battle against some German tanks from my father's colleague. She was the best at blowing up the targets.'

He stopped and we gawped some more.

'But you know I think I prefer to be living here in this place. It is very friendly and warm.'

Finding myself astonished by what he had said, I burbled

for a little while before turning to Olivier and asking him whether he was looking forward to the downhill competition as I had heard from his mother that he might well be selected for the village team.

'Oh yes, *monsieur*, but I really prefer the freestyle,' he mumbled quietly. 'You know what is that?'

'What that is?' I corrected. 'Yes, I do, but you know there is a big problem about the competition? Someone has stolen all the equipment so my friends say that it may not be possible to go ahead with it. Shame, isn't it?' I looked at the two youngsters.

Before I could gauge his reaction, Olivier had hurled the penknife that he now kept habitually in his hand across the table, and had rushed across the room and out of the door leaving Alexei and I looking at each other in astonishment. Mireille was in the kitchen, and I went in to see her and told her what had happened. Oh, she said, she would go and find him and get him to explain himself. No, I suggested. It would be easier to leave it for the time being. He was probably tired, and heaven knew I was. Perhaps we would just come back on Saturday afternoon. Bemused, I strolled back to the hotel with Alexei, who was going to meet his personal ski instructor, before heading up in the direction of Mon Repos.

As I trooped up the hill patting Monsieur Job's horse on the rump, the three of us making our way slowly up through a new snowfall to home, I could not help but wonder what had caused Olivier's reaction. Maybe it was just that he was a budding 'freestylee' as Guy and company liked to describe themselves in deeply phoney Jamaican accents. He was probably just upset that there was to be no competition.

My neighbour, who I had come across as I was mentally preparing myself for the climb, was his normal industrious self. After we crossed the piste and he had glared at a number of skiers who were doing their little best to avoid skiing under Hortense's hooves, he asked me if I was interested in helping him saw some logs. Obviously I wasn't, but I so much enjoyed the old man's company that I offered to accompany him to his woodshed. Woodworking and forestry were integral to the peasant life of the mountains. When, once upon a time, there had been few other distractions in the winter months, the evening hours had been passed constructing furniture and pieces of farm machinery from raw timber. Almost more impressively, the villagers also produced bowls, spoons, ladles and plates to be hung on their homemade dressers. Now, although all of modern life's necessities could be bought at the hypermarket further down the valley, Monsieur Job still enjoyed producing little bits and pieces out of the most uninspiring offcuts of wood. Whilst I set about sawing up a small forest of logs, he fashioned me a bottle stopper, useful only in the unlikely event that I found myself with a half-empty bottle on my hands. As the worn clasp knife whirled and whittled and it began to take shape in his small calloused hands, he began to reminisce.

Like many French men and women, he seemed to have an almost encyclopaedic knowledge of his country and also, more particularly, his region. As the little, tumbling pile of sawdust rose at my feet he gave me a brief, actually not so brief, history of the Alps and the Savoie. Although I became mightily confused by the numerous dukes of the area, it became clear that this corner of modern day France had over the centuries been equally considered Italian and Swiss. Only in 1860 had it been subsumed into the French Republic, and even in a recent survey, twenty-two per cent of the population had voted for the area to become an independent state.

As the first blisters swelled on my hand, he returned to his favourite subject – the war years. In hushed tones he told me, the first person to have heard the story in thirty years, that before he had met and married the present Madame Job, he had been in love, totally infatuated, with the daughter of the neighbouring farmer. They were the same age and had known each other since they had sat in the same pram outside his parents' farmhouse. When the war came, she too had joined the Maquis and had helped to accompany the fugitives over the border. They had been very much in love, he and Delphine, he knew they had, although things were not like today and they had never clearly expressed their feelings. He had planned to propose to her on their return from Switzerland, but as they had made their way through the Gorges de Collette they had been ambushed by the Gebirgstruppen. As they scrambled for the shelter of one of their secret caves, Delphine had taken a bullet in the leg. Monsieur Job had rolled and tumbled back down the slope and grabbed her under the arms. It had been so difficult to keep his footing as he dragged her back to safety. Just as he was trying to stand up again a sniper had shot her in the chest, in the heart, and she had died in his arms. Only a few days later had they been able to rescue her body, frozen in its beauty.

Sometimes, the old man, unbeknownst to his wife, would visit her grave and leave a few flowers from his meadows. If he thought there was nobody looking he would kiss the black and white enamelled photograph that lay on her tomb and cry. Ridiculous, he said, it was after all more than sixty years ago. He wiped his nose, wobbled his hairpiece a little and handed me my perfectly carved bottle stop. Still, he said, Madame Job was a *brave femme* and what was more she was a fine cook.

'On va manger?'

Oh, yes, I said, as the first of my blisters burst. I was starving.

'*Excellent, moi aussi,*' he agreed, as he reached into the chicken coop, pulled out a beady-looking hen and whirled it around by the neck until it was dead. Tucking it under his arm he invited me in for a *petit jaune*.

Considerably more pastis was in evidence when eventually I met up with Norbert the Mayor for our lunch in the elegant wood-lined dining-room of the Hotel Chamonix. Unfortunately, I had discovered only a few days before that it was to be a business lunch, and Norbert had asked me along in the role of translator and, it soon turned out, peacemaker. About half an hour after we had commenced our aperitifs and had discussed the relative merits of the English and French football teams – and I was left in no doubt about which side was superior – the other guests arrived in the form of Dimitri and his nervous secretary. By now the restaurant was murmuring with well-heeled diners who had decided to take a hard-earned break from the rigours of the slopes. Our table, fortunately, it transpired, was tucked away in an alcove, and I spent much of my time trying to hide behind a large potted aspidistra, as heads started to turn and the odd piece of silver-plated cutlery was dropped.

In fact, proceedings were initially nothing but cordial. Dimitri even presented him with a gift, which his secretary had produced with some pride and aplomb from his briefcase.

'I am very fan of France,' announced Dimitri solemnly, as the mystified Mayor started to pick open the wrapping. 'You have the great wines and cheese and then you have the good cooking and beautiful country and the "dawly burds" but . . .' Here, he stood up, handing his dark glasses to the secretary. 'One thing you French people you can never do very good. Yes, that is gherkin! Only Russian gherkin is good.'

Norbert blinked in amazement at the small glass jar with

its hand-written Cyrillic label, and then the challenge sunk in and he waved over a nervous-looking waiter, whispered furiously into his ear and waved his hands a good deal. The poor man rushed off in the direction of the swinging doors of the kitchens as one of his colleagues appeared demurely with a frozen bottle of vodka on a tray. Dimitri waved at him to start pouring. Norbert was about to react and demand something Gallic be served but manners got the better of him, and I suspect a curiosity about the effects of the Russian spirit. He had something of a nose for all things *spiritueux*. Soon the first waiter returned with a jar, this time of French gherkins which was placed alongside the competition. Solemnly, the two men took a bite of one of each of the mini, shrivelled, pickled cucumbers and pronounced their verdicts, which were unsurprisingly partisan. Nevertheless glasses were raised in a toast.

'So,' Dimitri smiled. 'Here is a toast to our business deal.'

'What business deal?' asked Norbert, his voice a whisper and his eyes bulging and swivelling slightly. This may, of course, have just been the vodka.

'You know, now we are going to buy this small village, yes?'

'*Non!*'

'Why? I will pay you good money. Double price if you want?'

'*Non! Jamais!* Never!'

Although both Dimitri and his secretary did a great deal of tablecloth smoothing and even at one stage offered to do a bullet-point presentation, which I mistranslated with explosive effect, Norbert was adamant that he would have nothing to do with their expansionist plans. Voices were raised and tempers inflamed, which three bottles of Côtes de Beaune 1984 did nothing to soothe. By the end of the meal, our mayor had come as close to cuffing the Russians around the ear as it is possible to do without being arrested for assault, and had sent them on their way before setting about a particularly good bottle of Marc de Savoie, a raisiny rocket fuel, so he said, that beat the hell out of the Burgundian version.

When eventually I managed to make an exit, Norbert's bellicose rhetoric ringing in my ears, it was past five o'clock, the hour at which I was supposed to be arriving at Mireille and Olivier's for our lesson. Unprofessional as I felt, I decided to cancel. Just as I was fumbling with my mobile phone in gloved hands – because in mid-February it was brutally cold – to make my excuses and try to rearrange a time, I narrowly avoided being run down by the big blue Renault police van. Wondering why an unknown female French voice was repeatedly telling me that I had dialled the wrong number, I waved at the officers on board as the slush slopped on my boots. Just as I was about to redial, I glanced up again and saw that huddling in the back, almost hidden by the puffy collar of his ski jacket, was Olivier. His eyes, which met mine for a moment, were glazed over with unhappiness. Watching the minibus drive on, I was momentarily rooted to the spot. What on earth had happened? Jerked into action by the flashing of the police van's indicator, I raced after it, realising that it must be heading in the direction of the station. Cancelling the call that I was about to put through to Mireille, considering it better to get to the bottom of the mystery, I raced up the side street, which under one of Norbert's new schemes doubled as one of the ski runs, transferring punters from the main slopes over to the bubble lift at the bottom of Mont Thierry.

My feet slipping freely on the compacted snow at one stage gave me the impression that I was just running on the spot. Grabbing hold of the shoulders of a number of passing skiers, I pulled myself up the narrow incline. By the time I had reached the small flight of steps up to the door of the *Gendarmerie*, I felt, in the thin air, that I had run a mini-marathon, and huffed and puffed loudly as I leant against the reception desk and whacked the silver bell with a gloved hand. Of Olivier there was no sign.

Some minutes later a young policeman appeared, looking extremely important with a clipboard in the crook of his arm. With an insouciance that young French men and women must be taught at civil service school, he managed to ignore me completely for at least four minutes, and at one moment even managed to find time to rummage around in the drawers of his desk. If he had pulled out a newspaper and had begun to do the crossword I would have been in no way surprised. Turning away, he gazed nonchal-antly out of the window at the tourists who ambled by chatting, enjoying themselves, unaware of the minor human crisis that was being played out in the small police station. When I had been ignored for the statutory amount of time, I developed a small cough which made itself heard every ten seconds or so. Finally, once our little game had been played out, the policeman shambled over as if he was about to give me a parking ticket. Skipping the pleasantries, I asked him where the boy was. '*Bonjour, monsieur*,' he said somewhat perfunctorily, and I fully expected him to tick off this section of the interview on his clipboard.

'Yes, yes, *bonjour, monsieur*. Maybe you can tell me where this young boy that you brought in just now has gone.'

'Are you his father?'

'No, what has that got to do with it?' I asked, and imme-diately realised what a stupid question it was. I could see the officer mentally go back five steps in his interview procedure and so decided to press on before he sat back down at his desk.

'No, no, I am not his father. I am his, er . . . He is, er . . . I am his uncle.' This was, whichever way you wanted to look at it, a lie, but I did feel avuncular towards Olivier and I was here to be on his side.

'One moment then.'

After he had left I had a bit of a snoop around, and under one of the frosted glass panels that lined the room I spotted Olivier's rucksack and his outsize snowboarding boots tapping nervously up and down.

Surprisingly quickly, an older policeman came to the desk looking grave. 'So, here is the situation, *monsieur*, this young boy was found behind one of the sawmills with some of his friends, and they had built themselves a ski course – you know, a freestyle course, quite a good one with an excellent half pipe. Anyway . . .'

'Well what's wrong with that? That's what kids around here do . . . Are you even . . .'

Somehow, with a superhuman effort, I managed to shut myself up.

'When we took a closer look, we discovered that they were using some of the material that was stolen from the storeroom behind the Café de la Poste.'

'Why did you just bring Olivier here? What about the other boys? What on earth makes you think that he was responsible?'

'Well, he admitted having picked the lock of the shed and stealing the contents. That's what made us think he was responsible,' replied the policeman, with an admirable stab at French irony.

'Oh, right . . .' Suddenly, I thought guiltily of the penknife I had given the lad and quelled a fleeting desire to do a runner.

'Anyway, he has just finished giving us a statement and then he will be free to go. We were going to ring his mother, but because you are here we can give him to you. He will have to come back, though. Shame, you know, to see a boy like that go to the bad. His father, you know, he was a bit of a hero in this area . . .'

'He hasn't gone to the bad, you moron. He's just very unhappy and it will take him some time to sort himself out. All we are asking is for some kind of compassion, you numbskull,' I chose not to say.

Olivier, still wearing his ski hat and goggles, trundled out of the office, and wordlessly we left, he and I. Whistling, the young policeman called us back, waving the boy's snowboard. I jogged back to pick it up and we made our way in silence down the main street through the village. Only when we were heading up the winding road to Mont Thierry did he stop and look at me.

'I only did it so that they would play with me again. They used to be my friends and now it seems as if I hardly know them. After you know, my dad and Philippe . . . I didn't want to talk to anybody. But now I do because that's what my *papa* would want me to do. But not like this . . . Oh, I didn't mean to do it. You have to believe me, Williams!'

Large teardrops, shining in the late afternoon sun, rolled down his face and he tried to wipe them away with the backs of his new Christmas gloves.

'It's okay, I do believe you. We'll just have to try and put this right, won't we?'

He nodded, and we plodded on for a few more yards before he stopped again and started to sob uncontrollably. I put my arm around his shoulders and surprised myself by how easy I found it to say 'there, there' in French.

'*Ça va aller, Olivier, tu vas voir, ça va aller.*'

'But my dad would have been so embarrassed by me. He would have been so angry.'

'Non, Olivier, non, *il aurait bien compris*, he would have understood.'

18

Jan Dark

When Olivier and I explained what had happened to Mireille and Alexei, who had been waiting patiently at the chalet, the former was unsurprisingly alarmed and angry, and when, on her instruction, her son had disappeared into his bedroom, she leaned against the wooden dresser in the kitchen and sighed. What was she to do? What would become of Olivier? Was this the first sign of things going to the bad? Maybe, I suggested, we should all give it twenty-four hours before we discussed the matter again, but I was sure that everything would come out in the wash. Promising to return the following day, I headed back for the village wondering whether it was true that, indeed, everything actually would come out in the wash and, equally to the point, whether you could actually say that in French.

The Café de la Poste was buzzing with excitement when I arrived feeling weary and in need of some refreshment. Jimmy was so animated he could hardly string a sentence together. 'Oh, yeah, dude, yeah, yeah, yeah, it was totally wicked, you'll never guess what. Oh, man.'

In fact, the confusion was such that I pretty much did

have to guess what. From what I could gather, Aubrey, friendly as he was with the mountain rescue team, had managed to organise a helicopter lift 'for the crew' up to the Crête des Dentelles. Once up there, way beyond the tree line, they had been in the deepest powder snow, carving virgin tracks back over into Switzerland.

All had gone to plan until they had strayed into a militarised zone and found themselves at the wrong end of a number of guns gripped in the hands of a French SAS battalion. The soldiers, unable to break off their exercise, insisted that the boys accompany them until the end. This involved bivouacking on the mountainside and eating rations out of mess tins as they watched machine guns being stripped down and reassembled which, naturally, they found absolutely fantastic. Although the soldiers would not admit it, the boys were convinced that they were actually there to spy on the Russians. Soon they would sweep down to arrest them and with a bit of luck there would be a gunfight.

It also transpired, only a little more mundanely, that the course of true love had not been running particularly smoothly in Mont St Bernard. To my surprise, young Guy was cutting a lonely figure at the bar staring into the bottom of a cup of cold hot chocolate as if hoping to spot there some indication of where his future lay. By his side lay a copy of a book entitled *Culture Shock! France – A Guide to Customs and Etiquette*.

'Hello, Guy. What are you up to? Good news, I have managed to locate your freestyle competition stuff.'

For the time being I did not want to go into the details of the case, although I was sure that in this small village the truth would soon surface. He expressed next to no interest.

'Well, I'll get it all back to you as soon as I can. Anyway,

so, what's new? Where is Amandine – working?' I knew
that this was by far the busiest week of February as it was
the French school holidays, and one of the county councils
in Paris had chosen Mont St Bernard as the destination for
some two hundred of their most disadvantaged children.
Luckily for them, the snow was at its best for the whole of
that season, and for two days now there had not been a
single cloud in the sky.

'I don't know where she is right now,' he grunted unhappily. 'I've been banned from seeing her. Her dad, you know
he's the mayor, right? Well he's none too happy that I've
been going out with her.'

'Oh dear, so what have you done to offend him then?'

'Well, it's really just the fact that I'm English, I think,' he
said, as he shook his head in disbelief at something so
strange. Then he went on to tell me of the scenes that had
ensued on his first and only trip to Amandine's house. She
had asked her mother if it would be all right to bring home
her new *petit ami*, her boyfriend, or as the French would
have it, her small friend. As Guy was at least six-foot four
this seemed a remarkably poor description.

All had gone very well to start off with. Monsieur le
Maire had been impressed by Guy's neat casual clothes –
which he had borrowed from one of the waiters at the Café
de la Poste and, to create a good impression that evening,
had exchanged for his normal post-apocalyptic attire.
Madame le Maire had been delighted by the bunch of
flowers that he had been holding when she had opened the
door to him. Actually, he had bought them for Amandine,
but it struck him in that moment that allowing her mother
to take them was rather an astute move. Certainly more
sensible than trying to wrestle them back from her, I
suggested gently. He smiled rather sadly and continued
with his story. It seemed that, although he had felt a bit in

the spotlight at first, stared at by Amandine's other much younger siblings as if he had just skied in from a different planet, things had gone smoothly and even his halting French had seemed to come quite easily. Bolstered by the presence of Nicolas, now a good friend, and the quietly supportive Amandine, he had even attempted to tell a joke.

Although I had made a point of trying to underline to all these youngsters at our occasional French-speaking lessons that trying to tell a joke in a foreign language is almost certainly doomed to failure, he had felt the moment appropriate. As the joke involved leprosy and prostitution I was inclined to disagree with him, but as luck would have it the medical vocabulary required to give the story its full impact was too much for him. When finally he was forced to ask the father the French word for 'the clap' and was told that it was *'applaudissement'*, he gave up and started to talk about cricket.

Amandine's mother was an excellent cook and Guy had eaten himself to a standstill, which was much approved of by the grandmother, who apparently took this as a sign of rude good health and great virility. Only when they had moved to the sitting-room to have coffee and one of Monsieur le Maire's home-distilled *eau-de-vie* – in this case made from pears called Williams, which apparently caused great hilarity at my expense – did things start to go, well, in this case, literally pear-shaped.

Charmed to have been invited into the bosom of this family, Guy's thoughts turned rather nostalgically to his own. Just in passing he happened to mention that his grand-father had been present at the Normandy landings, where, and he promised he didn't actually say this, the British had rescued the French. The mere mention of French and any other nationality in the same sentence, and I could have told him this after the scenes I had witnessed at the Hotel

Chamonix, was enough to send Amandine's father into a towering rage. Hurling himself across the room, he pulled an antique sword mounted on the wall from its scabbard and proceeded to chase the unfortunate Guy, first of all several times round the sitting-room, and then straight through the hallway and out of the front door.

'And all the time he kept shouting this thing at me and I just didn't understand what he was going on about.' He shook his head at the memory.

'Well, what was it that he was shouting?' I asked, feeling very sorry for the young guy. I too had memories of trying to avoid incensed parents, and had once spent two very long and cold hours on somebody's balcony in a state of undress that was not at all appropriate for late February when the incident had taken place.

'Well, I don't really know. I'll probably get it wrong, but it sounded something like "jandark", "jandark" all the time. He just kept going on about it.'

Even though I could see that it annoyed him, I could not help but laugh.

'Do you mean "Jeanne d'Arc"?'

'Yes, that's it. That's it. "Jandark, jandark." What's all that about then?'

'Well, Jeanne d'Arc is Joan of Arc in French. It sounds like he's got some sort of historical gripe with the British,' I laughed, wondering briefly whether Guy had ever heard of Joan of Arc.

Guy was no fool.

'Joan of Arc? You are joking, right? What was the guy on?'

'One too many *eaux-de-vie* by the sounds of it.'

'Yeah, but that is so out of order. Joan of Arc! That was like more than a hundred years ago.'

19

All Downhill From Here

To raise Guy's flagging spirits, and also to tie up the unhappy episode of the theft, Mireille and I insisted that Olivier return the equipment to him in person. This the boy was extremely unwilling to do. Initially, I believed this was simply out of embarrassment at having to face up to what he had done. Later, though, I realised that his shame ran much deeper than this. Guy and the other freestyle skiers were his heroes. He had often watched them at a distance admiring their cool tricks and their style. To have to face his idol and admit his misdemeanour was almost more than he could bear. But he did it, and Guy, with surprising maturity, accepted the boy's apologies with good grace, shook his hand and told him that it was, 'all right, mate.' Smiling, kind-heartedly, he offered to take him up to the snowpark to train with the other freestylers. Olivier accepted immediately and asked whether he could bring his friend Alexei.

'Sure you can, dude. No worries.'

On the morning of the downhill ski championship in late March, I discovered that Margie was not the only person to have come to grief on the slopes of Mont St Bernard. Recently, the weather had got considerably colder, and it was quite normal for temperatures to plunge to minus ten degrees Celsius at night and only float around zero in the middle of the day. Of course, for most of us skiers these were ideal conditions. Although your skis clattered on the frozen surface of the pistes first thing in the morning and any attempt to stop or slow down jarred and jolted every part of your anatomy from your knees up, by the time the sun shone fully on the valley at around two in the afternoon the skiing was perfect.

This was why I had recently adopted a routine which rarely involved me sticking my nose out of Mon Repos before midday, and then only to ski the few hundred metres down into the village. Throwing my skis over my shoulder with more or less practised ease, I would clunk along in my boots to the door of Gaston's restaurant. Now it was too cold to sit on the terrace, so instead I would have lunch with friends at one of the rough wooden tables that were laid out in front of a roaring log fire. As the downhill ski competition was undoubtedly the most important date in the Mont St Bernard sporting calendar – although the youngsters said that it would soon be replaced by the freestyle and snowboarding competition – that particular morning I made quite certain that I arrived at my table in good time.

Sipping the second of two robustly strong coffees and staring out of the window, I spotted Guy jogging in his ski boots towards the lifts. Although he was not competing, he was as keen as anyone to get to the race as he knew that Amandine was a favourite to win her category, and as by mayoral decree he had not seen her for nearly a week, this was a golden opportunity for him to make contact with her again.

Dipping a sugar lump into the last of my coffee, I overheard Emilie telling some local customers how some of the *remonteurs* and *pisteurs* had connived to strand Sergei and two of the bodyguards on the chair-lift overnight just as the Parisians had been. Strangely, I felt sorry for the men, particularly after they had helped out at the bar-room brawl. So involved had I been in hearing about the plight of the men on the chair-lift that I had not been keeping an eye on the clock. I had suddenly realised that if I was not going to be late for the race I needed to get a move on. Waving goodbye to Gaston, who raised one of his moustaches a millimetre by way of recognition, I picked up my skis, which seemed an awful lot heavier than they had before a four-course lunch, and headed for the *télécabine* that would take me as close as possible to the race meeting. I wasn't entirely sure where the course had been laid out, but I guessed, as it turned out correctly, that I would only have to follow the noise to find myself at the bottom of the run.

There wasn't really anybody about when I pushed back the doors of the little perspex bubble that had taken me to the top of the mountain. All the more reason for me to hurry up as the first races must already have started. Outside in the snow, I wandered a few yards to get my bearings, then threw my skis down on the ground and, in the approved fashion, whacked my boots with my ski sticks in order to dislodge any compacted snow that would prevent the binding from fitting properly. The last thing I wanted was to have one of my skis come adrift as I was watched by a huge crowd. Skimming quickly down a narrow track I joined the wider piste, and as I did so, to my surprise, Père Jean shot across me in his black ski suit. He was an enthusiastic skier and I had regularly seen him out on the slopes. More than once we had stopped and caught up on news over big cups of coffee. As he passed me I wondered whether it was true, as it was widely reported, that about his person he carried a small bottle of holy water and a miniature Bible, just in case he was required to deliver the last rites on the side of the mountain. Shifting along at that speed he was either trying to catch someone before their last gasp, or probably more likely he was just late for the race too. He waved cheerfully when he saw me and gave me a rather unecclesiastical thumbs-up.

Of course I should have just followed him, but no, instead I decided that I would cut through the trees, thereby taking off a whole bend of the piste, which would enable me to re-emerge in front of him in a thoroughly childish fashion. I could hear the cheers of the crowd and my pulse quickened. I tucked my sticks under my arms and bent my body down until my chin was almost touching my knees. Now I was really flying, and although the mountain here was rather steeper than I had ever remembered it, I felt good, I felt confident.

That was until I was passed by a figure that was not only going at least twice as fast as I was, but was quite clearly – I could tell from his attire and the number on a piece of card pinned to his back – competing in a downhill ski race. His body language told me that he was somewhat alarmed by my appearance and, although I could not read his facial expression as he was wearing a full-face helmet, he shouted something as he went past. It did not sound particularly friendly but then he was travelling at some speed.

Sometimes when I had been skiing alone, I had imagined what it must be like if you literally had to ski for your life – from an avalanche, say, or a team of assassins. Ridiculous and fanciful I know, but now suddenly very real. On one side of the slope was mountain, and if I had learnt anything about skis it was that they were of no use at all when it came to trying to go upward. On the other side was orange-plastic safety netting twice the normal height, which prevented any out of control sportsmen from disappearing into the trees, but sadly also prevented anybody who had, through no fault of his own, strayed into the middle of the race track from sneaking off again without anybody noticing. As the width of the entire piste at this point was not much more than ten or twelve feet, there was not really anywhere to hide. Did they let the next skier go before the competitor in front had arrived? I wondered. How long did it take them to get down anyway? And at what point in the course had I suddenly got involved?

There was not really very much time to consider my situation and so, as if pursued by the hounds of hell, I pressed on, hurtling round the next corner at a speed that must have put me in contention for at least a position in the top ten. What I saw around the other corner, however, very nearly brought me to a grinding halt. Laid out below me like a giant jigsaw was a sea of faces all looking up expectantly, all ready to cheer the next competitor to the finish line.

Should I try and get down as quickly as possible and then hope to disappear into the crowd before anybody could stop me, thereby taking the fairly sizeable risk that I would go head over toe at some stage between now and the bottom? In the end, I played the role of neutral observer pretending every few yards to have spotted something fascinating amongst the pine trees. By the time I actually did reach the finish line I had managed to disguise myself so effectively with my hood, headband, hat, goggles and scarf that I thought it extremely unlikely my own mother would have recognised me.

'Look, what is this? We 'ave ze new competitor. He is from the *Royaume-Uni*! It is Williams!' This last exclamation, pronounced in the unmistakable tones of our resident disc jockey and radio presenter, Jay-Pee, went up at the end in a crescendo before the amplified tones of one of his dreadful tunes swept the valley.

Most of the crowd were fully involved in following the progress of the skiers and most of them never listened to Jay-Pee anyway, so I only had to undergo a small amount of teasing from some of the younger members of the audience. I even managed to keep a smile on my now revealed face when some of the little boys and girls from my ski class set up their own impromptu competition to see who could best imitate the skiing style of Williams.

Thankfully, it turned out that I had only intruded into the completion of the warm-up runs, and the timed competitive descents were only now about to start. The contest was ordered by ascending age and after the descent of some kamikaze six-year-olds, some of whom I recognised from Madame Brassard's class, it was the turn of the *benjamins*, the ten-year-olds. Despite my understandable desire to keep a low profile, I found myself edging towards the front of the crowd. Olivier was the last competitor in his category, but it had not been at all certain that his name had been added back onto the list. Some of the organisers, small-minded functionaries that seem to surface on committees the world over, had decided to wield the paltry power that they possessed and punish Olivier for his misdemeanour by banning him from the race. Despite the fact that they had been in smug agreement about their decision as they had left one of the meeting rooms at the back of the Hotel Chamonix, they would surely have reconsidered had they seen the effect that this had had on the boy. Already withdrawn and ashamed, he now became so inhibited that he rarely left his bedroom, and when he did, his pale face and red eyes had shocked all of us. Fortunately, Norbert had become aware of the situation and with a unilateral, if not lordly, sweep of his arm had had the boy reinstated in a moment. Now I could see Olivier's face on the close circuit television, pale still, but excited as he pulled on his goggles and flexed his knees at the start gate. When the green light flashed up, he launched himself down the slope and the noise of cheering, yammering and clanging of cow bells roared across the mountainside. When he came into view around the last turn – a particularly tight one I happened to know – he was travelling well. When he swung to a stop in a great wave of snow and pulled off his helmet, he was only pipped into second place by a couple of hundredths of a second. After he had been released from a long and warm hug by his mother, he was surrounded by a small crowd of boys and girls his age, who took it in turns to cheer him, put their arms around his shoulders and kiss him resoundingly on both cheeks as cameras flashed and he beamed just as brightly. Alexei, who appeared to have made it to the ski meeting without his normal escort of bodyguards and was wearing the small medal he had won for his ice-skating performance around his neck, came over to his new friend and shook him warmly by the hand. When I showed Olivier a thumbs-up and winked, he waved back furiously, smiling and crying, and I was happy for him. I did not even mind it when he called out 'Salut, Williams' in front of several thousand people. Somehow, we all knew that despite the other excitements and the other achievements of the day, Olivier's race would have been the most important of all.

Finally, it was the turn of Monsieur le Maire, wearing his Republican sash over the top of a rather dated, faded ski suit, to give away the prizes. As at least a third of the twenty-odd cups were presented to a member of his more or less close family, he could consider it an afternoon's work well done. In such good humour was he that he even smiled benevolently when Guy slid over and scooped up Amandine before giving her a congratulatory kiss. After a couple of bottles of cheap champagne had been sprayed from the podium, an enormous array of cakes, tarts and sweetmeats was produced by a team of women dressed in lacy and embroidered traditional costumes. The mountain air alone had been enough for us to build up a mighty appetite, and before long the crowd was seated at the wooden trestle tables with plates piled high with calories. Steaming enamel pots of coffee made their way up and down the benches. Monsieur and Madame Job were sitting in the middle of a throng of neighbours and waved to me cheerfully as I made my way towards a tea urn that had been thoughtfully provided for *les Anglais*. They were both dressed in their Sunday best and Monsieur Job was looking particularly jaunty in what appeared to be a brand new flat cap made of Highland tweed. He was a great fan of the Scottish for some obscure historical reason, but also because they, like him, he claimed, were mountain folk.

'You see,' he called. 'This is the real life of the mountains. Not with all these tourists.' As if on cue, a brass band with feathers in their hats struck up a French folk song, and before long the circular area of snow that had been the end of the racetrack was filled with dancing couples. Quite bravely I asked Madame Job for the pleasure of a dance, which she, after a great deal of laughing and clucking with her friends, accepted.

Feeling a little weary after the experience, I thanked her very much and accepted an offer of a lift up the hill back to Mon Repos in their horse and sleigh. Once they had ridden back down the hill in the *télécabine* and I had skied to the bottom, we met up again and made our way to the village surgery, behind which Hortense, their pretty Percheron horse, was stabled. As we walked past, I glanced in through the misty window of the waiting room and could see that as usual the two young doctors who ran the practice were doing a thriving trade. Just as we were about to clear the corner, the electric doors slid silently open and a very recognisable figure dressed in a fur hat was pushed out in a wheelchair. Margie's arm was strapped up in a very high-tech sling, but this had apparently done nothing to improve her mood.

'So why the hell do I need to be in a wheelchair if I've just dislocated my arm? It's not like I haven't done it before! Two hundred and fifty Euros is outrageous! Bloody outrageous!'

There seemed to be no arguing with the implacable male nurse who was pushing her wheelchair. He looked as if he would be strapping her into a straitjacket if he had any more nonsense from her. She was still belly-aching as she was rather unceremoniously hoisted into the back of an ambulance, which with a spurt of snow from its wheels and a quick burst from its siren drove away into the night.

Once Hortense had made her surefooted way back up to Mon Repos there was hardly any time to put our feet up. Within half an hour we needed to get on the road down the valley towards Issy and the Stade Municipal – the indoor stadium – for the great ice-hockey encounter. Again, the Jobs had offered me a lift, and I soon found myself sitting relatively comfortably on the straw bale in the back of their blue, corrugated 2CV van. Monsieur Job was a furiously keen ice-hockey supporter having played a great deal in his youth. Of course, in his day, as he was eager to point out, it had been real ice hockey on real frozen lakes. I could perfectly well see that this would add an extra dimension to the excitement of the game. We arrived in good time and I helped Monsieur Job unload his banner which, as it read *Allez les Bleus de Mont St Bernard*, was of a fairly impressive length and required three people to support it. He also had a small canvas bag of trumpets, horns and rattles, which he dispensed to members of the supporters' club, and his own pride and joy: an aerosol foghorn, which I made the mistake of standing next to for the first five minutes.

The stadium, if not exactly the Enormodome, was quite a sizeable venue, yet there was not a square inch of space on the concrete benches that scaled up the walls to vertiginous heights on either side of the rink. The fact that these seats were cold and made of stone, and therefore liable to engender all sorts of unfortunate effects if sat upon for too long, mattered not in the slightest. Not for one moment of the seemingly endless game were they used for their intended purpose. More often than not they were used to leap upon in joy or off again in dismay; they were useful to drum upon, or in Monsieur Job's case beat your new Highland cap against, or, in the case of one fervent supporter, your head, in frustration at the idiocy of the referee.

Matters were not much improved by the appearance of the Russian party, who appeared to be more interested in ice hockey than even the most fervent French supporter. They found themselves seats rink-side, and the bulk of the bodyguards surrounding Dimitri obscured the view of a large part of the playing area. Monsieur Job became even more over-excited than he already was, bellowing at them to move out of the way. Alexei somehow slipped away from the group and joined Mireille, Olivier, Aubrey, Sophie and me. Grabbing my arm, he looked up at me. He had good news. He had spoken to his father recently and tried to explain to him how unpopular he was becoming. At first Dimitri had just shrugged, but when he had realised how upset his son had become, and how fond the boy was of the village and its population, he had relented. No longer would he try to take over the whole community, but would instead content himself with the purchase of the Hotel de l'Aigle Brun for long weekends. To his son's surprise, he had telephoned Norbert there and then for a meeting. Despite the fact that Sergei and the other bodyguards were poised outside the door of Norbert's office ready to burst in should there be any raised voices, when the two parted they did so on friendly terms. Dimitri had even offered to buy a cup to be presented at the freestyle competition. It was agreed that it should be presented by Dimitri to the person who had done the most to promote the reputation of Mont St Bernard.

Fairly shortly after we had arrived, the game had got under way and it had become very clear to me within minutes that I was unlikely to work out the rules for myself. Given the general levels of nervous excitement, it was almost certain that I would not learn them from anybody else in the audience either. So it was that I contented myself with cheering and booing in synchronised perfection with the rest of the Mont St Bernard supporters. Apart from anything else, so fast is the game of ice hockey that it is almost impossible to keep track of where the extremely dangerous-looking puck has most recently lodged itself. There was a large, high, Perspex screen between the audience and the rink, but when emotions were running particularly high towards half-time, I began to wonder whether this was for the benefit of the public or for the protection of the heavily padded players.

Whatever the case, some of the younger English members of the audience found it extremely and, I have to admit, rather repetitively funny to refer to 'flying pucks'. This in itself would not have been too bad had I not been asked on at least four occasions by French friends to explain what it was their Anglo-Saxon counterparts found so amusing. I muttered something about *'l'humour anglais'* and smiled inscrutably, hoping that this might bring the matter to an end. It simply meant that every time our team recorded some success, the French supporters would throw their arms around their English friends and scream, '*Yes, yes, flying pucks!*' I even saw Madame Job at it at one stage.

By half-time I was feeling quite bruised, and poor old Nicolas, who was actually playing, could barely stand up on his skates. Despite the fact that he was agile and fast, if ever he found himself sandwiched between either two members of the opposition, who were a bunch of ugly brutes, or just one player and the side hoardings, he stood no chance. When at one stage he was swept clean off his feet by a devious swipe of an opposition stick and banged his head hard on the icy surface, we rose as man and woman to demonstrate our indignation. On more than one occasion, if it had not been for the neon lighting, the soft drinks machine at the entrance and the clicking of phone cameras, you might well have believed yourself to be in the Colosseum of Ancient Rome.

To my consternation and the palpable trepidation of my French companions, we noticed at the beginning of the second half that Guy and Jimmy had come on as substitutes for *le petit Nicolas* and one other of our heroic players. If things went badly, I didn't fancy the reaction of Monsieur le Maire at the next council meeting, and nor did I fancy Guy's future chances with Amandine, who was sitting fretfully in the manager's dugout. Very fortunately, they both acquitted themselves well, although I wasn't aware that they had done much training, apart from a couple of not entirely sober turns around the little ice rink in Mont St Bernard after a long night at the Licebox. When they crashed back onto the players' bench after they in turn had been substituted, and pulled off their plastic helmets, I could not help but detect a degree of relief on their faces as they waved and winked at us from the other side of the pitch.

As the sun comes up in the morning, so was it certain

that Jay-Pee was responsible for the sudden bursts of music that blared out of the PA system without any due warning. Yet again, his feel for playing exactly the wrong thing at any given moment was without fault. Shortly after we went into the lead in the fourth half, we were blasted with snatches from a song the chorus line of which was 'Things can only get better . . .' As only a few minutes before, the cheerleaders, who featured Emilie and Sophie, my non-ski instructor, and a very large number of pom-poms had made their first appearance, he was on this occasion doubly wrong.

There were so many bells ringing, horns blaring, drums beating and whistles being blown that it was quite impossible to work out which stage in the match we had reached. Utterly confused, I only realised that the contest had come to an end when everybody stood up and walked out. We were back in the Café de la Poste by the time I had worked out the score. It transpired that the match had been drawn for the first time since the war, but this did not dampen spirits and toasts were made late into the night.

Unfortunately the 2CV was feeling a little weary by the time we tackled the hill back up toward home but Monsieur Job persevered at the steering wheel, whilst Madame Job and I got to the back of the vehicle and started to push through the thigh-deep snow. Such were our efforts that I happened to notice as we neared their farm that Madame Job's shoulder had left a sizeable dent in one of the flimsy rear panels. Monsieur Job's adrenalin levels were going bananas, so I decided that this was not the moment to mention the damage to the car and instead invited them in for a nightcap. Having purchased a bottle of Armagnac for such an occasion, I was mighty thankful for its restorative qualities as my neighbour started to reel off the results of all the other seventy or so ice-hockey encounters between the two villages.

My manners deserted me when he began to recite the
names of the players in each of those individual encounters, and without a great deal of grace I shovelled them
back out into the snow. They did not seem to mind in the
slightest, and headed off in the direction of home whirling
their rattles and blowing on their whistles for some time to
come. Hortense was also tired and whinnied with irritation
at having been woken by these hooligans. How long
Monsieur and Madame Job carried on celebrating I am not
exactly certain, as I conked out in the armchair in front of
the wood-burning fire within minutes, lulled to sleep by a
rousing chorus of *'Allez les Bleus'*.

20

La Fête Savoyarde

By the time of the freestyle-skiing competition, brown earth had begun to make its way back up the mountain and there was a definite *fin de saison* feel about the village. Within a few days eighty per cent of the *commerces* – the shops, the restaurants, even the bank and the Post Office – would be closed; not opening their doors again until the next influx of tourists in early June, the owners would take a relaxing and well-earned break. After the last set of visitors had left on the coming Saturday, Mont St Bernard would be little more than a ghost town, although as I headed across the village centre towards the lift that would take me back up Mont Thierry, that was difficult to imagine. Intensely focused competitors gripping their skis or their snowboards carved their way through the crowds like Moses through the Red Sea, the waves parting silently but for the odd quiet comment of admiration. Guy, Jimmy and Nicolas were just ahead of me in the queue, but I did not disturb them as they were deep in a conversation that I was confident was in a language I could not speak. When their turn came to enter the *télécabine* bubble up the hill, they rudely refused the suggestion of the lift attendant that they should share with three competitors from Issy, and once they'd dumped their skis in the rack on the outside of the bubble they climbed in and pulled the sliding doors closed. Artists in the privacy of their dressing room.

Up at the top, the atmosphere was carnival-like, and the owners of the Beauvoir had decorated the outside of the restaurant with streamers and flags that flew gaily either side of a giant banner which read *'Toute première compéti-tion freestyle de Mont St Bernard'*, and below that, painted out, I could see where English members of the committee had attempted two or three different spellings of 'Inau-gural' before opting instead in bright red letters for 'First Freestyle Competition Ever in Mont St Bernard'. Beneath the banner was a most professional-looking podium, where later the winners would receive the adulation of the already very sizeable crowd.

With crushing inevitability Jay-Pee was present with his turntables, but it transpired that Jimmy had convinced him to change his tunes. Threatening to reveal the disc jockey's latest indiscretion at the Licebox to his mother, of whom apparently Jay-Pee was terrified, Jimmy had managed to convince him to play music only selected by the freestyle committee. As a result, hip-hop, drum 'n' bass, R&B and dance music blasted across the valley. Actually, it was godawful, but probably better than having to listen to bloody 'Dancing Queen' six times an hour. Jay-Pee discov-ered that his dancing style was not at all suited to these new rhythms, and he could only stand by impotently and watch Sophie, who was wearing an absolutely dynamite new outfit, gyrate with a number of young men who were most certainly young enough to be his sons. Jimmy and I groaned simultaneously and went off to sit on a snowdrift, enjoying the sensation of being good losers together.

Monsieur le Maire, whose sash had got badly rucked up

at the back in the process of a photo opportunity with the young dancers, was having to be repaired by his wife. He did not look like he was enjoying himself at all and, once Madame le Maire had finished her ministrations, he stomped off in a huff to join his friends at the *buvette*, an impromptu bar erected in the snow that was already doing brisk business despite the fact that it was only just past ten in the morning. Just as Norbert was about to take his first sip of a particularly good white vin de Savoie, his mobile rang and he hunted around in various pockets before he located it. It was Dimitri. He was bringing the cup. Before long he appeared clutching something that would have looked more in place behind seven-inch secur-ity glass at the Tower of London.

Despite the fact that they were both competing, Nicolas and Guy had appointed themselves as the bilingual Masters of Ceremonies. They appeared on the balcony of the Beau-voir and greeted the crowd as if they had just stridden onto the stage at Wembley Stadium. We were introduced to the panel of judges, whose average age must have been about nineteen, and the games commenced.

Each of the different disciplines was more alarming than the last. One was simply a ski jump but, in a freestyle compe-tition, rather than simply lifting off the end of the lip, gliding through the air and landing softly with legs gracefully bent, now the contestant was required to perform any number of turns, twists and other contortions before landing. Watching them against the sun with one eye closed you might imagine that they were stuck in the middle of one of the rather faster washing-machine cycles. This, though, was nothing compared to the course that required a timed ski down a mogul field that was bumpier than an armadillo before shooting along a near-vertical wall of ice and performing some sort of gymnastics before, it was hoped, coming to a halt in front of the judges' desk.

Very fortunately, I am of a generation of skiers who has not had to face any of these particular manoeuvres as a test of manhood, and therefore have managed to avoid having to risk life and limb day in day out in winter sport's equivalent of the assault course in a boot camp. Still, all the competitors who were not immediately hospitalised seemed to enjoy themselves, and lapped up the congratulations and applause, the whistles and the weird hand gestures, the hugs and kisses that they received from the crowd. Not even the competitors from Issy seemed to be annoyed that, here again, most of the prizes were scooped up by Nicolas and a number of his more or less direct relatives. It was Nicolas, too, who was awarded the best all-rounder prize and presented with the jewel-encrusted cup that Dimitri had ordered from Cartier in Geneva. According to Aubrey it was worth more than an average *pisteur* earned in a season, but he smiled anyway and did not seem to mind too much.

Just as Jay-Pee cranked up the hip-hop equivalent of 'Congratulations and Celebrations', Guy and Amandine came flying hand in hand down the ski jump, performed a perfectly synchronised backflip against a cobalt blue sky, landed effortlessly and skied off down the mountain.

After the last echoes of the cheers had rumbled away down the valley, everyone set off in the direction of the *Salle de Fêtes*. For after all, now was the most important occasion of the day: *La Fête Savoyarde*.

La Gastronomie Savoyarde is renowned all over the world. Heaven knows why. There are only three stock ingredients: cheese, cured ham and potatoes. Very rarely, only on special occasions, two or three pieces of lettuce make their appearance for a star turn, but otherwise, whether it is Fondue or Tartiflette, Tarte Savoyarde or Raclette, one way or another it is just the same old potato, cured ham and cheese. But the saving grace of this cuisine is that there is always tons of it and, at the banquet at the Beauvoir that Monsieur le Maire had laid on, the tables were groaning.

Rather as Asterix and Obelix fête their adventures with a huge feast so here, amongst friends, we were celebrating a season in the snow. Jay-Pee, in the same way that the Bard Cacofonix is found trussed to a tree so that he cannot play, fretted as his turntables were unplugged and replaced by a diminutive accordionist in the shape of Monsieur Job.

Once the music was over and Monsieur Job, seated at the far end of one of the long tables, had disappeared behind the clouds of smoke that poured from his enormous festive pipe, Nicolas and the gang came up and surrounded me as I sat with Sophie and Angus, her ridiculously tanned new boyfriend.

'Come on, Williams,' pleaded Olivier and Alexei. 'Come on, come outside. We want to take your photograph. Come on.'

Half-skipping, half-tugging they pulled me toward the door that led out onto the gleaming snow, followed by the rest of the gang. Dimitri and Norbert chatted cheerily, and Sergei and the bodyguards, thawed finally after their night on the chair-lift and none the worse for it, hoovered up the contents of the bar. They then embarked on a bout of energetic Franco-Russian folk dancing with the 'dawly burds' to the cheers and applause of the sizeable audience.

'Now, come on, just come down that small ski jump there and we can take your picture.'

Under normal circumstances I might well not have considered it to be a small ski jump, but so bound up was I by the lads' enthusiasm and the festive nature of the day that I skipped sideways up the piste until I found myself at the top of the short run. Without a second thought I set off, bending my knees in the approved fashion when I hit the upward-turning curve of the lip of the jump. Suddenly I was airborne, defying gravity, soaring above the earth, above me only the hot sun. Then just as quickly it was all over and the snow rushed back towards me. Spreading my arms out wide to ensure my balance, I waited to make contact with the ground again, wondering idly who it was that I would shower with snow when I came to a halt. For some reason, however, when I made contact with terra firma again my skis decided to stop dead, but were on the other hand more than happy to relinquish me from their bindings. Thus I was projected through the air some ten yards before performing a technically perfect face plant in a snowdrift underneath the spiky pine trees, and the clicking of camera shutters echoed across the valley of Mont St Bernard.

Epilogue

F inally, the snow released its grip on the village of Mont
St Bernard until all that was left, high above the tree
line, was the silver sheet of glacier, gleaming like a faraway
magical kingdom on the summits of the Crête des Dentelles.
Soon, in the mild sunshine of spring, a tapestry of flowers
spread across the meadows and the hills were alive with
the sound of music. The sound of music, in this case, blaring
from the open windows of the ten or so Hummers as they
pulled out of town, Dimitri and Alexei waving their
farewells to their new friends. Mireille and a brave-looking
Olivier were amongst them, of course, clutching large
farewell jars of caviar outside the Hotel de l'Aigle Brun.
Even Sergei looked mildly emotional behind his dark glasses
as he gave a mock-American salute to Gaston when the
driver pulled away. The owner of the Café de la Poste raised
one eyebrow a micro-millimetre by way of *au revoir*.

Jay-Pee had wanted to organise a goodbye *boum* – that
strangely explosive French term for a party – but somehow
the *fin de saison* atmosphere had not been conducive to
further hilarity. Instead, a last quiet, or at least fairly quiet,
evening had been spent in the Café de la Poste. Ice-cold

vodka and several gigantic wickerwork-bound flagons of *marc de Savoie*, that had been hauled up from the deepest of cellars, had been consumed without moderation. Monsieur Job had then produced his ancient but amazingly well-maintained accordion, and one of the 'dawly burds', sitting on a barstool under the unflinching gaze of Gaston, had sung mournful Russian love songs, which Dimitri's secretary had tried rather unsuccessfully to simultaneously translate, or at least until the singer threw one of her seven-inch stilettos at him.

Nevertheless, the effect had been sufficiently moving for their employer, Dimitri, to become uncharacteristically tactile and rather tearful. The mayor of Mont St Bernard, due, perhaps, to the emotion of the moment, had seemed to lose control of his limbs and had been last seen being hauled out of the door and into the street by his daughter and future son-in-law, his mayoral heels dragging in the slush.

By the early hours of the morning only the younger generation had been left – and me. Even now the hike up to Mon Repos was sufficient excuse to stay in the cosy bar and when Aubrey, at some stage, had offered to drive me home, I had been quite relieved that he couldn't find his keys, remember where he had left his van or where it was that I lived. Dawn had broken before finally I had set off hoping that I might encounter Monsieur Job and Hortense plodding up the hill.

Even a few days after the departure of the Russians, I was still not feeling quite myself and it was with something of a trembling hand that I handed back a letter to Olivier. He had asked me to check it for mistakes in his English before he sent it off to Alexei in Moscow. The two, now firm friends, had agreed to remain pen pals until Olivier and Mireille could go out and stay in Russia. The French boy was wired with excitement at the idea – particularly as he had been told any number of stories by Alexei – all of them highly far-fetched. They surely did not really plan to build a bull-fighting arena in the grounds of their house and import matadors from Spain? Did they? Not simply because his father had imported several thousand bottles of Rioja and wanted somewhere authentic to drink it? Surely not.

Some time very soon, Mont St Bernard will have to face another invasion from Anglo-Saxon hordes, but this time they will not be wearing anti-UV fluorescent face cream and woolly hats with Viking horns, and nor will they be brandishing sharp-looking skis and sticks. This incursion will be altogether more soberly-attired in tweed and dark suits, and summer dresses and elegant hats – all dressed up for the wedding of Guy and Amandine. Norbert will be presiding over the civil side of the ceremony, having undergone an intensive programme organised by his family. This is all in an attempt to cure him of his more strident Anglophobic tendencies before the arrival of the guests.

Père Jean will of course be directing the religious ceremony in the little white church with its copper cupola. The bells will ring out prettily across the valley as the young couple step out and are showered with rice. No one knows, quite yet, whether the long trestles with their smart white cloths and table decorations of fir cones and mountain flowers will be laid out at the Beauvoir or the Hotel Chamonix. Whichever venue is chosen, the view will be superb. Aubrey is going to do the catering and is thinking – 'just for a laugh' – of asking the now repaired Margie whether she would like to wait tables.

Although Guy has some studying to finish off in England, he will soon return and, after the wedding, take up the job that Gaston has offered him as the new DJ at the Licebox.

Jimmy, who had decided to carry on working full-time at the Café de la Poste, is much looking forward to his friend's return. He and Aubrey will then be able to advise Gaston about the 'most wickedest, most phatest sounds' with which to entertain, or rather to assail, future visitors to Mont St Bernard's 'Premier Nitespot'.

Jay-Pee took his early 'retirement' from the turn-tables with good grace. Now, he says he will be able to concentrate on public broadcasting and erecting more loudspeakers in the streets of the village. The local population can hardly wait.

Finally, however much I was interested in the destinies of all my friends, and however affectionate I felt towards my adopted community, I knew I had to go. Yes, my new, if rather sketchy, career awaited . . .

Sometimes, prior to other departures from other corners of the world, I have been tempted to slip away in the middle of the night rather than have to say goodbye, but when I did bid farewell to my friends here (after a very good lunch on the terrace of Chez Gaston), it was more of an *au revoir* than an *adieu*.

'So, we will see you next season, Williams?' Mireille asked, as she kissed me elegantly on both cheeks, and Olivier enthusiastically shook my hand, his eyes twinkling.

'Who knows?' I laughed, and sighed as I gazed across the valley and up the slopes to the highest peaks of the mountains of Mont St Bernard. 'You just might.'